FIELD SPORTS & UPPER CLASSES 10

SHOOTING 13

CRICKET
— OFFICERS POP'Y WITH, 1860S

'THE ARMY ISN'T *ALL* W

CULT OF GAMES & PS 18

VITAI LAMPADA 19

SPORTS, GAMES & DEV OF LEADERSHIP QUALS 20

To My Father –

Thomas Philip Campbell Jr.

1937–1996

And to the professionals who go to war not for an ideal,

but because it is their job.

'The Army Isn't *All* Work'

Physical Culture and the Evolution of the British Army, 1860–1920

JAMES D. CAMPBELL
University of Maine, USA

Routledge
Taylor & Francis Group

LONDON AND NEW YORK

First published 2012 by Ashgate Publishing

Published 2016 by Routledge
2 Park Square, Milton Park, Abingdon, Oxon OX14 4RN
711 Third Avenue, New York, NY 10017, USA

First issued in paperback 2017

Routledge is an imprint of the Taylor & Francis Group, an informa business

British Library Cataloguing in Publication Data
Campbell, James D.
  'The Army Isn't All Work': Physical Culture and the Evolution of the British Army,
  1860–1920.
  1. Great Britain. Army – Physical training – History – 19th century. 2. Great Britain.
  Army – Physical training – History – 20th century. 3. Great Britain. Army – Sports –
  History – 19th century. 4. Great Britain. Army – Sports – History – 20th century.
  5. Military sports – Great Britain – History – 19th century. 6. Military sports –
  Great Britain – History – 20th century.
  I. Title.
  355.5'0941'09034–dc23

Library of Congress Cataloging-in-Publication Data
Campbell, James D., 1964–
  "The Army Isn't All Work": Physical Culture and the Evolution of the British Army,
  1860–1920 / James D. Campbell.
     p.   cm.
  Includes bibliographical references and index.
  1. Great Britain. Army – Physical training – History – 19th century. 2. Great Britain. Army
  – Physical training – History – 20th century. I. Title. II. Title: Physical culture in the
  evolution of the British Army, 1860–1920.
  U325.G7C36 2012
  355.5–dc23   2012010737

ISBN 13: 978-1-138-10888-2 (pbk)
ISBN 13: 978-1-4094-3696-6 (hbk)

Contents

List of Figures   *vii*
Acknowledgements   *ix*
"Vitaï Lampada"   *xiii*

Introduction   1

PART I: *MENS SANA IN CORPORE SANO*: THE ORIGINS OF THE ARMY GYMNASTIC STAFF AND REGIMENTAL SPORT, 1860–1880

1   Officer Sport: Aristocrats and Schoolboys   9

2   The Other Ranks: Health, Morals and Morale   23

3   The Army Gymnastic Staff and Regimental Sport   33

PART II: "PLAY UP AND PLAY THE GAME": PHYSICAL TRAINING AND ARMY SPORT, 1880–1908

4   "A Marvellous Improvement in the Rank and File": Physical Training at the Turn of the Century   47

5   "No Better Pastime for Soldiers": The Expansion of Army and Regimental Sport   65

6   "They Have Taken to Our Manly European Games": Military Athleticism and the Empire   79

PART III: "TRAINING FOR SPORT IS TRAINING FOR WAR": 1908–1914

7   Physical Training and National Preparedness   103

8   Maturity: The Institutionalization of Army Sport   113

9   The War Game: Mobilization and "The Death of an Army"   129

PART IV: "THE GREATER GAME": ARMY PHYSICAL CULTURE IN
WARTIME

10   Civilians to Soldiers: Sport and Fitness in Kitchener's
     New Armies   145

11   "Make Them Tigers": The Army Physical and Bayonet
     Training Staff   157

12   "The Greater Game": Wartime Recreational Training   175

Epilogue: "Raise the Tone": The Formation of the Army
Sport Control Board   193

Select Bibliography   203

Index   217

List of Figures

1.1   Polo Tournament, Secunderabad, c.1897 (courtesy of the
      Council of the National Army Museum, London)   17

3.1   The Gymnasium at Aldershot, 1868, from the *Illustrated
      London News* (author's collection)   36

3.2   Class of Staff Instructors in the Gymnasium at
      Aldershot, *c.*1894   39

4.1   Recruit Physical Training, Royal Irish Regiment,
      Buttevant, 1898 (courtesy of the Council of the National
      Army Museum, London)   53

4.2   Bayonet instruction class, Army School of Physical Training,
      Aldershot, c.1894 (author's collection)   57

4.3   Colonel George Malcolm Fox, Inspector of Gymnasia,
      Aldershot, 1895 (author's collection)   59

5.1   Football match, India, *c.*1890s (courtesy of the Council
      of the National Army Museum, London)   69

5.2   2nd Battalion Grenadier Guards All-Army Tug-of-War
      Championship Team, 1894–1895. The team captain, Pioneer
      Sergeant Jones (center), has his Gymnastic Staff Instructor's
      brevet above the stripes on his right sleeve (courtesy of the
      Council of the National Army Museum, London)   72

5.3   Boxing match, India, *c.*1890s (courtesy of the Council of the
      National Army Museum, London)   76

5.4   Gymnastics display at Northumberland Fusiliers Regimental
      Sports, East London, South Africa, January 1, 1900 (courtesy
      of the Council of the National Army Museum, London)   77

6.1   Indian Army horseback wrestling (Imperial War Museum)   84

6.2   45th Sikhs Tug-of-War, sports day, 1918 (Imperial War Museum)   98

7.1   Gymnastic Staff Instructors gymnastic display, *c.*1895 (author's collection)   110

8.1   Cricket match, 14th (King's) Hussars NCOs vs. 7th Dragoon Guards NCOs, Canterbury, May 9, 1906 (courtesy of the Council of the National Army Museum, London)   115

8.2   7th Dragoon Guards Association Football Team, 1907 (courtesy of the Council of the National Army Museum, London)   119

8.3   Northumberland Fusiliers Officers vs. Sergeants football, Mhow, India, 1913 (courtesy of the Council of the National Army Museum, London)   127

9.1   9th Battalion, the London Regiment Recruit PT, December 1914 (Imperial War Museum)   135

10.1   1st Battalion, the Wiltshire Regiment football after coming out of the line, 1916 (Imperial War Museum)   153

11.1   Bayonet Assault Course, France, *c.*1918 (Imperial War Museum)   169

12.1   Pillow fight, Guards Division sports day, c.1918 (Imperial War Museum)   181

Acknowledgements

In 1996 I undertook a research project to discover whether there was a connection between the changes in the British Army between the Crimean War and the First World War, and the appearance in Britain during that same time of what we know now as Modern Sport. I began this project at the suggestion of my graduate advisor, Dr. William Baker of the University of Maine. He is an historian of Britain, but first and foremost he is an historian of sport and all the ways in which sport has been a part of peoples' lives and their societies since ancient times. I suspect that he had little interest in supervising the research of someone who thought he was really only interested in the Victorian British Army and the *Boys Own* tales of how it spread the benefits of British civilization around the globe. After many years of work, of wrong turns and exhilarating discoveries, and hopefully some maturing (but not a loss) of that original fascination with the Soldiers of the Queen, that research project is now this book.

It has taken far longer than I had ever intended for this manuscript to reach publication. Many thanks to the editors, readers, and staff of Ashgate Publishing who have made this possible. It was more difficult than I had thought it would be to undertake this effort while still serving as an active Army officer. Military duties, including the untimely intervention of the ongoing war, have a way of interrupting what has really been an intellectual hobby. I can say, however, that among other things my enforced sabbatical in Afghanistan allowed me to get a lot of reading done, and to see first hand the results of the spread of the British Army's physical culture. In the spring of 2006 while waiting to leave a small forward operating base in Helmand Province, in the first-ever Coalition Forces convoy to the then still-obscure town of Sangin, I spent some time watching our Afghan National Army partners play cricket in a dusty and windy patch of desert. It was a poignant event for me on several levels.

In an endeavor such as the completion of a book project like this, one realizes very quickly that without the assistance of many people, completing the project would be impossible. I have a long list of people to whom I owe much—I only hope that I can eventually repay some of them with more than a citation at the beginning of a manuscript. More than any other person, I owe a deep debt of gratitude to Dr. Baker. He started working with me when this project began as a Master's thesis—largely as the result of his suggestions. Little did either of us know that there would be such fertile ground in that field as to lead me to develop the topic into what has become this book. Dr. Baker's ideas, encouragement, admonishment, and superb editing have made this document what it is.

There are many others at the University of Maine who have contributed in a large way to this project as well. Dr. Richard Blanke's critical eye and promptings about comparison with Continental armies forced me to carefully maintain focus on the validity of sources and ideas. Dr. Janet TeBrake encouraged me to understand the connections between the British Army and its imperial counterparts, as well as the influence of the Army on the subjects of the Empire. Professor Robert Whelan, with his own interest in the nature of military leadership, and in how soldiers deal with the environment of war, was a kindred spirit and a check on many of my ideas. And finally, my mentor from King's College London, Dr. David McLean, gave timely suggestions as to sources, and his prodding me to pursue a complete and in-depth review of those sources led me to discover much material that might otherwise have escaped me. I thank Dr. Mclean especially for his personal commitment to my project.

There are many others who deserve my thanks. Dr. William TeBrake, past Chairman of the Department of History at the University of Maine, and his successors, Dr. Scott See and Dr. Nathan Godfried, hired me to teach American Military History and Sports History. My experience doing that has made this manuscript more informed. I also thank my brother Ned Campbell and his wife Emily Hayes Campbell, for their hospitality, interest, and encouragement on my many research trips to London. I am grateful to my friends and colleagues while I was assigned to the Army ROTC battalion at the University of Maine, for their interest, encouragement, and solicitude in allowing me to focus on things other than strictly military business. Thanks also to my colleagues in the Maine Army National Guard, for their friendship and for abiding my obsession with historical esoterica that was no doubt trying, at times, for focused military professionals.

My great friend and comrade Major Charles Dobson, late of the 1st Battalion Worcestershire and Sherwood Foresters, was not only important in helping me to understand the sometimes confusing nuances of British military culture, but he was also an invaluable sounding board for many ideas during our shared time in combat in Afghanistan. Charles is a Rugby football man, but he did grudgingly acknowledge the role played by other sports, as well as PT, in the British Army.

I would also like to thank the staff of the Reading Room at the National Army Museum in London. They run a superb institution. Their patience and helpful attitude allowed me to make the most of several all-too-brief visits— that museum will always be one of my favorite places. Ms. Emma Lefley of the Picture Library was extraordinarily kind and her assistance allowed me to procure many of the obscure and hopefully interesting images that appear in the book. Thanks also to the staffs of the Imperial War Museum Reading Room and

Photo Archive, the British Library, and the British National Archive (formerly Public Record Office) at Kew. I cannot forget the assistance of the Director and the Secretary of the Army Sport Control Board, Major General (ret) S.W. Saint-John Lytle, CB, and Lieutenant Colonel (ret) Barry Lillywhite. Lieutenant Colonel Lillywhite provided me with not only a ride around Aldershot but also a kind tour of the Board's facilities, and Major General Saint-John Lytle gave me access to the Board's historical files—something it was clear that few outsiders, if any, had ever had before. I owe a great debt to the staff of the Royal Army Physical Training Corps Regimental Association, and to the Commander and staff of the Army Physical and Adventurous Training Group, Aldershot. They also helped me in getting around Aldershot, and were gracious in their treatment of the curious U.S. Army officer who wanted to know all about their Corps.

Mr. Jim Pearson, a former Physical Training Corps NCO and Honorary Curator of the Royal Army Physical Training Corps Museum, proved to be perhaps the best source of material I could have hoped for. He gave unstintingly of his time, guided me around the school (despite his being aged over 80, I was sweating while trying to keep up with him), and allowed me unfettered access to all of his materials. His tour of the museum gave me an appreciation for the history and proud traditions of the Corps, and put into context the sometimes disjointed material I had accumulated. Most importantly for me, Mr. Pearson made me copies of original documents, and found for me the only extant original typescript copies of the Staff's War History, reports produced during the First World War, and the original correspondence associated with those documents. I cannot adequately express my thanks to Jim for his trust and kind assistance.

Finally, I would like to thank my wife and children. My wife has supported my fascination with the history of the British Army for almost thirty years, and has been the most important person in pushing me through the endurance race that completing this project has become. She is my life. My children have grown up around this document—they are probably unsure what their father will be like when it is no longer a daily part of our lives.

COLONEL J.D. CAMPBELL
August 2011
Tampa, FL

"Vitaï Lampada"

There's a breathless hush in the Close to-night --
Ten to make and the match to win --
A bumping pitch and a blinding light,
An hour to play and the last man in.
And it's not for the sake of a ribboned coat,
Or the selfish hope of a season's fame,
But his Captain's hand on his shoulder smote --
"Play up! play up! and play the game!"

The sand of the desert is sodden red --
Red with the wreck of a square that broke; --
The Gatling's jammed and the Colonel dead,
And the regiment blind with dust and smoke.
The river of death has brimmed his banks,
And England's far, and Honour a name,
But the voice of a schoolboy rallies the ranks:
"Play up! play up! and play the game!"

This is the word that year by year,
While in her place the School is set
Every one of her sons must hear,
And none that hears it dare forget.
This they all with joyful mind
Bear through life like a torch in flame,
And falling fling to the host behind --
"Play up! play up! and play the game!"

Sir Henry Newbolt

Introduction

July 1, 1916, dawned sunny and hot in Flanders, with a thick haze of smoke and dust from the Allied artillery barrage that had been blasting the German lines for seven straight days. The deafening roar of cannon fire heralded the beginning of the Somme offensive, the baptism by fire of Britain's New Armies. The million volunteers of this force had flocked to the colors to replace the original, professional British Expeditionary Force (BEF), the "Old Contemptibles" who had been all but wiped out in the bloody combat of 1914–1915. In the early morning hours of that day, Britain's mostly untested infantry battalions waited to advance, crammed shoulder to shoulder in the first-line trenches. Officers and NCOs gave last-minute instructions and motivational speeches to their soldiers, in all likelihood partly to gear up the men and partly to prepare themselves for the experience that lay ahead. In one of those battalions, the 8th Battalion, East Surrey Regiment, those preparations took a somewhat different form: Captain W.P. Neville, a company commander in the East Surreys, had set up a contest among his four platoons. He issued each platoon a football, purchased on his last London leave, and offered a prize to the first platoon to kick its football into the German front lines after going "over the top." A survivor of that day's fighting recalled zero hour:

> As the gun-fire died away I saw an infantryman climb onto the parapet into No-Man's Land, beckoning the others to follow. As he did so, he kicked off a football. A good kick. The ball rose and traveled towards the German lines. That seemed to be the signal to advance.

That kick-off was most probably made by either Captain Neville or one of his platoon commanders. Captain Neville was killed immediately after leaving his trench, but two of his company's footballs survived, and are preserved today in English museums. A monument was later erected at the Somme to commemorate this feat of military athleticism, and the celebrated military artist Richard Caton Woodville immortalized the event in his painting *The Surreys Play the Game.*[1]

---

[1]   Paul Fussell, *The Great War and Modern Memory* (New York: Oxford University Press, 1975), pp. 27–28. This incident is also referred to in Modris Eksteins, *Rites of Spring: The Great War and the Birth of the Modern Age* (New York: Anchor Books, 1989), p. 124.

Historians and writers who repeat accounts of this well-known episode use it as an example of the innocence of the pre-1916 British Army, the amateurish delight of citizen soldiers at the prospect of going off to glorious war. This incident also serves as a metaphor for the end of the Victorian Age, an age, like the soldiers at the Somme, about to be consumed in the inferno of the First World War. But this incident, and others like it,[2] also highlights for many the unrealistic, almost ridiculous approach to war of the contemporary British Army, and allows observers of the period one more opportunity to shake their heads at the unprofessional, aristocratic British officer corps—"The Donkeys"—who were more concerned with horses, drinking, and sport than with the modern application of military science.[3] Any officer, so the familiar line goes, so obsessed with games that he would consider as proper military leadership the ludicrous act of starting a major attack by kicking a football must be totally out of his element, and the widespread stories and reports of incidents similar to this one in the first years of the war only serve to confirm for many the backward state of British military thinking and leadership. A sports-mad, upper-class officer corps, unconcerned with modern training and doctrine, hopelessly bound up in the conservative traditions of the mid-nineteenth century, is how the British Army's leadership is most often portrayed in accounts not only of the First World War but of the years before as well, leading all the way back to the Charge of the Light Brigade.

Is this an accurate assessment of the "contemptible little army," as it was described by the German Emperor William II?[4] Had Britain's preoccupation with Kipling's "flannelled fools" and "the muddied oafs at the goals" and the cult of athleticism led to an army woefully unprepared for "modern" war? Clearly, the answer to these questions is no. The BEF that arrived in France in 1914 was,

---

[2]   Other, similar incidents are described by Fussell in *The Great War and Modern Memory*. I am indebted to Miss Sylvia Nash of Aldershot, England, editor and writer for the British Army sports newspaper *Scoreline*, for these accounts: On September 25, 1915, at the Battle of Loos, the London Irish Rifles passed a football between them on their way across No Man's Land, and on the first day of the Somme campaign the 16th Battalion, Northumberland Fusiliers left their trenches following a high-kicked rugby ball. Some of these stories may be apocryphal, but their prevalence and contemporary acknowledgment lend them an air of credibility.

[3]   The most glaring example of this kind of portrayal is, of course, Alan Clark's *The Donkeys* (London: Random House UK [New Edition], 1992). Another popular version of this story is contained in Barbara Tuchman's *The Guns of August* (New York: The Macmillan Co., 1962). Even in more balanced accounts such as in Lyn Macdonald's books *1914* (New York: Atheneum, 1988) and *1915, The Death of Innocence* (Baltimore, MD: Johns Hopkins University Press, 1993) there is a tendency toward presenting this view of the Army's senior leaders.

[4]   Anthony Livesey, *Great Battles of World War I* (London: Marshall Editions Ltd., 1989), p. 14.

as a contemporary described it, the best army ever to leave Britain,[5] and the effect that army had in the opening months of the war was far beyond that which its small size would have suggested. Not only did the "Old Contemptibles" make their mark on the war, but their heirs in the New Armies and Territorials who replaced them throughout 1915 and 1916 managed to take on for the Allies the brunt of the fighting in France and outside Europe for the rest of the war, after revolution withdrew Russia from the fighting, and Verdun and the Nivelle Offensive made the French Army an unsure partner.

Rather than sport having a negative effect on the readiness of the British Army, the physical culture that evolved in the Army after 1860 made a significant contribution to military effectiveness. Moreover, the operation of the Army's sport and physical training schemes provide strong indicators of growing officer professionalism and concern with proper training throughout the period from the end of the Crimean War to 1920. From its origins as a means of keeping the soldiers from drink and the officers from duty, between 1860 and 1920 physical culture in the British Army developed into a systematic, institutionalized form of combat-oriented training that had its own published doctrine and regulations, and a proponent agency embodied in the Army Gymnastic Staff (later the Army Physical Training Staff). As early as 1865 the Queen's Regulations specified a required course of physical training to be taken by all new recruits and older soldiers, backed up by centrally trained instructors at the battalion level.[6] By the 1890s virtually all British military installations had a gymnasium or other physical training facility, and by the first decade of the twentieth century most had standard athletics fields and football and cricket pitches. All these developments were part of a deliberate program constructed by the Army hierarchy to improve the physical and spiritual wellbeing of the British soldier, enhance unit morale and *esprit de corps*, and develop individual initiative and leadership qualities. These functions were designed to contribute to a well-trained and efficient force with the fighting spirit to win Britain's wars, and parallel other efforts at modernization and professionalization that evolved simultaneously.

During the First World War the pre-war schemes of physical training and command-sponsored games acted as a powerful means of assimilating civilian–soldiers, and then ensured that they were physically and mentally prepared for the rigors of fighting, from Mesopotamia to Ypres. The sports programs of the pre-war Army continued to expand, contributing to the morale, welfare, and fighting spirit of Tommy Atkins and his imperial brethren, ensuring that they were able to stay the course and continue the fight until the Armistice in 1918.

---

[5]   Tuchman, *The Guns of August*, p. 202.
[6]   Orders published in the *London Times*, Thursday, May 11, 1865.

These same programs had been used since the middle of the nineteenth century to improve the military effectiveness of Britain's imperial troops, and to inculcate them with the same ethos of athleticism that was a seminal part of the British Army's philosophy of training and leadership. The bonds thus forged by this common set of values helped unify and homogenize the otherwise potentially disparate partners of the Commonwealth Forces.

The story of the development of British Army sport and physical training between 1860 and 1920 is inextricably tied to the larger story of the late Victorian and Edwardian Army itself. That saga is essentially one of a continuing process of reform and modernization, sometimes a fight against entrenched and seemingly insurmountable obstacles, including those of public apathy or enmity, a conservative hierarchy and government penury.[7] These efforts at reform were overwhelmingly successful. Most historians of the Army in the sixty years prior to the Great War tend to focus on the political reformers who worked to change the Army from without, but between the Charge of the Light Brigade and the Battle of Mons the British Army also substantially transformed itself from within. In the face of not insignificant obstacles the Army changed itself from an anachronistic and frequently ineffective instrument into perhaps the best trained and most professional army in the world.[8]

The role of military physical culture in that process of remaking the Army is only a small piece of the whole, but a critical one. The recognition of the importance of physical fitness for combat readiness and soldier welfare came early on in the post-Crimean War period, and so the establishment of formal physical training programs was one of the earliest manifestations of this reform movement. The growing interest in scientific training methods that resulted in successive updates to doctrinal literature and regulations throughout the period was evidenced early on in the wholesale adoption of the physical training scheme. Moreover, the contemporary debate surrounding the type and extent of physical training is closely related to debates over everything from recruitment, length of service, and overseas postings, to education, race relations in the Empire, and national image.[9]

---

[7] For an excellent synopsis of the problems and reforms within the late Victorian army, see Brian Bond, "The Late Victorian Army," *History Today* Vol. II No. 9 (Sept. 1961), pp. 616–624. A more comprehensive work outlining the reforms and general civil–military relations during the Victorian period is Edward M. Spiers, *The Army and Society, 1815–1914* (London: Longman Group Ltd., 1980).

[8] Livesey, *Great Battles of World War I*, p. 14.

[9] See Edward M. Spiers, *The Late Victorian Army* (Manchester: Manchester University Press, 1992), for a detailed discussion of these questions—the recruitment problem was perhaps the single most troublesome one for the Army during this period, and virtually all debate concerning reform touched on it. For the relationship between recruiting and physical training, see Lieutenant Colonel A.A. Woodhull, "Recruiting and Physical Training

Though considered by the Army leadership from the beginning as a component of physical training, Army sport has a distinctly different set of circumstances from those of formal physical training that surround its adoption and widespread popularity. The story of Army sport is but a chapter in the story of the explosion of sport and leisure pastimes in late nineteenth-century Britain. Many social currents acted on and contributed to the development of Army sport, including public-school athleticism, working-class leisure, traditional upper-class sporting pastimes, and the growth of amateur and professional sporting leagues and associations in Britain. Army teams were among the charter members of the Football Association and the Rugby Football Union, and the first Army Superintendent of Gymnasia was one of the founders of the English Amateur Athletic Association.[10] The role of sport and games in the late Victorian Army was a much more hotly debated topic in civilian and military circles, and sport was never as widely accepted as an element of the army's preparation for war as was formal physical training; the debate over the proper place of sport and games in military training continues today, in the British Army and elsewhere.[11]

This book will do two primary things. First, it will document the origins and development of institutional physical training in the late Victorian Army, and the ways in which the Army's gymnastic training evolved into what by 1918 was viewed as perhaps the most important building block of the process of making a civilian into a fighting man. Second, it will assess the nature and extent of British military sport, particularly regimental sports, during this period and into the First World War. Each of these areas is quite closely related. As the responsible agency for physical training, the Army Gymnastic Staff played a large role not only in fostering sport and games, but through its trained instructors it organized and coached unit teams, arranged tournaments and sports days, and assisted in the construction of pitches and grounds. Both sport and formal physical training have similar dynamics regarding officer education, officer-enlisted relations, regional variations, and doctrinal bases. And both of

---

in the British Army," *The Journal of the Military Service Institution of the United States* Vol. 16 (1895), pp. 37–47.

[10]   Lieutenant Colonel E.A.L. Oldfield, *History of the Army Physical Training Corps* (Aldershot: Gale and Polden Ltd., 1955), p. 4. Here again I am indebted to Miss Sylvia Nash for providing me with the proofs of her unpublished work on the history of Army Rugby, in which she outlines the founding of the Rugby Union and discusses the role of teams from Army units, most particularly the Royal Engineers, in the early years of that body.

[11]   Tony Mason and Eliza Riedi's excellent new book, *Sport and the Military: The British Armed Forces 1880–1960* (Cambridge: Cambridge University Press, 2010), deals with the subject of sport alone. It does not include the other pillar of military physical culture, formal physical training, in its central analysis of the often controversial influence of sport in the British Army and Navy.

these areas had a symbiotic relationship to Army reform during this period. The genesis of scientific physical training lies at the root of the movement for reform itself, and the success and expansion of both physical training and sport in driving up the morale, health, and overall effectiveness of the Army acted as a catalyst for continued innovation and reform.

A complete examination of British Army physical culture, including both physical training and sport, provides more than just a window into important movements within the British military. Because of the important social and cultural position held by the British Army in the late Victorian and Edwardian period, through such an examination one can also gain a greater understanding for the ways in which British society influenced the military and vice versa. Sport, games, and physical training in the British Army between 1860 and 1920 were a crucial part of training and modernizing the military, and their nature and practice clearly suggest that a country's military, at any given period, is a fundamental reflection of that country's society.

PART I

Mens Sana in Corpore Sano: The Origins of the Army Gymnastic Staff and Regimental Sport, 1860–1880

Chapter 1

Officer Sport: Aristocrats and Schoolboys

I am sure that I am not exaggerating when I say that whether at cricket, boating, boxing, hunting, racing, shooting with rifle or gun, we invariably held our own. ... We suffered under one grievous misfortune ... we never in my time, excepting in the rebellion in Ceylon, were engaged in any campaign. We have fought with every kind of wild animals, but never with human beings.

Johnson Wilkinson, East Yorkshire Regiment (15th Foot)[1]

Being a good sportsman, a good cricketer, good at rackets or any other manly game, is no mean recommendation for staff employment. Such a man, without book lore, is preferable to the most deeply-read one of lethargic habits.

Colonel Garnet Wolseley (later Field Marshal Viscount Wolseley, Commander-in-Chief of the British Army), 1869[2]

During the nineteenth century and well into the twentieth century, British Army officers were of primarily upper-class origins, with a majority coming from landed families. Those officers not coming from such a background quickly conformed to the social mold of their peers, or were ostracized and, more often than not, hounded into leaving the service. These facts have been well established in numerous detailed demographic studies of the Victorian and Edwardian officer corps.[3] With the officer corps firmly rooted in the social and cultural traditions of the rural upper class, it would naturally follow that the values and pastimes of that class would dominate the British officer corps, and they did. One of these class characteristics that dominated the life of the British officer was a passion

---

[1]   Byron Farwell, *Mr. Kipling's Army* (New York: W.W. Norton & Co., 1981), p. 203.

[2]   From Colonel Garnet Wolseley, *The Soldier's Pocket-Book for Field Service* (1869), quoted in Byron Farwell, *Eminent Victorian Soldiers* (New York: W.W. Norton & Co., 1985), p. 206.

[3]   Several excellent works cover the subject of officer demographics, pastimes, and social proclivities in great detail, most notably Gwyn Harries-Jenkins, *The Army in Victorian Society* (London: Routledge & Kegan Paul, 1977), and Edward M. Spiers, *The Late Victorian Army* (Manchester: Manchester University Press, 1992). Additionally, see Farwell, *Mr. Kipling's Army*.

for sport—mainly field sports and competitive games. This passion was a major factor in the Army's decision to institute a formal physical training program, and is a primary reason for sport and physical training becoming so widely embraced as integral aspects of training in the late Victorian Army.

Field sports—hunting, fishing, shooting, horse racing—are occupations traditionally practiced by the European upper classes. In many respects these pastimes largely defined the rural upper classes in Britain before the world wars. Major estates were maintained at great expense solely for the purposes of sport, with the owners of these estates spending enormous sums of money to manage and record hunting pursuits and provide for small armies of gamekeepers, stables of horses, packs of hounds, and even "Earth Stoppers," men who were employed to see to the maintenance and wellbeing of fox lairs and new litters of pups within the estate.[4] Sport has been viewed by historians as a significant means of fostering upper-class identity and unity, and these elements of sport clearly apply to nineteenth-century Britain's overwhelmingly gentry-derived officer corps.

For centuries, field sports and athletic pursuits have been associated with the profession of arms. Many of these sports originated as means of military training, and so have enjoyed an accepted place in the lives of warriors down to the present day. These pastimes, however, occupied a place so central in the lives of Victorian British Army officers that it is in some respects difficult for us to fathom today. The average officer spent the vast majority of his time occupied with sport, more so than any other single activity, to include his military duties. The pursuit of sport, even during wartime, had a long history in the British Army: it was a widespread practice among the officers of the Peninsular Army to maintain personal and unit packs of hounds. Wellington himself kept a pack of hounds until his dogs and his huntsmen were captured by the French.[5] Some regiments maintained packs of hounds that followed them from posting to posting, following the tradition maintained by their forebears in the Peninsular Campaign. The Green Howard Hounds were an Army institution, started just after the Indian Mutiny and lasting for nearly a century.[6] Outside the unit hunts, the imperial community maintained hunt clubs across the Empire. In addition to numerous clubs in Ireland, such clubs as the Peshawar Vale Hunt Club in India and the Cape Foxhounds in South Africa were well established and extremely popular. General Sir Evelyn Wood said that he normally hunted forty-six days

---

[4]   F.M.L. Thompson, *English Landed Society in the Nineteenth Century* (London: Routledge and Kegan Paul, 1963).

[5]   Farwell, *Mr. Kipling's Army*, p. 206.

[6]   Ibid., p. 206.

per year, but due to his "heavy work load" during the South African War he was only able to hunt twelve times that year.[7]

Another officer recorded in his diary kept during that war,

> a prodigious slaughter of fowl, buck, antelope and Cape Buffalo when he was based at Naauwpoort, regular hunting with the Cape Foxhounds at Wynberg, and 140 days of polo in South Africa: "What with polo three days a week, and hunting three days, and a shoot on Sundays, I managed to keep myself pretty fit!"[8]

Officers were afforded ample opportunity to indulge their passion for sport because of the prodigious amount of leave time available to them. These men were granted leave in a way that would seem astounding to an army officer of today. Officers could be granted leave for sometimes six months or more during the year, and they also had the option of going on half pay for any length of time to tend to personal business or for other reasons, such as to serve in the government. Commanders would routinely authorize extended leaves for the purposes of hunting or other sporting activities, and actively encourage subordinates to engage in sport and games, even while on active service.[9] Hunting could supplement the meager fare available to soldiers in more remote stations within the Empire, and aside from this rather obvious function, most officers saw sport as a way to alleviate boredom and promote good health.

Officers especially took advantage of this liberal leave policy in Ireland. Ireland was for many a posting where the average officer had little to do but play games and engage in field sports. There it would appear that most of these men did almost nothing but ride to hounds, fish, and attend race meetings. Reflecting on his Irish service in the early 1880s, Sir Edward May fondly remembered the regimental races, hunting, and cricket: "Such sport I have never had before or since."[10] Major General J.F.C. Fuller recalled of his time at the Curragh, "it was a delightful life, mostly duck shooting and hunting in the winter, and tennis and cricket in the summer."[11] In his *Personal Adventures and Anecdotes*, retired Colonel J.P. Robertson relates the history of his time in Ireland before the Crimean War as a pleasant series of social engagements, yachting trips, and fishing expeditions, only occasionally disturbed by civil unrest. He admits that,

---

7   Ibid., p. 206.

8   Lieutenant Edward Longueville, quoted in Spiers, *The Late Victorian Army*, p. 97.

9   For details on leave, see the works referenced in note 3 above. I will address leave and its relation to sporting activities in the context of professional development further on.

10   Spiers, *The Late Victorian Army*, p. 219.

11   Ibid., p. 107.

while stationed at Enniskillen, he only attended to his military duties every other day, as on alternate days he was busily occupied with salmon fishing.[12]

Even more so than Ireland, India was the true military sportsman's paradise. Officers posted to India could look forward to a strong likelihood of participation in combat operations, and reaped the benefits of a much lower cost of living than that in either Ireland or England. The primary attraction of India, however, was sport. Lieutenant General Adrian Carton de Wiart thought India tawdry. Full of "revolting smells and noises," its only attraction was that he knew it to be "a wonderful centre for sport."[13] Most memoirs and regimental journals provide a vision of the officer's life in India that centered almost exclusively on sport. As Johnson Wilkinson, an officer in the East Yorkshire Regiment recalled,

> I am sure that I am not exaggerating when I say that whether at cricket, boating, boxing, hunting, racing, shooting with rifle or gun, we invariably held our own. ... We suffered under one grievous misfortune ... we never in my time, excepting in the rebellion in Ceylon, were engaged in any campaign. We have fought with every kind of wild animals, but never with human beings.[14]

The time spent planning, participating in, and recording sporting exploits would certainly suggest that officers were full-time athletes and sportsmen, and only part-time soldiers. Winston Churchill, describing his first trip to India as a subaltern in the 4th Hussars, said that, after making suitable living arrangements, he and his fellows in the regiment were able to devote themselves to "the serious purpose of life. This was expressed in one word—Polo." Churchill states that the officers of the 4th Hussars spent more time on polo than on any other activity, with the possible exception of "duty."[15]

Lieutenant General Lord Baden-Powell's memoirs of his service in India are largely taken up with accounts of his sporting activities, primarily polo and pigsticking. He was also an avid big game hunter, and spent a large part of his career on various shooting expeditions in Africa and India. According to Baden-Powell, when posted to India his regimental duties occupied an infinitesimal

---

[12]   Colonel J.P. Robertson, *Personal Adventures and Anecdotes of an Old Officer* (London: Edward Arnold, 1906), p. 132. See also General Sir Alexander Godley, *Life of an Irish Soldier* (New York: E.P. Dutton & Co., Inc., 1939). Godley's memoirs are full of his sporting exploits in Ireland, with many fascinating photographs of various hunts and shooting parties.

[13]   Farwell, *Mr. Kipling's Army*, p. 208.

[14]   Ibid. p. 203.

[15]   Winston S. Churchill, *A Roving Commission: My Early Life* (New York: Charles Scribner's Sons, 1930), p. 106.

amount of time compared to that spent on sport, and he argues that time spent hunting or playing polo was far more valuable for his career than that spent on his relatively minimal regimental duties. His advocacy of the outdoorsman's life and the sporting ethic would be incorporated as an integral element in the scouting movement he founded, and all of the various books and pamphlets he wrote for Boy Scout consumption are peppered with anecdotes and lessons from his hunting and outdoor experiences.[16]

Regiments and individual officers in India kept detailed records of their hunting expeditions and their "bags": the game books and hunt club records of some units record a vast destruction of native fauna that would be unthinkable, if not impossible, today. The 2nd Battalion Gordon Highlanders game book from their time in India between January 1902 and December 1912 records that officers shot:

> 674 big game of thirty-six species, including three elephants, six tigers, twelve panthers and eighty-four boars. They also shot 27,293 small game, including 4,256 pigeons, 7,549 ducks and 9,354 snipe. The officer with the "best bag" killed ninety-nine head of big game of twenty-five species in four and a half years.[17]

Service in Africa was also a prime opportunity for many officers to engage in sport. Although more recently colonized and therefore more primitive, the sporting promise of Africa was well recognized by many Victorian soldiers. The wide variety of terrain, climate, and fauna was conducive to a full range of sporting activities, from hunting with the Cape Foxhounds, to snipe hunting in Tunisia, and hippopotamus and elephant hunting in Kenya. Baden-Powell, in *Sport in War*, describes a series of exciting encounters with lions during his service in the Matebeleland campaign. While on various scouting missions in hostile territory, he thought nothing of suspending operations for as much as a full day to track, shoot, and skin lions. He always made a special point of allowing his bearers to take parts of the lion for medicinal and shamanistic purposes.[18] General Sir Alexander Godley described in his memoirs "great sport" hunting jackals with

---

[16]   See Sir Robert Baden-Powell, *Indian Memories* (London: Herbert Jenkins Ltd., 1915). Baden-Powell's other works that fall into this category are far too numerous to list here.

[17]   Farwell, *Mr. Kipling's Army*, p. 207. These game books and hunt club records are a fascinating window into the life of the late nineteenth-century Empire. Many of these documents exist both in regimental museums and at the National Army Museum in London. The enormous amount of game killed by British officers alone leads one to wonder that there is any animal life left in India at all.

[18]   Lieutenant General R.S.S. Baden-Powell, *Sport in War* (Toronto: George Morang & Co., 1900).

the regimental hounds during his service under Wolseley in Rhodesia. Godley's account of that campaign is strongly colored by his wonder at the amount and variety of game available for shooting in the region, as well as his concern for the care and training of the regimental hounds.[19]

These sporting activities continued well into the First World War, often causing bewilderment and consternation among friend and foe alike. French and German soldiers thought this British attachment to sport archaic, unmilitary, and even immature.[20] Yet despite censure from allies and ridicule from enemies, the King's officers persisted in behavior that they firmly believed set them at a level far above that of their detractors. In December 1914, the Northumberland Hussars organized a pack of hounds at Steenwerck, and "meetings were as frequent as 'the exigencies of the Service' permitted." King Edward's Horse, while acting as infantry in 1915, had a pack of beagles smuggled across the Channel to them under the tutelage of a famous huntsman, George Heasman, attached from the 3rd Hussars. Heasman's dedication to his craft was legendary, and he and his pack are the subject of many humorous anecdotes. On one occasion, Heasman and his pack were:

> toiling through the mud on a cold scent, just forward of a field battery, at the moment when one of its guns elected to "poop off." With the bang of the discharge, down went the beagle's sterns and off they bolted into the thickening mist, heading for every point of the compass. It was then that the outraged little Hussar rose up in his wrath, to demand of the peccant Battery Commander, "How *dare* you make that damned noise when my hounds are running?"—a blazing irrelevance which would have brought a grim smile even to the lips of the Iron Duke himself.

These sporting proclivities were not unique to cavalrymen. In 1917 the First Battalion Royal Fusiliers had a well-known pack, under the care of their Transport Officer, Captain Jack Weston. The British enthusiasm for sport around Ploegsteert Wood in Belgium caused the authorities to post a sign there

---

[19]   Godley, *Life of an Irish Soldier*, pp. 38–58.

[20]   Lionel Dawson, an Englishman, acknowledged this view of British behavior: "To the foreigner the Englishman's methods of enjoying himself, or of participating in war, had always been as incomprehensible as his refusal to be perturbed by adverse circumstances." Dawson, however, argues that this sportsman's mentality within the British officer corps produces more "gallant and confident leadership" than any other army in the world: Lionel Dawson, *Sport in War* (London: Collins, 1936), pp. 13–16.

in 1915 that read: "In future machine guns must not be employed to shoot hares in No-Man's-Land."[21]

In addition to hunting and shooting, officers enthusiastically took to team games, especially cricket, football, and polo. These games each held similar attractions to those of field sports. Cricket is an ancient and revered game with origins deeply rooted in rural England, and so was a familiar and traditional game for the upper-class officer. Football, especially Rugby football, demands a high degree of fitness and agility, as well as a large amount of physical courage and teamwork, all desirable qualities for a soldier. Polo combines these aspects of football with the requirement for skilled horsemanship, another requisite attribute for both the rural gentry and the nineteenth-century soldier. Additionally, the expensive requirement for a string of ponies lent polo an air of exclusivity that was attractive to the more snobbishly inclined officers, particularly those in the cavalry.

Polo was extremely popular during the late nineteenth century, especially in India. A British officer, Lieutenant (later Major General) John F. Sherer, is generally credited with the development of modern polo in India during the 1850s.[22] The first Indian matches with English participants have been variously reported as occurring in 1859 and 1862.[23] From modest beginnings, this game became incredibly popular, spreading like wildfire through the cavalry regiments and even into some infantry regiments. In 1913 the polo team of infantrymen from the Northumberland Fusiliers posted impressive victories against teams from the 14th Hussars and local Indian clubs, while losing to the civilian Bhopal club in the Mhow Gymkhana.[24]

Polo was brought to every corner of the Empire by enthusiastic soldiers, and its introduction in England has been variously credited to the 10th Hussars and to the 11th Hussars. An account of the first game in England played by members of the 11th Hussars at Aldershot in 1870 tells how "contestants rode their ordinary chargers and hockey sticks were used to belt an ordinary billiards ball rather aimlessly from one end of the ground to the other."[25] Described by

---

21 All of the abovementioned anecdotes from the First World War are contained in Reginald Hargreaves, "Divertissement," *The Cavalry Journal* Vol. 31 (Jan–Nov 1941), pp. 204–225.

22 Horatio A. Laffaye in *The Encyclopedia of World Sport*, 3 vols., ed. David Levinson and Karen Christensen (Santa Barbara, CA: ABC-CLIO, 1996), II, p. 758.

23 These two dates come from Hargreaves, "Divertissement" and Baden-Powell, *Indian Memories*, p. 32 respectively.

24 *St. George's Gazette, Journal of the Northumberland Fusiliers* Vol. 31 No. 362 (February 28, 1913).

25 Laffaye, *The Encyclopedia of World Sport*, II, p. 758. Also Hargreaves, "Divertissement."

Baden-Powell as "the finest game that has ever been invented,"[26] polo in the Army received official sanction from the Prince of Wales and the Commander-in-Chief, the Duke of Cambridge, in 1872.[27] From 1878 regular inter-regimental tournaments were held, at least up until the outbreak of the Second World War.[28] By the late nineteenth century it is possible that polo was by far the most popular sport among army officers, and certainly so among cavalrymen.

Winston Churchill, while a subaltern with the 4th Hussars in India, was once inspired after an inter-regimental tournament to give a speech on polo to a crowded officer's mess. There "he proceeded to show how it was not merely the finest game in the world, but the most noble and soul-inspiring contest in the whole universe," which earned him a standing ovation. After the cheering died down, however, "one in authority arose and gave voice to the feelings of all when he said, 'Well, that is enough of Winston this evening.'" Churchill was then subdued by his brother officers and pushed under an overturned couch with two large lieutenants sitting on it to keep him quiet. He quickly escaped, though, with the comment, "It's no use sitting on me, I'm India rubber," a statement he managed to repeatedly prove valid even after his polo playing days were long past.[29]

Cricket's widespread popularity among officers began in the 1860s,[30] but military matches had been played between Army and Navy officers as early as 1802.[31] Reports of cricket matches at Lords between Guards officers and members of the House of Commons and with members of other regiments occupy a large share of the text of early volumes of the *Journal of the Household Brigade*. A cursory reading of one of these volumes leaves the impression that Guards officers, when not involved with social dinners, hunts, or horse racing, were entirely occupied with either playing or watching cricket matches. Rare indeed was the regiment that did not have an eleven composed of officers and the occasional enlisted soldier, even before the period covered by this study.

Team games and field sports in the officer corps went beyond being mere leisure pastimes. They were professionally important as well. The social aspects of sport and games could have an important bearing on a man's career, both in

---

26   Baden-Powell, *Indian Memories*, p. 32.

27   Hargreaves, "Divertissement."

28   Records of these and virtually all other Army sporting events are contained in *Army Sport Records, 1880–1939* (published by the Army Sport Control Board, War Office, 1939). I also make this statement based on the dates of various regimental polo books (9th Lancers, 1883–1950, 1st Bn the Suffolk Regiment, 1883–1931) and the list of the Indian Cavalry Polo Tournament Nominees and Runners–up (1883–1939) in the archives of the National Army Museum.

29   Baden-Powell, *Indian Memories*, pp. 35–36.

30   Hargreaves, "Divertissement."

31   Eric Parker, *The History of Cricket* (London: Seely Service & Co. Ltd., 1950), p. 222.

Figure 1.1   Polo Tournament, Secunderabad, c.1897 (courtesy of the Council
of the National Army Museum, London)

the Army and outside it. Race meetings, hunts, and test matches were gathering
places for upper-class society, and as members of that society these opportunities
for officers to mingle and establish networks of friends were crucial. The social
and professional importance of sport is indicated in *The Journal of the Household
Brigade*'s 1876 volume. This journal catered to the elite of the officer corps, and
this particular volume contains nineteen sections; of those, eight deal entirely
with sporting topics, and of the remaining eleven only four deal with what could
be described as purely "military" subjects. The rest cover social activities other
than sport.[32] Even as late as 1906, the April number of *The Black Horse Gazette*,
journal of the 7th (Princess Royal's) Dragoon Guards, devoted more than half
of the issue to covering sport, games and athletics: four pages of this sporting
coverage consisted of accounts of race meetings, polo matches, and an article
describing the East Kent Fox Hounds.[33]

---

[32]   *Journal of the Household Brigade*, 1876.
[33]   *The Black Horse Gazette, Journal of the 7th (Princess Royal's) Dragoon Guards*,
Vol. IV (April 1906).

Clearly, not only was sport the major interest of most officers: after the abolition of purchase in 1870, the success of an officer's career often depended on his attachment to it. Lord Baden-Powell saw his participation in polo and pigsticking outings as an important means of furthering his promotion prospects,[34] and the fact that comments could be made on an officer's efficiency reports like "a good man to hounds"[35] suggests that sport was far more than a pleasant diversion to many. An officer's place in society, his relationship to senior officers, his connections, relatives, and friends, all could influence promotion, duty assignments, and whether or not he would see active service. Therefore sport, as the single most important social activity of officers, could often be just as, if not more, important to career progression as garrison duty performance.

This passion for sport and games had other roots beside the traditions of the landowning gentry. Officers were not only primarily members of the rural upper classes, but as a corollary to that membership they were almost to a man products of public schools. As former schoolboys they were naturally subject to the cult of games and athleticism that stemmed from nineteenth-century British public schools.[36] This obsession with games carried over into their lives as officers, and was one of the most central factors in the development of late Victorian Army sport.

Much has been written about the cult of games in Victorian Britain. The effects of this upper- and middle-class obsession with athleticism were far reaching—from the use of sport and games to assist in British cultural proselytization across the Empire, to the effect of athleticism in de-emphasizing academics and thereby eroding Britain's competitive edge in technology and industry.[37] The debate over the cult of games within the Army is no different. Games were seen alternately as essential to the maintenance of a superior corps of leaders, and as a pernicious and unprofessional obstacle to military efficiency.[38] As products of the public schools, officers were as a group perhaps

---

[34]   Tim Jeal, *The Boy-Man: The Life of Lord Baden-Powell* (New York: Wm. Morrow & Co., 1990), pp. 111–113. Jeal describes young Baden-Powell's joy at being asked to various social occasions due to his prowess at pigsticking, and clearly points out the professional implications of this rise in social status.

[35]   Farwell, *Mr. Kipling's Army*, p. 72.

[36]   For the connection between Army officers and the public schools, see Jeal, *The Boy-Man*, chapter 3; Farwell, *Mr. Kipling's Army*; Spiers, *The Late Victorian Army*; and Harries-Jenkins, *The Army in Victorian Society*.

[37]   The two best treatments of the cult of games in Victorian Britain are books by J.A. Mangan: *Athleticism in the Victorian and Edwardian Public School* (Cambridge: Cambridge University Press, 1981) and *The Games Ethic and Imperialism* (New York: Viking, 1986).

[38]   See Tony Mason and Eliza Riedi, *Sport and the Military: The British Armed Forces 1880–1960* (Cambridge: Cambridge University Press, 2010), chapter 2, for a detailed

more influenced by athleticism than most other comparable groups in British society. Most officers went directly from the school to Sandhurst, where the public-school atmosphere held sway well into the last century, and then into the relatively closed, all-male environment of the regiment.[39] This progression (or lack thereof) tended, for most officers, to make the atmosphere of the mess a mere continuation of the public-school experience.[40] The enforced closeness of the regiment, and the conservative values and mores of the officers' mess all contributed to a powerful carry-over of public-school attitudes and traditions into Army life. The very close relationship between sports, the public-school culture of athleticism, and the Army is brought into sharp relief in the famous Sir Henry Newbolt poem "Vitaï Lampada," where images of a schoolboy cricket match and the battle of Abu Clea in the Sudanese desert are intertwined with the exhortation to "Play Up and Play the Game."

This heavy public-school influence was manifest in many ways. Hazing, pranks, and strong peer pressure for conformity within the mess were continuations of elements of public-school life that made the officer corps more homogeneous, and contributed to both its strengths and weaknesses. The aversion to serious study and a "tradesmanlike" approach to the profession were attitudes derived from the public school, and detracted significantly from efforts to increase officer professionalism throughout this period.[41] On the positive side, the deep camaraderie and boyish, at times almost fanatical lack of physical fear that characterized a striking number of contemporary British officers have roots in this school-influenced atmosphere of the mess.

Knowledge of the central role the games ethic played in officer culture is critical to an understanding of why sport and physical training became so crucial to the late Victorian Army. Aside from the social importance of sport and games for officers, these men carried with them into the Army their fundamental belief in the value of sport and games for building character and "manliness." Strong character and physical prowess were then, and still are, generally accepted as essential parts of the successful combat leader's makeup, and so it followed that

---

examination of officer sport and its critics.

[39] Many contemporary accounts of life at Sandhurst reflect this public school atmosphere, most notably Winston Churchill's. For a good history and general description of life at Sandhurst in the Victorian period, see Hugh Thomas, *The Story of Sandhurst* (London: Hutchinson & Co., 1961).

[40] Jeal, *The Boy-Man*, chapter 3.

[41] See Brian Bond, "The Late Victorian Army," *History Today* Vol. II No. 9 (Sept. 1961), pp. 616–624, and Jay Luvaas, *The Education of an Army: British Military Thought, 1815–1940* (Chicago, IL: University of Chicago Press, 1964). Luvaas discusses efforts to increase professionalism and modernize training and doctrine, and makes reference to these public-school attitudes as obstacles.

games and sport would be seen as crucial to the professional development of the British officer. It is impossible to overestimate the importance of this idea when attempting to understand the development of Victorian and Edwardian military physical culture. Officers at the highest levels of the Army firmly believed that participation in games and field sports gave young officers the essential traits required to lead British soldiers—moral and physical courage, physical fitness and mental agility, loyalty and team spirit. An active, fit officer who revels in outdoor pursuits, one who can properly function as a member of a team, and one who is willing to sublimate personal success and fame for the greater glory of the team possesses highly desirable attributes for a military leader, attributes that armies still search for and try to inculcate in their leaders today. For the purposes of understanding Victorian military physical culture, it is largely irrelevant whether or not we in the twenty-first century entirely agree with the efficacy of the ideas constituting the philosophy of athleticism; the fact is that, in the Victorian and Edwardian Army, the primary and most successful means for developing these desired leadership qualities were seen to be participation in sport and games. These pastimes, therefore, were not only viewed as important means of social indoctrination, but as some of the primary elements of officer training and development.

The contemporary literature arguing this view of sport and games is extensive, with military writers consistently pointing out the military training value of sport and games. Following a negative report of the 1902 Military Education Committee on sport in the Army, Major R.G. Burton of the Indian Army responded in *The United Services Magazine* with an article fiercely defending the military training value of games and hunting. He pointed out the importance of team games in inspiring *esprit de corps*, and "inculcating the powers of judgment and decision." He then went on to argue the usefulness of hunting in training officers for war:

> Of all sports big game hunting deserves most encouragement, for there is no recreation in which the qualities most required in war are so largely needed to ensure success, and are so prominently developed. This sport, in fact, which has been well termed the "image of war", is war in miniature.

Burton writes of the training in the use of ground, scouting, and observation gained through hunting, as well as the courage and physical stamina required. In this article, and one he published in a later issue, he even goes so far as to suggest that tiger hunting mimics the strategy and tactics used in modern combat. Fanciful, perhaps, but in his points about the training value of planning and conducting hunting expeditions Burton was certainly correct.[42] Of the warlike dangers of tiger hunting there could be no doubt: in the May 1894 issue of *The Thistle*, the journal of The Royal Scots, the lead editorial lamented the untimely passing of His Excellency Sir James Dormer, K.C.B., Commander-in-Chief of the Madras Army—the second British officer killed by a tiger since the regiment's arrival in India.[43]

In General Sir Alexander Wardrop's hunting diary he listed the detailed preparations, amounts and type of equipment and stores, and specific instructions to servants necessary to undertake various hunting and shooting expeditions in India. Wardrop's diary reads just like a military operations journal or an operations order—undeniable evidence of the military applications of hunting in the Victorian period.[44] This value was clearly recognized by those commanders who encouraged their subordinates to take leave in order to go hunting; the general lack of officer training opportunities in garrison combined with the recognized professional development aspects of sport were strong inducements for a liberal leave policy:

> When Captain John Adye, newly posted to Aldershot, asked his commanding officer, Major Thomas Studely, for leave to go hunting, he was told: "As long as there is one subaltern left in barracks to do the work on a hunting day I do not want you to ask for leave. Always go."[45]

Baden-Powell strongly believed in the value of sport as military training, particularly pigsticking and polo, those being "an exceptionally practical school for the development of horsemanship and of handiness in the use of arms while mounted."[46] In 1906, Captain R.F. Legge of the Leinster Regiment argued that:

> An officer should be alert, active, keen, resolute, resourceful and physically strong; his powers of observation quickened by special training, his fibre hardened by a rigorous course of physical exercise and active sports.

---

[42]   Major R.G. Burton, "Some Ideas on the Training of an Officer," *The United Services Magazine* Vol. 25 (new series) (1902), pp. 637–642, and "The Strategy and Tactics of Tiger Hunting," *The United Services Magazine* Vol. 28 (new series) (1903–1904), p. 402.

[43]   *The Thistle* Vol. II No. 2 (May 1894), p. 1.

[44]   "The Hunting Diary of General Sir Alexander Wardrop," unpublished, National Army Museum archives. Wardrop also authored a book on pigsticking: *Modern Pigsticking* (London: Macmillan, 1914).

[45]   Farwell, *Mr. Kipling's Army*, p. 69.

[46]   Baden-Powell, *Indian Memories*, p. 31.

He emphasized that there was no better way to conduct that "special training" than shooting and hunting.[47] As for team games, these were again seen to be invaluable training for leaders. Major A.J. Richardson stated that "proficiency at games of skill argues a well-balanced mind," and put a twist on a well-known statement by adding, "If Waterloo was not won on the playing fields of Eton, and I don't think it was, neither was Colenso lost there."[48] Finally, in a 1907 justification for retention of a more upper-class officer corps, Viscount Esher put it this way:

> If he [the officer] is rich, he can devote his day to any form of sport, or to any of those manly games, which differentiate the British regimental officer from the officers of all other armies, and for certain purposes, are invaluable training for war.[49]

Field sports and team games were not only essential ingredients in the social life of the Victorian Army officer, but they were seen as necessary and valuable elements in his training for war. That these pastimes could be used as means to build character, and could foster *esprit de corps*, teamwork, and courage, was a widespread belief and was accepted practice as early as the 1850s. The role of sport and team games in maintaining a fit and healthy officer, inured to the hardships of vigorous outdoor life, was recognized and those activities actively promoted and encouraged by the Army's leadership, often to the point of coercion. For such a fundamentally important element in the philosophy of the leadership and hierarchy of the Army to remain exclusively applied to officers was unthinkable—it was only a matter of time before those recognized benefits of sport, team games, and "rigorous physical exercise" would be applied across the entire Army. For those men interested in reforming and improving the Army after the debacle of the Crimea, those benefits would necessarily need to be provided to the men of the "other ranks."

---

[47]   Captain R.F. Legge, "Some Ideas on the Military Education of the Officer," *The United Services Magazine* Vol. 33 (1906), pp. 415–420.

[48]   Major A.J. Richardson, "That Idol—Education," *The United Services Magazine* Vol. 31 (1905), p. 545.

[49]   Viscount Esher, "A Problem in Military Education," *The United Services Magazine* Vol. 34 (1907–1908), p. 484.

Chapter 2
The Other Ranks: Health, Morals and Morale

... it is not the fault of the system that the Army hospitals are so full as they are. Fifty per cent of the cases would not be there if soldiers would manfully determine not to allow themselves to be led into excesses of ANY KIND. They would be better men physically and morally. The vicious man is never an athlete, and conversely the athlete is always a well conducted man.

Surgeon-Captain J.R. Forrest, 1896[1]

Reform—of government agencies, bureaucracy, social life, and institutions—was a rallying cry for much of liberal, middle-class Britain in the mid-nineteenth century. A dizzying number of voluntary societies, charitable associations, hospitals, schools, reading rooms, and other similar and like-minded organizations sprang up during this period with aims ranging from the emancipation of women and trades unionism to electoral reform and working-class education. Part of this mid-century liberal reforming zeal was applied to that bastion of conservatism, the Army. Given both incentive and moral fervor by the mismanagement, disease, and poor leadership within the Army during the Crimean War, reformers across the political spectrum sought to upgrade and improve the Army. These movements for reform aimed at eliminating flogging, combating the perennial "recruiting problem," restructuring Army administration and command hierarchy, abolishing the purchase system, and, most important for this study, improving the health, living conditions, and morals of the British soldier.[2]

---

[1]   Alan Ramsay Skelley, *The Victorian Army at Home: The Recruitment and Terms and Conditions of the British Regular, 1859–1899* (London: Croom Helm, 1977), p. 60.

[2]   These reforms and the political and social context in which they occurred are dealt with extensively in Skelley, *The Victorian Army at Home*; Gwyn Harries-Jenkins, *The Army in Victorian Society* (London: Routledge & Kegan Paul, 1977); Edward M. Spiers, *The Late Victorian Army* (Manchester: Manchester University Press, 1992) and *The Army and Society, 1815–1914* (London: Longman Group Ltd., 1980); Byron Farwell, *Mr. Kipling's Army* (New York: W.W. Norton & Co., 1981); and Brian Bond, "The Late Victorian Army," *History Today* Vol. II No. 9 (Sept. 1961), pp. 616–624. For more recent and detailed scholarship on reform of diet, hygiene,

The shocking reports of death from disease and infection during the Crimean War, coupled with similar revelations about mortality and disease among soldiers in peacetime garrisons, contributed to a wide range of reform efforts. Each of these was designed to improve the lot of Tommy Atkins and make him better able to fulfill his functions of Imperial policeman, enforcer of the *Pax Britannica*, and container of domestic unrest. Most of these reform efforts succeeded in some measure, but none more so than the efforts to provide the soldier with a healthy alternative to drinking and whoring, one that would make him stronger and more resistant to disease and privation, and raise his daily existence out of the doldrums of garrison life. This effort manifested itself in several ways: soldier education programs, barracks building, and refurbishing campaigns. Along with the officers' advocacy of sport, games, and physical activity, this effort was the second primary factor contributing to the adoption of a formal program of gymnastics and physical training for the Army.[3]

At the end of the Crimean War, cries for reform of the Army echoed throughout official Britain, and among the most vocal of those calling for reform was Florence Nightingale. Nightingale was, at the time, at the apex of her fame and influence, and she headed the efforts to initiate fundamental change in the Army's medical systems and in the living conditions of the soldiers. Through lobbying by Nightingale and others, most notably Mr. Sidney Herbert, the Palmerston government was induced to create the Army Sanitary Commission. The membership of this commission was largely selected by Nightingale, and it was given a mandate to investigate and recommend solutions to medical and sanitary issues brought to light during the Crimean War.[4]

---

and healthcare within the British services, see Yuriko Akiyama, *Feeding the Nation: Nutrition and Health in Britain before World War One* (London: Taurus Academic Studies, 2008), especially chapter 6.

[3] For a superb and detailed study of the problems of drinking, vice, and the health within the Army in India, see Douglas M. Peers, "Imperial Vice: Sex, Drink and the Health of British Troops in North Indian Cantonments, 1800–1858," in David Killingray and David Omissi, eds., *Guardians of Empire: The Armed Forces of the Colonial Powers c. 1700–1964* (Manchester: Manchester University Press, 1999), pp. 25–52.

[4] See F.B. Smith, *Florence Nightingale: Reputation and Power* (New York: St. Martin's Press, 1982), and Elspeth Hurley, *Florence Nightingale* (New York: G.P. Putnam's Sons, 1975). These two books offer conflicting interpretations of Nightingale and her work; Smith is more inclined to view Nightingale in the same manner as portrayed by Lytton Strachey in *Eminent Victorians* (New York: Harcourt, Brace and Co., 1918), and Hurley's view of her is far more positive. In Farwell's *Mr. Kipling's Army*, he argues that Nightingale may have even delayed significant reform through her confrontational methods that irritated the Army hierarchy and may have caused them to "dig in their heels" on sanitary and health issues.

The history of the Sanitary Commission is well known. The work of that body has been thoroughly documented, and need not be repeated here.[5] In short, the major efforts of the Commission focused on restructuring and professionalizing the Army Medical Department by raising the pay and status of Army surgeons, eliminating the regimental hospital system, and creating one uniform hospital system Army wide. The Commission also began a complete overhaul and construction program intended to create more sanitary and hygienic barracks.

This rebuilding and construction program was needed to eliminate unhealthy living conditions for soldiers that, in the years prior to the work of the Commission, were abominable. Barrack rooms were more often than not grossly overcrowded, with married soldiers' wives and children living right in the rooms among the men. Rooms were poorly ventilated or not at all—chronic shortages of wood for heating led men to keep windows more or less permanently closed. Soldiers rarely bathed, and were not given to keeping bed linen or clothing clean, and so the resultant body odor combined with the stink from open urine tubs kept in the barrack rooms made the air so foul that soldiers were sometimes overcome when they exited the barracks in the morning. On some military installations, Sanitary Commission inspectors likened barracks conditions to those of a slave ship, and some buildings were forcefully and immediately declared uninhabitable.[6]

Sanitary Commission efforts successfully eliminated the worst of these conditions: by century's end the cases of death and hospitalization from cholera, fevers, and other infectious diseases resulting from poorly ventilated, unsanitary, and vermin-ridden barracks were dramatically reduced.[7] These efforts roughly coincided with similar efforts to improve public housing conditions and sanitation across Britain in the late nineteenth century. The Sanitary Commission made attempts to improve the diet of soldiers as well, advocating newly designed kitchens and more hygienic cooking and messing techniques.[8] In addition to these other efforts, in 1858 the Sanitary Commission strongly recommended that some form of physical training be adopted by the Army in order to improve the overall health and physical conditioning of the soldier. This recommendation was based on several findings, including the recognized benefits of exercise in improving the soldier's physical strength and therefore his

---

[5]   Skelley, *The Victorian Army at Home*, chapter 1. In this chapter, titled "The Health of the Rank and File," Skelley provides perhaps one of the most detailed and complete analyses of Sanitary Commission work available. Again, see also Akiyama, *Feeding the Nation*.

[6]   Ibid., pp. 32–41.

[7]   Ibid., pp. 40–41. Also see Spiers, *The Late Victorian Army*, pp. 140–141.

[8]   Ibid., p. 141. Also Skelley, *The Victorian Army at Home*, pp. 63–68. Hurley, *Florence Nightingale*, pp. 171–172, 179.

resistance to disease, and the increasingly lower physical standards found among new recruits during this period.[9]

The problem of obtaining sufficient recruits to man Britain's all-volunteer Army was chronic throughout the nineteenth century. Most of the famous Cardwell reforms of the 1870s were aimed at alleviating the recruiting problem—introduction of short service, creation of two-battalion regiments that were territorially associated, reducing the number of battalions overseas, and creating stronger links between the Militia, Volunteers, and the Regular Army.[10] The Army was clearly not the most attractive profession for young men, what with a twelve-year minimum term of service prior to the Cardwell reforms that practically amounted to life in the ranks, low (almost non-existent) pay, abysmal living conditions, rigorous discipline including the lash, low social esteem, and a monotonous and dreary daily routine only occasionally broken up by the prospect of death or dismemberment. Given these facts, the average young man was a hard sell for the recruiting sergeant. In an article published in 1900, the author, "Linesman," listed the reasons for most young men to take the Queen's shilling:

(1) Betterment of condition, i.e. attainment of work and food in lieu of precarious or entirely absent ditto. (Common.)

(2) Desire of Glory. (Rare.)

(3) Attraction offered by handsome clothes, and consequent admiration and increase of importance among companions. (Common, much more so than clothing committees have any notion of.)

(4) To escape from consequences of crime, or from quarrels at home, or from uncongenial work. (Fairly common in towns, less so in agricultural districts.)

(5) From genuine desire of a soldier's life and work, and desire to adopt it as a profession. (Rare.)

"Linesman" posits that the first and third reasons provided more soldiers than the others, with the first giving more than the others combined.[11] As the century progressed and Britain became increasingly urbanized, the Army found that its previous strong base of recruits from rural Britain and Ireland began to disappear, and more and more recruits began to come from the urban lower classes. For example, by the time of the Crimean War the Highland regiments

---

[9]   Skelley, *The Victorian Army at Home*, p. 58.

[10]   Spiers, *The Late Victorian Army*, pp. 1–28. Also Farwell, *Mr. Kipling's Army*, pp. 153–164.

[11]   "Linesman," "The British Soldier", *Journal of the Military Services Institution of the United States*, Vol. 26 (1900), p. 71 (this article is a reprint from the *United Services Magazine*).

began to obtain more recruits from urban and industrial areas like Glasgow and the Clydeside than from the Highlands themselves. Additionally, in the wake of the potato famine in Ireland and the subsequent rural depopulation there, the source from which the Army had traditionally procured the vast majority of its new soldiers dramatically dried up.[12]

This changing demography also tended to provide recruits who were smaller, less healthy, and much less physically fit than the rural farmboys who had stocked Wellington's army. As this recruiting problem worsened, most notably during the Crimean War, the Army was forced to progressively lower its physical standards for new recruits. For example, between 1869 and 1900 minimum height requirements for new enlistees fluctuated based on the need for soldiers, but on the whole they declined. In 1869 the minimum height requirement was 5 feet 6 inches, and in 1900 it had dropped to 5 feet 3 inches.[13] In the Crimea and during the Indian Mutiny, commanders found that these new soldiers were often physically unable to perform the duties required of them, and that they were far more susceptible to sickness and disease than men recruited from rural districts. Recognition of this problem and the desire to rectify it led to the Army's leadership to look to the example of the continental armies of France and Prussia, where physical drill and gymnastics programs had been in place for a number of years, and by the late 1850s plans were being discussed for the institution of some form of formal physical training.[14]

The last major influence on the institution of formal physical training in the Army was a moral one. Ever since the demise of Cromwell's fiercely puritan New Model Army, Britons looked on their professional army in many cases, quite rightly, as a mob of low-bred, immoral, criminally minded ruffians whose main occupations were drinking to excess and contracting venereal diseases. The Duke of Wellington himself described his soldiers as "the scum of the earth,"[15] and as late as the end of the nineteenth century even Kipling, that staunch cheerleader

---

[12]   Spiers, *The Late Victorian Army*, p. 131. For an extensive study of the demography and recruitment patterns in Highland regiments, see Diana Henderson, *Highland Soldier: A Social Study of the Highland Regiments 1820–1920* (Edinburgh: John Donald Publishers Ltd., 1989).

[13]   Spiers, *The Late Victorian Army*, p. 122. See also A. Leith Adams (Surgeon-Major, London Recruiting District), "The Recruiting Question, Considered from a Military and a Medical Point of View," *Journal of the Royal United Services Institution* (1874), pp. 55–98.

[14]   "Report on Gymnastic Instruction in the French and Prussian Armies, August 1859," WO 33/14, National Archives. See also Skelley, *The Victorian Army at Home*, chapters 6 and 7 ("The Recruiting Problem" and "Patterns of Recruitment").

[15]   Farwell, *Mr. Kipling's Army*, p. 209. Wellington went on to say that, if the French were not frightened of them, they damn well scared *him*.

for Tommy Atkins, described British soldiers as "blackguards."[16] The efforts of Britain's reforming classes to improve the lives of various social groups like factory workers and working-class women were bound to be eventually directed at this goldmine of iniquity, and by the middle of the century various programs were in full swing to raise the traditionally low moral standards of the British soldier.

Attempts at moral reform took two forms: private and official. Numerous private individuals and charitable organizations founded Soldiers' Homes, libraries, and missions in areas close to military installations. The first of these Soldiers' Homes was founded by the Reverend William Carve Wilson at Portsmouth, in 1855. It only lasted until 1859, but it is commemorated by a monument erected by grateful non-commissioned officers and soldiers.[17] A later home was opened by a Wesleyan minister, Charles Henry Kelly, at Chatham in 1861, followed by centers at Aldershot and in Ireland in 1877.[18] These "homes" generally sought to provide alternative off-duty activities to the consumption of alcohol and the frequenting of brothels. They provided soft drinks and tea, bible classes, parlor games, and often a small lending library. These Soldiers' Homes were somewhat successful in raising the tone of the average garrison town, and although their exact rate of success in forestalling debauchery is impossible to estimate, they almost certainly had an impact. By the middle of the 1870s, homes such as these had gained official recognition and support from the Duke of Cambridge and the Prince of Wales, and their future seemed assured.[19]

Along with the foundation of Soldiers' Homes, several attempts were made by religious organizations and like-minded officers to spread the temperance movement within the Army. Henry Havelock, the General made famous by the Indian Mutiny, formed a temperance club in his regiment, the 13th Foot, that came to be known as "Havelock's Saints."[20] Throughout the late Victorian and Edwardian periods temperance societies existed in the Army, at home and abroad. But just as these societies had mixed to little success in reforming the drinking habits of civilians, drinking remained an important fixture in the lives of British soldiers despite efforts at temperance reform. Arguably, drinking only declined appreciably with the introduction of short service in 1870, when a slightly better class of recruits began to enter the Army. These men were in general better educated and more inclined to favor slightly finer off-duty pursuits than

---

16   Ibid., p. 70. The statement runs thus: "Speaking roughly, you must employ either blackguards or gentlemen, or, best of all, blackguards commanded by gentlemen, to do butcher's work with efficiency and despatch."

17   Ibid., p. 199.

18   Spiers, *The Late Victorian Army*, p. 145.

19   Farwell, *Mr. Kipling's Army*, p. 200.

20   Ibid., p. 213.

the "old sweats" of the long-service Army. The infusion of short-service men beginning in the 1870s has been used by historians to explain a general rise in the moral caliber of the Army and, almost certainly, at least partly accounts for the popularity of Soldiers' Homes, temperance societies, and regimental schools and reading rooms.

These last two features were part of official efforts at providing soldiers with opportunities to better themselves and avoid the occasion of sin. Between 1825 and 1838, through fear of subversive propaganda (mostly Fenian, a recognition of the overwhelming numbers of Irishmen in the ranks), all books had been banned in Army barracks. The only exceptions to this rule were a list of twenty-eight volumes that had been approved by a committee of bishops. In 1838, however, an Act of Parliament mandated reading rooms for all barracks, despite the fact that at that time most soldiers could not read. As the number of literate soldiers increased, especially toward the end of the century, these reading rooms expanded both in size and in number. By 1900 it could be said that all regiments and garrisons had libraries, albeit of varying size and quality. Soldiers, like the rest of British citizens, read most of the popular authors of the day, including Balzac and Dickens. Private Frank Richards said of his compatriots in the early 1900s:

> as for the Decameron of Boccaccio, in my time every soldier in the British Forces in India who could read had read this volume from cover to cover. It was considered very hot stuff.[21]

The government also attempted to raise the educational level of soldiers by establishing regimental schools, providing for facilities, materials, teachers, and instruction in crafts and various useful trades. In this respect, government provision of education for soldiers and their dependents was well beyond anything done for civilians. From 1860 the number of soldiers unable to read or write steadily declined, from 19 percent in 1861 to only 1.9 percent in 1889.[22] This statistic is partly affected by the fact that as the century progressed more literate men enlisted (also reflecting the rising literacy rates in the country as a whole), but the Army's efforts to improve the educational level of its soldiers were undeniably successful. Whether or not these efforts bore fruit in the area of decreasing drunkenness and other intemperate behavior, however, is highly debatable.

Another significant area where the government attempted to legally influence the off-duty behavior of soldiers was in the realm of sexual activity. This attempt to regulate carnal pursuits was in part motivated by moral concerns, but

---

[21]   Ibid., p. 198.
[22]   Skelley, *The Victorian Army at Home*, p. 89.

primarily by a serious concern to lower the incidence of venereal disease among
soldiers. By the 1860s the frequency and severity of venereal disease was having
a crippling effect on the Army's readiness, one that gained national attention.
The problem of venereal disease gained notoriety not only because of its impact
on military readiness, but because of the financial requirements of treatment
and the touchy issues of morality raised by it. In 1860 the incidence of these
diseases was 369 cases per every 1000 men, as opposed to only 78 in the Navy, 70
in the French Army, and 34 in the Prussian Army. Clearly this problem, largely
an import from India, was so severe as to effect national security—venereal
disease accounted for the equivalent of the loss of two full battalions per year.
The year 1862 was particularly bad, with the number of men hospitalized rising
to 26,787, or 33 percent of the forces in the United Kingdom. This outbreak
was what prompted the government to enact the notorious Contagious Diseases
Acts, designed to restrict prostitution. Whether as a measure to protect society
from the Army, or vice versa, the blatant inequity and difficulty in enforcing
these laws led to their repeal in 1886.[23]

In addition to the Contagious Diseases Acts, a wide variety of remedies were
attempted to control this problem, including the abovementioned Soldiers'
Homes and reading rooms, and in India some units even set up regimental
brothels where the women were periodically certified as "clean" by Army
medical officers. One of the stated goals of short service when it was introduced
was to reduce the requirement for enforced celibacy among enlisted men. For a
brief period soldiers were fined for contracting venereal disease, but this practice
was quickly discontinued when it was discovered that men were avoiding sick
parades and attempting home remedies, usually to their detriment. The problem
of these diseases continued to plague the Army well into the twentieth century,
although by 1900 the number of cases had dramatically declined from that in
the 1860s. Although the causes for this decline are impossible to accurately
pinpoint, all of these remedies must have had a positive effect on the problem.[24]

The most lasting, and in a sense most revolutionary solution attempted for
the problem of immoral and dissolute behavior among the "other ranks" was
the institution of mandatory gymnastics and voluntary regimental sports. Aside
from the recognized benefits of physical training to the health and physical
capabilities of soldiers, the belief of the Army's leadership in the moral and
character-building effects of exercise, sport, and games argued for their adoption
as a formal means of training. By getting soldiers out of the barracks, canteens,
and whorehouses and into the gymnasium and onto the games field, officers

---

23   Ibid., pp. 53–58. Skelley provides a detailed discussion of the problem of venereal diseases
and the efforts to contain them, including the Contagious Diseases Acts.

24   Ibid., pp. 53–58.

believed that they could improve the fighting capabilities of their men while also improving their minds, morale, and moral fiber. At the same time, given the Army's philosophy of athleticism, it logically followed that, if sport and games improved the leadership, war fighting spirit, and character of officers, they would certainly do so for the enlisted men.

By the end of the 1850s, the arguments for creating a formal, institutionalized program of physical training for all ranks were overwhelming. Concerns over the health of soldiers, the declining physical capabilities of recruits, and the destructive and immoral behavior of enlisted men combined with philosophical beliefs about the benefits of sport and games to create a powerful demand for such a program. In 1859 the War Office sent Colonel Frederick William Hamilton and Dr. Logan, Inspector General of Hospitals, to France and Prussia to investigate and report on the gymnastic training systems in their armies. They reported that France had had a system in place since the 1840s, with a central gymnastics training school established in 1852. The Prussian army had instituted formal military gymnastics training in 1842. Concluding the report, Colonel Hamilton strongly advocated that Britain adopt gymnastics training for the Army, to both supplement drill and relieve the boredom of soldiers.[25]

Therefore, acting on these arguments, in 1860 Major Frederick Hammersley and twelve handpicked NCOs from various units in the Army were sent to Oxford University for a six-month course in gymnastics run by Mr. Archibald McLaren, the famous innovator in physical education whose system was then believed to be the most progressive in Britain. McLaren was included in the special War Office Commission tasked with investigating the feasibility of establishing a gymnastic training program for the Army, and he would eventually write the first Army instructor's manual of physical training and fencing. Major Hammersley and his twelve NCOs were to become experts in the conduct of modern physical training, and would form the cadre to train the rest of the Army in those methods.[26] This small group was designated, somewhat ambitiously, the Army Gymnastic Staff, and would later adopt the fitting motto *Mens Sana in Corpore Sano*, "A sound mind in a sound body."

---

[25] "Report on Gymnastic Instruction in the French and Prussian Armies, August 1859."

[26] Lieutenant Colonel E.A.L. Oldfield, *History of the Army Physical Training Corps* (Aldershot: Gale & Polden Ltd., 1955), p. 1.

Chapter 3
The Army Gymnastic Staff and Regimental Sport

The object of the system of gymnastic instruction approved for the Army, as laid down in the book of instructions, dated February, 1862, is to develope [*sic*] and increase the physical powers of the soldier ... After the forming of recruits the object of gymnastics training is to harden and strengthen the trained soldier, so as to enable him to cover 1,000 or more yards at a rapid pace, and leave him in a good wind, and able to use his bayonet efficiently.

Regulations for Military Gymnasia, 1865[1]

... there remain a good many hours which may be more or less utilized to the soldier's advantage. Some of these are given to gymnastics and out-door games, the importance of which, both from physical and moral points of view, is so much insisted upon, that they form no small part of the education we expect our sons to get at the public schools and universities, so that we may fairly claim them as valuable to our men also.

Major General C.F. Chapman, C.B., late Quartermaster General of India[2]

In 1860, when the Army Gymnastic Staff was formed, there was a strong and widespread consensus among the Army's leaders about the benefits and necessity of a physical training program for soldiers and young officers alike. Just how that program was to be outlined and implemented was not generally agreed upon, nor was the extent to which physical training and its partner, organized sport, would be incorporated into the Army's training regimen. This debate over the proper place of physical training and sport continues to the present, and not just in the British military community.[3]

---

[1]   Published in the *London Times*, Thursday, May 11, 1865. This is a paraphrase of the more detailed instructions published in the *Queen's Regulations* of that year. The verbiage differs slightly from the *Queen's Regulations*, and the contents of the two vary in some slight ways.

[2]   Major General C.F. Chapman C.B., "Citizen Soldiers of the First Class Army Reserve," *The United Services Magazine* Vol. 2 (1890–1891), p. 570.

[3]   As an Infantry company commander in Germany from April 1992 to October 1993, I was constantly faced with this dilemma—I had soldiers who were participating in All-Army

Commanders throughout the Victorian Army had to balance the requirements for gymnastic training with those for dismounted drill, musketry, guard details, riding instruction, field days, and the myriad other tasks of regular soldiers. They also added to this list of training activities their desire to provide soldiers with opportunities for wholesome recreational sports. A few years after the founding of the Army Gymnastic Staff the task of determining how and when soldiers would undergo physical training became relatively simple— beginning in 1865, the Queen's Regulations provided detailed instructions for gymnastics training that outlined the required minimum program for all ranks. This program was immediately popular and within just a few years of its formation the Gymnastic Staff had been enlarged and had grown into an accepted and permanent institution, with gymnasia being constructed at Army posts across the Empire.

After completing the course of gymnastics at Oxford University that began in September 1860, Major Hammersley was offered the newly created position of Superintendent of Gymnasia, to be posted at the just-established School of Gymnastics in Wellington Lines, Aldershot. Frederick Hammersley was an officer whose career had great potential for success; commissioned into the 14th Foot (The Buckinghamshire Regiment) on July 1, 1842, he had distinguished himself in the Crimea. He served in the trenches at the siege and fall of Sebastopol, and earned Sardinian and Turkish decorations along with a brevet to Major.[4] After being offered the position in Aldershot, the young Major wrote to his father, asking for advice, and his father responded with some discouraging comments. He wrote that he hoped his son would not be tempted by the prospect of an "easy berth" to accept this job that seemed "hardly fit for a gentleman, much less an officer, who aspires to military distinction." He concluded his letter by urging his son not to hastily commit to a position "which appears to me analogous to that of Mr. Angelo, the Fencing Master." Luckily for the Army, Major Hammersley, "a man of outstanding ability," who was described by a contemporary as a "practical athlete with one of the finest physical developments I have ever seen," went against his father's advice and accepted the new position. Through his hard work and dedication over the next sixteen years, gymnastics training in the Army was firmly and successfully established. Incidentally, Major Hammersley did achieve his desired distinction and promotion.[5]

---

wrestling tournaments when they were desperately needed for gunnery training, and I was also constantly arguing the case with the battalion's medical staff for training in unarmed combat and contact sports.

[4]   *Hart's Army List*, 1869.

[5]   Ibid.: Hammersley was promoted to Lieutenant Colonel on January 1, 1868. See also Lieutenant Colonel E.A.L. Oldfield, *History of the Army Physical Training Corps* (Aldershot:

Major Hammersley was initially assisted by the twelve NCOs who had attended the Oxford University course with him. These men, now affectionately known as the "Twelve Apostles" by their successors in the current Army Physical Training Corps, first established the School of Gymnastics at Aldershot and then trained subsequent instructors for units and gymnasia throughout the Army. Their working uniform consisted of red shirts, ordinary blue uniform trousers, blue socks, and boots. More practical uniform or distinctive insignia for the Gymnastic Staff did not yet exist.[6] According to the first regulations published in 1865 for gymnastics training, unit instructors were to be selected by their unit chain of command for attendance at courses held in Aldershot beginning on 1 January and 1 July of each year. These men were to be "subjected to a strict medical examination as to their physical powers and fitness for the duty," unmarried and under 25 years old, and if cavalrymen they had to be certified as "good swordsmen."[7] After undergoing this selection process, would-be gymnastics instructors attended a six-month course of gymnastics and physical training, including long-distance cross-country running, fencing, boxing, and various conditioning drills involving rope climbing, trapeze work, and the negotiation of obstacles while carrying packs and rifles.[8] At any time during this course men deemed "inefficient" by the new Superintendent of Gymnasia and his staff would be removed from the course and returned to their units. Those who excelled might be offered the chance of promotion and assignment as members of the Gymnastic Staff at Aldershot.[9]

Upon completing the School of Gymnastics, graduates returned to their regiments and took up duties as instructors at one of the many new gyms being built throughout the Army. Directed in 1862, the first of these gyms was built at the Aldershot school, the second at the Curragh in Ireland, followed by facilities at Chatham in 1864 and at Shorncliffe in 1867. The gym at Aldershot was subsequently demolished and a new one built in 1894, which is still in

---

Gale & Polden Ltd., 1955), pp. 2–3.

[6]   Ibid., p. 6.

[7]   *Queen's Regulations* (1865), Section 10: Gymnastic Training, p. 227.

[8]   *Illustrated London News*, March 18, 1868, pp. 266–7. On page 267 there is a very busy picture of Gymnastic Staff students being put through their paces in all of this training—it is unlikely that all of these events would occur simultaneously as depicted, but the illustration is valuable nonetheless, as it is perhaps the only extant image of the school's original facilities and apparatus (see Figure 3.1).

[9]   *Queen's Regulations* (1865), p. 227.

Figure 3.1   The Gymnasium at Aldershot, 1868, from the *Illustrated London News* (author's collection)

daily use at the current Army Physical Training Corps School.[10] The Chatham gymnasium is the oldest Army gym still in use.[11]

Each of these new facilities, in addition to its non-commissioned officer staff, had an officer assigned as Superintendent of Gymnasia,[12] who had also been trained along with the NCOs at the Aldershot school. This officer's job was to oversee the course of instruction at his post, ensure that the facilities were properly maintained, and supervise compliance with the physical training regulations. Every Superintendent of Gymnasia was required to report regularly

---

[10]   Oldfield, *History of the Army Physical Training Corps*, p. 3. I am indebted here also to Mr. Jim Pearson, a retired member of the Army Physical Training Corps and former curator of the Corps museum at Aldershot. Mr. Pearson was good enough to spend an entire morning with me and gave me much of the material cited in this section, as well as a fascinating tour of the PT school and the Fox Gym, built in 1894. The gym is still in vigorous use—while we walked through, PT Corps instructors were putting a class of potential instructors through their paces on climbing ropes and the vaulting horse.

[11]   *Mind, Body and Spirit: The Annual Journal of the Army Physical Training Corps* No. 79 (1995/96), pp. 30–31.

[12]   Major Hammersley was appointed Inspector of Gymnasia for the Army and promoted to Lieutenant Colonel in 1871; all of the officers in charge of local gyms were assigned as Superintendents.

to Major Hammersley.[13] Many of these men were gifted athletes in their own right, and went on to be major influences in the growth and spread of Army sport. Major Hammersley himself devoted much of his spare time to the propagation of amateur sport and athletics; he became the first chairman of the Amateur Athletic Association in 1866. His work with the National Olympian Association, which was formed to oversee all athletic organizations in Britain, resulted in the passing on to the Army Gymnastic Staff the Association's motto of *Mens Sana in Corpore Sano*.[14]

The gymnastics training program for the Army had been finally decided upon based on the report submitted by the War Office's Committee on Gymnastic Instruction for the Army. This committee recommended in 1864 that gymnastic training for recruits should be mandatory, and compulsory for trained soldiers in the Infantry. They further added that gymnastics for trained cavalrymen should be voluntary, but swordsmanship instruction must be mandatory. They also recommended that Superintendents of Gymnasia should be appointed to all imperial stations (outside of India), including Quebec, Halifax, Malta, and Mauritius.[15] The result of these recommendations was that gymnastic instruction for all new soldiers lasted for three months, and initially took precedence over all other training for the first two months—musketry, fencing, and riding instruction would not occur until recruits had satisfactorily completed their first two months of gymnastics training and their squad and platoon drill.[16] This requirement was later amended, however, so that by 1874 cavalry and infantry recruits did not undergo gymnastics training until after completing preliminary recruit training, including musketry and riding. This change probably came largely at the demand of cavalry commanders, who required a significantly longer time than the infantry to train recruits in their basic skills and duties.[17]

---

[13]   *Queen's Regulations* (1865), p. 232. Major Hammersley did not have to perform all of his duties alone: on August 11, 1865 he was assigned a clerk, and in 1867 Captain Bathe of the 5th Fusiliers was detailed by the Aldershot command to assist him. After Hammersley's promotion to Lieutenant Colonel in 1871 he was given Major Hallows as permanent Assistant Inspector (Minute 1, "Report of the Committee on Gymnastic Training for the Army, 1864," WO 33/14, and Oldfield, *History of the Army Physical Training Corps*, p. 3.

[14]   Ibid., p. 4.

[15]   "Report of the Committee on Gymnastic Instruction for the Army, 1864," WO 33/14. Members of this committee were: Mr. Douglas Galton, Major General Frederick William Hamilton, E.A. Parkes M.D., E.R.S (Prof. of Hygiene), A. Horsford (Deputy Adjutant General), Major Hammersley, Archibald Mclaren, Inspector General of Hospitals T.G. Logan, and Mr. B.H. Matindale.

[16]   "Regulations for Military Gymnasia," *London Times*, May 11, 1865.

[17]   Lieutenant Colonel Evelyn Wood, "Mounted Riflemen," *The Journal of the Royal United Services Institution* Vol. XVIII No. LXXIX (March 4, 1874), p. 17.

Initial recruit training consisted of one hour per day at the gymnasium spent on various tasks such as the use of dumbbells and the vaulting horse, designed primarily to strengthen the recruit's upper body. This being the age of the "strong man," more modern concepts of overall cardiovascular fitness had not been introduced, and a man's fitness was seen to be mainly a function of the size of his chest and arm muscles.[18] Recruits were given a careful medical examination before and after their initial training, with regular medical supervision required during the daily sessions. Details of recruits' height, weight, chest, and arm measurements were taken before and after the course, and if recruits were not found to have made satisfactory progress in their development, they were required to perform additional remedial training.[19] Men who had made normal progress were expected to be able to execute ten pull-ups, fourteen dips on the parallel bars, jump 3 feet high, and run a mile in 7 minutes or less without undue fatigue. These standards are very similar to what the modern soldier is expected to do, and are clearly well beyond the abilities of the average civilian. In his 1869 annual report, Major Hammersley stated that virtually all recruits had vastly improved their health and muscular development, and "in the winter months especially showed significant weight gains as a result of their training."[20]

The course prescribed for trained soldiers—those men who had completed initial training, but were not yet 30 years old—was slightly different from that designed for new recruits. Every infantryman under ten years' service underwent a course of gymnastics for three months each year, meeting every other day for an hour, "taking care that guards and other garrison duties are not interfered with." Classes consisted of squads of no more than fifteen men each, and they went through a similar series of exercises to that of the longer and more difficult instructor's course. "In order to further encourage the men," at the end of each course the local Gymnastic Staff instructors identified potential new instructors from each class; "three or four of the most efficient" would be retained to go through a second, voluntary course that could result in their being appointed assistant instructors. From this group local commanders and Superintendents of Gymnasia selected men for the Instructor's Course at Aldershot.[21]

---

[18]   Oldfield, *History of the Army Physical Training Corps*, pp. 1–2.

[19]   *Queen's Regulations* (1865), p. 231.

[20]   "Report of the Director of Gymnastics, on the Gymnastic Instruction of the Army, for the year 1869," *Parliamentary Papers*, 1869–1870, pp. 575–581, and Alan Ramsay Skelley, *The Victorian Army at Home: The Recruitment and Terms and Conditions of the British Regular, 1859–1899* (London: Croom Helm, 1977), p. 60. Skelley cites *Instructions for the Physical Training of Recruits at Regimental Districts* (1896), and Hammersley's *Report on Gymnastic Instruction* (1870).

[21]   *Queen's Regulations* (1865), pp. 231–232.

Figure 3.2   Class of Staff Instructors in the Gymnasium at Aldershot, *c.* 1894

This carefully designed program, closely and diligently supervised by a dedicated, professional new staff, met with applause and wholehearted support from the Army (although clearly some of the men subjected to its rigors must have been less than pleased). In 1866 Queen Victoria herself visited the School of Gymnastics at Aldershot, and expressed her satisfaction with the results of the program. In 1871 Major Hammersley was promoted to Lieutenant Colonel—the Army Gymnastic Staff was an unqualified success.[22] By 1880 it was poised to fully participate in what would amount over the next twenty years to a virtual revolution in British military affairs.

Formalized sport and games for all ranks had a slower start than the Army's gymnastic training scheme, but by the end of the 1870s the late Victorian explosion of military sport and games had begun, supported and encouraged by the Gymnastic Staff and aided by the institution of what was to become the annual Royal Tournament, and the formation of organized Rugby and Association football leagues both within the Army and for civilians.[23] In the first

---

[22]   *Illustrated London News*, March 18, 1868, pp. 296–297, and Oldfield, *History of the Army Physical Training Corps*, pp. 5–6.

[23]   For further details on the formative years of Army sport, see Tony Mason and Eliza Riedi, *Sport and the Military: The British Armed Forces, 1880–1960* (Cambridge: Cambridge University Press, 2010), chapter 1.

twenty years after the founding of the Army Gymnastic Staff physical training and organized sport across the Army had taken firm root, fundamentally transforming the life of the Victorian soldier, and opening the door for further changes in the next forty years that would make a British soldier's life in 1908 virtually unrecognizable to a soldier of the 1850s.

On Wednesday May 22, 1872, a group of officers from the Coldstream Guards played a cricket match on the grounds of Phoenix Park, London. All that month teams from the Household Brigade had played a series of matches against teams from the Lords and Commons, the Royal Engineers, the Rifle Brigade, and the Royal Artillery. These matches were played almost entirely by officers and gentlemen from the various organizations represented, with the exception of Household Brigade team mainstays Sergeant Simpson of the Grenadier Guards and Corporal-Major Robinson of the Household Cavalry. In all the play that month up to the twenty-second, the only other rankers present were Private Jordan from the Rifle Brigade, Corporal Hawkins from the Grenadiers, and Bombardier McCanlis from the Royal Artillery. The match on May 22, however, was different. That match was played by officers from the Coldstream Guards on one team, and by non-commissioned officers and men from the regiment on the other.[24]

This match may have been only one in the long series of games played by the Household Brigade during the 1872 cricket season, but it is remarkable in that it marks one of the first times such a large number of "other ranks" played in a recorded game, and one against regimental officers at that. Significantly, cricket is one of the first modern British leisure pastimes in which people from different social classes participated together, and this trend was followed in the Army as well. The 1870s were when organized sporting events open to all ranks first widely occurred, and this cricket match in the Coldstream Guards is an example of what would eventually become a hallmark of British Army sport during this period: all-ranks-integrated teams and competitions. These rank-integrated sporting events at first seem incongruous given the contemporary distinction and absolute lack of fraternization between officers and men. Traditionally, officers had virtually no personal contact with soldiers, and those that did were often considered odd. Lord Kitchener was never known to address a soldier in the ranks other than to give him an order. Field Marshal Sir William Robertson, a former ranker himself, said of the British private:

> In not a few regiments his officers saw little or nothing of him, except when
> on parade or at stables, they showed no interest in his personal concerns and

---

24 *Journal of the Household Brigade* (1872), pp. 148–165.

sometimes did not even know his name, although he might have been under his command for weeks.[25]

A notable exception to this common trend was Lord Baden-Powell, who, among his other eccentricities, enjoyed the company of his men and often took a personal interest in their lives.[26] The walls of rank distinction, however, did not extend to the games field. By the mid- to late 1870s it was becoming increasingly common for officers and soldiers to play games together.[27] This egalitarian spirit stemmed in part from the requirement for new subalterns to undergo recruit physical training in squads alongside the privates.[28] Additionally, the amateur games ethic that was so important as an element of military philosophy insisted on the egalitarian nature of sportsmanship and athleticism—it did not matter who played, as long as they did their best and acted as a "good sport." Perhaps the most important reason for this cooperative spirit is that as officers felt that sport and games were essential to building character and *esprit de corps* among the men, they needed to provide leadership and an example to soldiers in those areas by participating in their games. As regimental sports became more widespread and popular toward the end of the century, the potential for conflicts between rankers and officers on the games field increased, but may have in many cases been avoided through an informal delineation of "officer" and "soldier" games. In many units soccer football became the special province of the ranker, and cricket of the officer.[29]

An important factor in the growth of regimental sport in the 1870s was the movement throughout British society to form associations and leagues to regulate play and provide for championships. The Football Association (F.A.) was formed in 1863, and the Rugby Union in 1871. The Army was heavily represented among the individuals and teams that initially formed these bodies, and something of this organizing and propagating spirit was transferred to

---

[25]   Byron Farwell, *Mr. Kipling's Army* (New York: W.W. Norton & Co., 1981), pp. 132–133.

[26]   Tim Jeal, *The Boy-Man: The Life of Lord Baden-Powell* (New York: Wm. Morrow & Co., 1990), chapter 3. In Jeal's book there is an interesting photograph of Baden-Powell participating in a gymnastics display with enlisted men of the Malta Garrison, where he was assigned as the Governor's aide circa 1892. Jeal also mentions in chapter 3 Baden-Powell's fascination with instructors of the Gymnastic Staff, whom he described as "magnificent specimens."

[27]   Farwell, *Mr. Kipling's Army*, p. 203–204.

[28]   *Queen's Regulations* (1865), p. 230, also "Regulations for Military Gymnasia," *London Times*, May 11, 1865.

[29]   "Ex-Non-Com," "The Soldier in Relation to Regimental Sport," *The United Services Magazine* Vol. XL (1909–1910), p. 35.

the nascent institution of regimental sport. An example of this representation is Major Hammersley's participation during the 1860s and 1870s in both the Amateur Athletic Association and the National Olympian Association. The Royal Engineers were pioneers in the field of football, with a team from the regiment as one of the founding members of the F.A., and Captain (later Major) Sir Francis Marindin of the Engineers served as president of the F.A. from 1874 to 1890. Teams from the Royal Engineers figured prominently in the early days of the F.A. Cup championship: the Royal Engineers were runners-up in the first cup final in 1872, again in 1874 and 1878, and won the cup final in 1875.[30] In 1871 two engineers won the Army international distinction in football when they were chosen to play for England; for the rest of the century international caps were regularly awarded to Army players.[31]

Football had deep roots in the Army, most likely because of the game's close association with British public schools. A game between the Guards and the cavalry reportedly occurred at Balaclava on March 27, 1855. Before the formation of the Rugby Union in 1871 there were several versions of the game with teams varying in size depending on which style of play was chosen, usually by the opposing captains just prior to the game. In the early years the Army usually conformed to the Eton game with eleven men to a side, but a club team was formed at the Royal Military Academy, Woolwich, using Rugby rules in 1860. From there Rugby football gained in popularity in the Army and matches were played throughout the 1870s, with teams such as the Royal Artillery Band having a successful season in Union play during the 1874/75 season. The famous Calcutta Cup was brought to England and presented to the Union by the Royal East Kent Regiment (The Buffs) after attempts to establish a league in India succumbed to the growing popularity there of polo.[32]

The Army carried football and cricket to imperial outposts all over the world. Cricket is now possibly more popular in South Asia and the Caribbean than in the British Isles. The Army took Association football to Ireland; the 94th regiment and the Argyll and Sutherland Highlanders fielded teams there that played against teams from Landsdowne and Dublin University. In 1879 during the Second Afghan War, a Rugby game was even reported as being played in the

---

[30] Geoffrey Green, *The Official History of the F.A. Cup* (London: The Naldrett Press, 1949), pp. 10, 17.

[31] Sylvia Nash, "The History of the Army Rugby Union," unpublished manuscript, p. 4. Many thanks to Miss Nash, who graciously provided me with a typescript copy of her first chapter.

[32] Ibid., pp. 1–7.

Bolan Pass into Afghanistan, between sides representing England and Ireland.[33] By the 1880s football of both styles came to be by far the most popular sport among soldiers, reflecting the enormous popularity of the game among the British working class. Some regiments, particularly those from Scotland, became almost obsessed with the game, at times taking more pride in won–loss records than in battle honors.[34]

In addition to the growth of regimental sport, the 1870s saw the institution of military tournaments and athletics meets, sometimes called Gymkhana, using the Indian term. These tournaments generally consisted of both standard foot races and other track and field events, and military skills competitions such as mounted combats, bayonet fencing, and tent pegging.[35] Tournaments often also included gymnastics competitions and displays, and tug-of-war contests as well, the latter being an extremely popular sport in the Army at the time. The largest and most famous of these tournaments was the Royal Tournament, held each year with participants from all the services.

This event originated in the 1870s, with a large tournament for charity arranged for members of home-based units of the Army at Lillie Bridge in London on June 9–10, 1876. Organizing committee members included Lieutenant Colonel Hammersley, Inspector of Gymnasia, Major General His Serene Highness Prince Edward of Saxe-Weimar, and Mr. J.G. Chambers of the Amateur Athletic Association, along with numerous other distinguished officers of the Army, active and retired. One of these was Colonel Goodlake, late Coldstream Guards, who was one of the first recipients of the Victoria Cross for his gallantry while serving as a captain at the Battle of Inkerman in the Crimea. Interestingly, two of the judges for mounted competition combats were Ressaldars (Native Indian officers) from the Prince of Wales' Own Bengal Lancers.[36]

This tournament consisted of foot races, gymnastic events, a "Marching Order" race, ring tilting, tent pegging, and mounted combats such as sword vs. sword, sword vs. lance, and sword vs. bayonet. Enlisted men featured prominently in these competitions, with rankers taking the majority of prizes

---

[33]   Ibid., pp. 1–7. Miss Nash's reference here is confused—she states that the game was played in the "Bhutan Pass," but I can find no reference to a British force entering Bhutan in 1879. There were numerous British and Indian forces in the Bolan Pass in 1879, so I can only assume she made this understandable mistake.

[34]   Farwell, *Mr. Kipling's Army*, pp. 202–203, also "Ex-Non-Com," "The Soldier in Relation to Regimental Sport," p. 33.

[35]   Tent pegging was a sport originally designed as a way for enlisted men to gain the benefits of pigsticking, and was seen as *de rigeur* for lancers; it involved riding full tilt down a course and attempting to spear a peg, driven part way into the ground.

[36]   *Journal of the Household Brigade* (1876), p. 93.

in all events, including Staff Instructors Sergeant Weaver, Sergeant Chesterton, and Sergeant Fitch of the Army Gymnastic Staff at Aldershot who won all but one of the prizes in gymnastics. This tournament was different from the (by that time) fairly common regimental sports days, in that it was held at a national level for all units.[37] Its success prompted the Inspector of Gymnasia, Major Gildea, to organize an "Assault-at Arms" tournament at the Albert Hall in 1878, which was so popular that the following year it was combined with the annual display given by the Volunteer Forces on Wimbledon Common. In 1880 the tournament was moved to the Agricultural Hall in London, and in succeeding years this event developed into the annual Royal Military Tournament. By 1914 it included the Navy and was dubbed the Royal Naval and Military Tournament. It continued to be held up to 1998, serving as a major advertising event for Britain's armed forces—it was finally discontinued by the government as a cost-saving measure.

By the end of the 1870s, both formal physical training and regimental sport were fixtures in the Army. Each had become an accepted mode of training and morale building by the vast majority of soldiers. From officers' aristocratic sporting interests, educational ideals about athleticism, and the moral reforming zeal of middle-class liberals, military sport and physical training had grown almost overnight into an integral part of the lives of British soldiers. This promising start for military physical culture was, however, merely a preliminary phase of the rapid and dramatic growth and popularity that Army sport and physical training would experience over the next forty years.

---

[37]   Ibid., pp. 93–97.

PART II
"Play Up and Play the Game": Physical Training and Army Sport, 1880–1908

Chapter 4

"A Marvellous Improvement in the Rank and File": Physical Training at the Turn of the Century

Gymnastics form an important and integral part of every soldier's training, and should always be kept up as enjoined by regulation. Assaults of arms (station and battalion) might be encouraged, and the sporting instincts of the soldier enlisted to excel in feats of arms, as well as in athletics, football, cricket, &c.

Colonel A.G. Raper, 1892[1]

This physical development of the soldier, in whom the fighting instinct is naturally strong, gives to the British Army much of the formidableness it possesses.

Lieutenant Colonel A.A. Woodhull,
Deputy Surgeon General, United States Army, 1895[2]

The years between 1880 and 1908 mark what is perhaps the greatest period of change and positive development in the history of the British Army.[3] Indeed, the same could be said of most major Western armies as well, with a significant

---

[1] Colonel A.G. Raper, "Notes on Organization and Training by a Regimental Officer," *The Journal of the Royal United Services Institution* Vol. 36 No. 167 (January 1892), p. 12.

[2] Lieutenant Colonel A.A. Woodhull, "Recruiting and Physical Training in the British Army," *The Journal of the Military Services Institution of the United States* Vol. 16 (1895), p. 47.

[3] This fact is widely accepted by historians not only as it applies to the British Army but to virtually all other major Western armies as well. For the British case, see Edward M. Spiers, *The Late Victorian Army* (Manchester: Manchester University Press, 1992); Jay Luvaas, *The Education of an Army: British Military Thought, 1815–1940* (Chicago, IL: University of Chicago Press, 1964); Brian Bond, *The Victorian Army and the Staff College 1854–1914* (London: Eyre Methuen, 1972); and M.D. Welch, *Science and the British Officer: The Early Days of the Royal United Army Services Institute for Defense Studies (1829–1869)* (London: The Royal United Services Institute for Defense Studies, 1998). For general works covering other Western armies, see Hew Strachan, *European Armies and the Conduct of War* (London: George Allen and Unwin, 1983) and Azar Gat, *The Development of Military Thought: The Nineteenth Century* (Oxford: Clarendon Press, 1992).

difference being that the British Army underwent this transformation while engaged in almost constant warfare in remote places around the globe. This period saw the last time British soldiers went into combat wearing the famous red coat, the last time they carried their colors into battle, and the last major cavalry charge in British history. During this time the British Army adopted quick-firing, breach-loading artillery, smokeless gunpowder, a magazine-fed bolt-action rifle, and the machine gun. The Army also abolished its old numerical regimental designations and amalgamated many famous old units to create a more modern two-battalion regimental system based on geographical association: for example, the 24th Regiment of Zulu War fame became the South Wales Borderers, and the 93rd of "Thin Red Line" fame amalgamated with the 91st to become the Argyll and Sutherland Highlanders. Near the end of this thirty-year period the Victorian Army underwent the wrenching experience of the South African War, which, among other things, acted as a powerful spur for further dramatic military reform and modernization.[4]

Along with these other significant developments, this period also saw the continued development of physical training in the Army. This improvement and integration of physical training in many ways paralleled other training and doctrinal innovations in the Army both before and after the South African War: increased emphasis on mobility, scouting and reconnaissance, musketry, and open-order tactics all appeared during this period. In 1880 the Army's physical training program and the Gymnastic Staff were accepted elements of the Army's overall training system, but they continued to grow in importance during the succeeding years as the movement for modernization and reform gained strength. More emphasis on total fitness as opposed to mere upper-body strength, a commitment to swimming as an element of physical training, attempts to adopt a more modern and efficient system of training based on Scandinavian models, and efforts to more fully integrate physical training and sport into the

---

[4]   The Haldane Reforms of the early 1900s were in a large part stimulated by the experience of the South African War, partly because of deficiencies noted in training and doctrine during the war, and partly from a recognition by the British Government that, because of the international situation during the war, it had to have closer ties with one or more of the continental powers. This recognition in turn drove the Army to focus on the possibility of a continental war, and therefore to move toward the reforms required to make the Army capable of fighting one. See Edward Spiers, *Haldane: An Army Reformer* (Edinburgh: Edinburgh University Press, 1980) and *The Late Victorian Army*, chapter 11 ("The Second Boer War: The Ultimate Test"), for an overview of this process. For a contemporary commentary on Army reform, see the Hon. H.O. Arnold Forster, *The Army in 1906: A Policy and a Vindication* (New York: E.P. Dutton & Co., 1906).

Army's complete training scheme all occurred between 1880 and 1908, along with continued construction of gymnasia and other training facilities.[5]

These efforts all indicate a growing professional maturity within the leadership of the British Army. British military professional journals flourished during this period, their pages containing lively debates on the full range of reform efforts, including all aspects of sport and physical training. Soldiers in other countries recognized these changes in Britain, and although most Western military eyes remained firmly focused on Germany, observers overseas took increasing note of Britain's military renaissance, including the system of physical training. During this period the United States Army adopted physical and sports training methods consciously modeled on the British system.[6]

This period of ferment and change within Britain's military establishment culminated in the area of physical training with the publication in 1908 of the Army's first comprehensive physical training manual, which was so well thought of by the soldiers in Holland whose own system was part of its inspiration that it was translated into Dutch.[7] By 1908 the Army was well on its way to becoming the modern, highly trained, and professional force that landed in France in the summer of 1914. The previous thirty years had transformed this organization almost beyond recognition, and the development of the Gymnastic Staff and physical training between 1880 and 1908 provides a clear example of this process.

In 1880, Lieutenant Colonel Hammersley's successor, Major G.F. Gildea of the 21st Foot, was succeeded as Inspector of Gymnasia by Lieutenant Colonel W.B.G. Cleather of the North Lancashire Regiment. Cleather was enthusiastic about his new appointment and determined to bring innovations to his new corps. He saw a need to modernize the Gymnastic Staff, and bring British military

---

[5] Lieutenant Colonel E.A.L. Oldfield, *History of the Army Physical Training Corps* (Aldershot: Gale & Polden Ltd., 1955), chapter 1.

[6] See Woodhull, "Recruiting and Physical Training in the British Army"; Lieutenant A.B. Donworth, "Gymnasium Training in the Army," *The Journal of the Military Service Institution of the United States* Vol. 21 (1897), pp. 508–515; Lieutenant G.A. Taylor, "Soccer Football for the Army," *The Journal of the Military Service Institution of the United States* Vol. 45 (1909), pp. 158–160; Captain James E. Pilcher, "The Place of Physical Training in the Military Service," *The Journal of the Military Service Institution of the United States* Vol. 16 (1895), pp. 295–303; Lieutenant E.L. Butts, "Physical Training of the American Soldier," *The Journal of the Military Service Institution of the United States* Vol. 16 (1895), pp. 499–512; and Major R.L. Bullard and Captain H.S. Hawkins, "Athletics in the Army," *The Journal of the Military Service Institution of the United States* Vol. 37 (1905), pp. 399–409. In 1914 the U.S. Army published its first manual of physical training, which, although not an exact copy, owed a lot to its British predecessor.

[7] Captain F.J. Starr, "War History of the British Army Gymnastic Staff," (first draft) unpublished manuscript, Army Physical Training Corps Museum File # 1664, p. 1.

physical training more into line with what was current practice in Europe and
with what was increasingly being demanded from commanders throughout
the Army.[8] The physical training program had changed little from its first
appearance nearly twenty years previously, and with its expanded acceptance and
implementation there was a growing recognition of its inadequacies. Numerous
articles appearing in British military professional journals in the 1880s and
1890s complained about the shortcomings of regulation physical training as it
then existed. All of the authors sang the praises of gymnastics and embraced the
absolute necessity of conducting this kind of training in order to prepare officers
and soldiers for war, but many complained that the system in place since the
1860s did not wholly satisfy the requirements of either recruit training or unit
training of "old" soldiers.

An example of one of these articles is one entitled "Battalion Command,"
published in the *Journal of the Royal United Services Institution* in September
1891. The anonymous author provided advice and philosophy based on
his experience on how to be a successful commander. He covered a wide
range of subjects interesting to the aspiring commander, such as discipline,
administration, and musketry. Given equal place with these traditional topics
was a discussion of his unit's physical training program and his feelings about the
Army system. In his view, the paramount goal of physical training for the soldier
was to enable men to "get alongside an enemy in good form," a paraphrase of the
1865 regulation's stated purpose of troops being able to cover 1,000 yards at a
good pace and then being able to use the bayonet efficiently. But the author then
deprecated the Army's system by pointing out that it was focused on increasing
the soldier's upper-body strength while neglecting his legs:

> Our physical training has always, as a rule, tended more to strengthen a man's
> arms than his legs, whereas the latter are the most important of the two, for it is
> the soldier's power of movement that is everything in war. This power is not to
> be gained by a march once a week. As far as my experience goes, the only way to
> attain it is to have running drill extending over some months.

The author then went on to give details of the program he implemented while in
command, which supplemented the required gymnastics training, consisting of
running and long footmarches. He also described ways in which soldiers' boots
could be made softer and therefore easier on the men's feet, a science with which
every infantry leader should be intimately familiar.[9]

---

8   Oldfield, *History of the Army Physical Training Corps*, pp. 7–8.
9   "Anonymous," "Battalion Command," *The Journal of the Royal United Services
Institution* Vol. 35 No. 163 (September 1891), p. 478.

"Battalion Command" is an important article in that it is indicative of the growing interest of many officers in the late nineteenth century in scientific training methods designed to improve combat effectiveness. This article was not written by a disinterested aristocrat in the mold of a Lord Cardigan but rather by a professional soldier in the mold of the contemporary Army's "Model of a Modern Major General," Lord Wolseley. The emphasis this author placed on physical training shows just how important this kind of training had become to the Army: the author's discussion of how to improve physical stamina follows only discipline, and is in turn followed by musketry.[10]

This particular author's dissatisfaction with the "strong man" program then in place was not uncommon. In "Notes on Organization and Training by a Regimental Officer," Colonel A.G. Raper again emphasized the importance of gymnastics as an integral part of every soldier's training, but advocated that gymnastics training be conducted only in the afternoons for trained soldiers, and then in close conjunction with a program of athletics, football, cricket, and "military sports," the events conducted at assaults-at-arms or military tournaments.[11]

Along with complaints about the lack of symmetry in the physical training program were admonitions that it was not enough. In September 1891, Colonel G. Hatchell lauded the recent change to the regulations that called for the recruit's course of gymnastics to be extended from one month to three: "No sounder move in the right direction was ever made." He went on to advocate, however, further changes to improve the effects of the program on "town recruits," whose lack of physical development was pronounced, and even hindered their ability to perform other basic drill.[12]

These and other suggestions and complaints did not fall on deaf ears. Two years after assuming duties as Inspector of Gymnasia, Lieutenant Colonel Cleather had organized a trip, suggested by his friend Mr. Nordenfeldt (of machine-gun fame) to visit Sweden and study the "Ling System" of physical training then in use by the armies of Denmark, Norway, and Sweden. Cleather departed England in July 1882, accompanied by ten officers and twelve NCOs of the Gymnastic Staff, who were required by the Liberal government to pay their own expenses for the trip. They were met in Sweden with what Captain Lloyd, one of the officers in the party, described as excellent hospitality, and were treated to a royal audience and several gymnastic and other athletic displays.

---

[10]   Ibid., p. 478.

[11]   Raper, "Notes on Organization and Training," p. 12.

[12]   Colonel G. Hatchell, "The Training of Our Recruits," *The Journal of the Royal United Services Institution* Vol. 35 No. 163 (September, 1891), pp. 959–960.

The British visitors put on several demonstrations of their own, impressing the Swedes with their strength, and most particularly their boxing prowess.[13]

On his return from Scandinavia, Cleather attempted to convince the Army hierarchy to adopt the Ling System, a series of free exercises performed in formation, in unison, usually to the accompaniment of music. The system would de-emphasize upper-body strength while encouraging overall fitness, but the enthusiasm of the Inspector of Gymnasia was only able to secure permission to institute "physical drill" with and without arms, free gymnastics, and light dumbbell exercises, with musical accompaniment. From this time on, units could conduct these forms of training in addition to, but not in lieu of, the standard instruction. The practice of performing drill to music soon became common; imagine a whole battalion in formation, performing bayonet exercises to the tune of some popular song of the day.[14] Many photographs exist of units training in this way. They are vaguely suggestive of today's aerobics classes, however unlikely the comparison may seem.[15]

In 1885 the Army Gymnastic Staff, now under the direction of Colonel G.M. Onslow of the 20th Hussars, passed a major milestone in its development. The Staff was recognized with the grant of official status as a separate corps, with distinctive insignia—crossed sabers surmounted with a crown. The officers assigned as Superintendents of Gymnasia and the Inspector and his staff were then grouped together in the Army List under the heading "Schools of Instruction."[16] In 1890 the Staff received another bonus in the form of yet another new inspector, Lieutenant Colonel George Malcolm Fox of the Black Watch, a veteran of the Battle of Tel el-Kebir.[17] Fox was the first in a series of Inspectors assigned from the Highland Brigade, and "there is not the slightest

---

[13]   Oldfield, *History of the Army Physical Training Corps*, p. 8.

[14]   Ibid., p. 9.

[15]   See Boris Mollo, *The British Army from Old Photographs* (London: J.M. Dent & Sons Ltd., 1975) and Phillip Warner, *Army Life in the '90's* (London: Hemlyn Publishing Group Ltd. [Country Life Books], 1975).

[16]   Oldfield, *History of the Army Physical Training Corps*, p. 9.

[17]   Interestingly, Lieutenant Colonel Fox is featured prominently in Alphonse de Neuville's famous painting of that battle, *The Storming of Tel el-Kebir*. In the painting De Neuville portrays Fox as being wounded in the shoulder, but in fact he was wounded in the thigh; an odd mistake for a military painter renowned for meticulous accuracy. In an account by Private John Gordon (related in *Mind, Body and Spirit* No. 79 [1995–1996], p. 122), then Captain Fox, commander of D Company, 1st Battalion The Black Watch, described his participation in the attack at Tel el-Kebir thus: the assault on the Egyptian trenches was well under way, "When I leaped to the top of the trench [and] I found myself on a platform with three friends all ready for me. The swing of my sword took off the head of one, the point of my sword killed another but before I could get at the third the beggar put a bullet into

Figure 4.1   Recruit Physical Training, Royal Irish Regiment, Buttevant, 1898 (courtesy of the Council of the National Army Museum, London)

doubt that the man who extended the greatest influence on the Army Gymnastic Staff was Fox."[18] This remarkable man had begun his service with the Gymnastic Staff as Assistant Inspector of Gymnasia at Aldershot from 1883–1887, and then again from 1889–1890.[19] Under his supervision while Inspector a major construction campaign began at Aldershot and elsewhere to modernize and expand the Army's physical training facilities. In these efforts Fox was aided by his Assistant Inspector, Captain (later Colonel) W. Edgeworth-Johnstone, another exceptional man who lent both distinction and notoriety to the Gymnastic Staff.[20]

Fox gave an early indication of the direction he intended to take the Gymnastic Staff at a lecture he presented on December 15, 1891 at the Aldershot Military Society. Colonel Onslow, the former Inspector of Gymnasia, was present at the lecture, and sitting in the chair was none other than Major General Frederick Hammersley, the founder of the Staff. In the course of the lecture Fox outlined some of the initiatives he wanted to undertake in continuing the modernization

---

my thigh." This incident may go a long way towards explaining Fox's later determination to ensure that all British soldiers were well trained in swordsmanship and bayonet fighting.

[18]   Lieutenant Colonel A.A. Forbes, Honorary Curator of the Army Physical Training Corps Museum, quoted in *Mind, Body and Spirit* No. 79 (1995–1996), p. 123.

[19]   In ibid., p. 123.

[20]   See Warner, *Army Life in the '90's*, p. 94. On page 93 there is an excellent photograph of Captain Edgeworth-Johnstone, posed in his fencing gear—a large, severe-looking officer with a magnificent mustache, even by contemporary standards. Also see *Army Sport Records 1880–1939* (published by the Army Sport Control Board, War Office, 1939). Captain Edgeworth-Johnstone was a decorated veteran of several campaigns with the West India Regiment (the only all-black regiment in the Regular Army), and was serving with the Royal Irish Regiment when assigned to the Gymnastic Staff. He served as Superintendent of Gymnasia for the Southern Military District until assigned as Assistant Inspector. In that position he was responsible for the direction of the Headquarters Gymnasium and the School where, given his qualifications, he likely did an outstanding job. He was recognized as one of the best all-round athletes in the Army. As a boxer he was twice Amateur Heavyweight Champion of England, and a holder of both the Army Championship and the Irish Championship. He played cricket for the Gentlemen of Ireland, and while at Sandhurst he captained the Royal Military College Rugby Team. In 1890 he won the Sabre vs. Sabre competition and the Challenge Cup at the Royal Military Tournament and at the Army Athletic Meeting at Aldershot. He also won the sabre competition at the British Amateur Fencing Association Championships in 1898 and again in 1900. Another fact about this extraordinary man—while his former comrades in the Army Gymnastic Staff were training soldiers in France during World War One, the now Lieutenant Colonel Edgeworth-Johnstone was the Commissioner of the Dublin Metropolitan Police, and was instrumental in crushing the 1916 Easter Rising. With men such as this responsible for the physical development of recruits and potential instructors, it is small wonder that the Gymnastic Staff and its program gained such wide popularity and respect.

of physical training. He argued that the responsibility for conducting unit physical training must be in the hands of the local unit commanders and not placed entirely on the shoulders of the Superintendents. He also argued that gymnastic training must be made mandatory for all soldiers, not just recruits. Given that the current system only allowed for roughly five percent of all trained soldiers to receive gymnastic training, without mandatory sessions for all soldiers year round, the significant gains made by recruits were often lost when soldiers arrived at their units. Besides the call for regular, mandatory training for all soldiers, Fox added that regular route marching, running, and "national sports and games" were integral parts of the program and must be kept up continually alongside gymnastics training. In this call Fox anticipated changes that would eventually be institutionalized with the publication of the first Manual of Physical Training in 1908.[21]

Under Fox's direction the old gymnasium at Wellington Lines, Aldershot was replaced by a newer gym along with several other buildings, and these were formally opened in 1894 under the title "Cranbrook Gymnasium."[22] These buildings still form the nucleus of the current Army Physical Training Corps School, the main gymnasium having since been renamed the Fox Gym in honor of its builder, while in 1994 the entire school was named Fox Lines.[23] Fox also oversaw the leveling of some waste ground adjoining the gym, which would later become an athletics field and football pitch. With expanded facilities the Gymnastic Staff began to expand its training role to include instruction in fencing, boxing, and bayonet fighting.[24] Boxing (under the influence of Captain Edgeworth-Johnstone, no doubt) eventually became an important element in the physical training of both recruits and trained soldiers; the British Army still includes boxing as a mandatory training event for all recruits.[25] Fox also introduced the spring bayonet, which allowed more realistic training in bayonet

---

[21]   "'The physical training of the recruit and drilled soldier,' with practical illustrations by squads, by Lieutenant Colonel G.M. Fox … on Tuesday, December 15, 1891, in the Prince Consort's and Military Society's Library, South Camp" (Aldershot: Gale and Polden, 1891), lecture # 36. British Library shelfmark C.193.a.257(36).

[22]   Oldfield, *History of the Army Physical Training Corps*, pp. 13–14.

[23]   *Mind, Body and Spirit* No. 79 (1995/96), p. 123.

[24]   Oldfield, *History of the Army Physical Training Corps*, pp. 13–14.

[25]   A Colour Sergeant from 3rd Battalion, the Parachute Regiment once described to me the practice in his regiment of "the mad minute": early in the first week of recruit training, trainees are paired off with another of roughly similar size and build, and then without prior instruction put into a boxing ring for a minute of fighting. Those who are hesitant to "go at it" are suitably encouraged by the instructors, a practice bound to quickly settle for the aspiring paratroopers any doubts they might have about the precise nature of their newly chosen profession.

fighting, and "bayonet fencing" became a popular tournament sport. In 1893 he brought to Britain two professional Italian fencing instructors, Professor Masiello and his protégé Signor Magrini. With the assistance of these men the Army instituted a program of fencing instruction that, under the control of the Gymnastic Staff, greatly enhanced efficient use of the *arme blanche*.[26]

In 1895 Lieutenant Colonel Fox introduced an amendment to the system of recruit physical training that allowed for classification of recruits according to size and physical abilities: men would be "squadded" with others of similar build and stamina, and based on their progress they could be moved to different squads after a periodic review.[27] All these innovations—those introduced by Cleather in 1882 and by Fox throughout the 1890s—went a long way toward modernizing physical training across the Army, but there was still room for improvement. The much-vaunted Ling System of free exercise was still not approved for use, and outmoded and even dangerous training techniques such as exercise to the point of extreme fatigue or even injury were still used by some of the more zealous, if misguided, instructors. Even after he took the Staff on its second Scandinavian tour after assuming duties as Inspector in 1890, Fox had been unable to convince his superiors to adopt the more progressive elements of the European training system.[28] And in spite of continued improvements, the increasingly scientific-minded officers of the Army wanted still more.

In an 1898 promotion essay published in the *United Services Magazine*, Surgeon-Captain J. Will of the Army Medical Staff advocated many changes to the way in which recruits were trained. He most strenuously advocated a program of progressively applied free exercises based on the varied needs of each soldier's state of health and development, and recommended that Gymnastic Staff Instructors be taught how to make appropriate assessments:

> [the instructor] ought to be acquainted with the elements of human anatomy and of the physiology of bodily exercise. He should be able to estimate the individual capacity and not regard his pupils in the aggregate, as is very often done, and he should also be able to interpret at once the signs of fatigue and the indications of suddenly developed breathlessness.

Will also emphasized the importance of adequate healthy rations to improved physical development.[29] To a soldier of today these recommendations seem

---

[26]   Oldfield, *History of the Army Physical Training Corps*, p. 14.

[27]   Surgeon-Captain J. Will, "The Recruit and His Physical Training," *The United Services Magazine* Vol. 17 (1898), p. 649.

[28]   Oldfield, *History of the Army Physical Training Corps*, pp. 10, 13.

[29]   Will, "The Recruit and His Physical Training," pp. 628–651.

BAYONET CLASS DRILL AT ALDERSHOT.

H ERE are the men of an Aldershot class going through individual practice under the eyes of their instructor—
man being pitted against man in a kind of friendly duel, to lunge and parry, and so on, until one of the men, as
we see in the photograph, has got the best of it. The instructor acts as chief umpire, checks and notes the points
made, stops any attempt at unfair play, prevents bad blood being shown, and criticizes faults all round.

Figure 4.2   Bayonet instruction class, Army School of Physical Training, Aldershot, c.1894 (author's collection)

commonplace—physical training instructors in most modern armies are given extensive instruction in anatomy and the "physiology of bodily exercise"[30]—but in 1898 these ideas, though perhaps not revolutionary, were quite progressive. Given the contemporary state of military literacy, it actually might have been difficult to find enough instructors capable of detailed anatomical learning. Despite this fact, however, Will's essay is, again, a strong indication of the late Victorian British officer's professional interest in training that would ensure the maximum combat effectiveness of the Army. The Army's physical training system was only a part of that training, but given its "newness" and high visibility thanks to men like Edgeworth-Johnstone, it acted as a touchstone for debate on modernization and rational methods.

Lieutenant Colonel Fox was replaced in 1897 by another Highland officer, Colonel the Honorable John S. Napier, of the Gordon Highlanders. Fox continued to have a powerful influence on the institution of physical training in Britain: from 1902 to 1903 he sat on the National Commission for Physical Directions and from 1902 to 1904 he held the position of Inspector of Physical Training for the Board of Education. He visited Scandinavia alone in 1908, and was made a Commander of the Royal Order of the Sword by King Gustav of Sweden in 1909. He was knighted in 1910 by King Edward VII.[31]

Colonel Napier, a protégé of the new Commander-in-Chief Lord Wolseley, was determined to complete the modernization of the physical training program and further enhance the stature of the Gymnastic Staff in the process. Under his direction more than eighty new gymnasia were erected throughout Great Britain, NCO and officer lounges were added to the Headquarters Gymnasium, and a visitor's gallery was constructed in the building to accommodate spectators for boxing competitions and other displays. These improvements at Aldershot were partially funded by gate money from the new athletic grounds.[32]

Colonel Napier also insisted on expanding the role of swimming within the training program, and with that goal in mind he set out to construct a modern swimming pool at the Gymnastic Staff's growing headquarters and school. Receiving no help from official sources, Napier used £12,000 of Royal Military Tournament Funds to construct a swimming facility that was still in use in the 1990s and has only recently been closed. From his time on, soldiers have been trained not only to swim as a recreational and stamina-building activity but also

---

[30]   Both at the United States Army's Physical Fitness School and at the British Army's Physical Training Corps School, soldiers are given extensive instruction in these topics.

[31]   *Mind Body and Spirit* No. 79 (1995/96), p. 123.

[32]   Oldfield, *History of the Army Physical Training Corps*, pp. 14–15.

COLONEL FOX: THE INSPECTOR OF ARMY GYMNASIA.

COLONEL G. M. FOX, Inspector of Army Gymnasia, is the officer specially in charge of the department of the Army which deals with the physical training and development of the soldier. Some of his best men—specially selected for the occasion from among the instructors at Aldershot Headquarter Gymnasium—are seen every year at the Tournament at Islington. The training of the Army in swordsmanship comes also within COLONEL FOX's supervision, and to him is due the credit of introducing the new system of sword exercise, based on Masiello's Italian method of fence, in place of the practice based on the French method, hitherto in vogue in the British Army.

Figure 4.3   Colonel George Malcolm Fox, Inspector of Gymnasia, Aldershot, 1895 (author's collection)

to swim in full clothing and equipment. This exercise has doubtless saved many soldiers' lives over the years.[33]

During Colonel Napier's term as Inspector of Gymnasia the war in South Africa took place. The effects of that war on all aspects of the British Army were profound, and have been dealt with in great detail in the historiography of the period. The role that physical training and the Gymnastic Staff played in the South African War and the subsequent reform movement is merely a part of that whole story, but one that is illuminating. The Gymnastic Staff was employed in vigorous training of the large influx of recruits required during the war, and although there is no record of an organized deployment of staff instructors to the combat zone (such as would occur in the First and Second World Wars), Colonel Napier was called to serve on Lord Roberts' staff and his post at Aldershot was temporarily filled, once again, by Fox, now a full Colonel.[34] Soldiers en route to the war conducted various forms of physical conditioning on board ship,[35] and while in South Africa units continued to engage in organized sports, games, and tournaments. The major effects of the war on the Army's physical training programs, however, came in the war's aftermath.

As the war drew to a close, Major C.B. Mayne of the Royal Engineers published an article in the *United Services Magazine* that strongly pointed out the vital importance of physical fitness for infantry to be successful, especially in the attack. He illustrated his argument with examples of recent skirmishes and attacks in South Africa that almost invariably took place over hilly and broken terrain. Major Mayne discussed in detail the precedent of vigorous physical training for the infantry in Sir John Moore's Light Infantry training program during the Peninsular Campaign of the Napoleonic Wars, and he argued that the Army should resurrect a similar program of practical cross-country maneuvers and running drill.[36] Running drill was already in vogue in some units: Major General Gatacre's command during the Nile campaign to reconquer the Sudan in 1898 conducted routine running drill as part of their training while waiting to move upriver.[37]

A year later an article entitled "Modern Military Training" appeared in *The United Services Magazine*, in which the anonymous author pointed out that the

---

[33]   Ibid., pp. 15–16.

[34]   Ibid., p. 17.

[35]   Mollo, *The British Army from Old Photographs*. Photograph #64 in this book shows soldiers in fatigues and boots performing "setting-up" exercises on the deck of a ship.

[36]   Major C.B. Mayne, "The Training of Infantry for the Attack," *The United Services Magazine* Vol. 20 (1899–1900), p. 278.

[37]   Edward M. Spiers, *The Victorian Soldier in Africa* (Manchester: Manchester University Press, 2004), p. 145.

British Army's experience in South Africa had been "productive of much good in rousing us and opening our eyes to many weaknesses in our system of training our troops," and he went on to describe some of these weaknesses and possible corrections. One of his most strident points was that mobility would be the key to any future conflicts, and that rapid mobility could only be obtained in two ways: a great number of mounted troops, and "high physical training of men and animals." He went on to provide four principles upon which he believed all future training should be based in order for the Army to make the most of its recent experience.

The first principle he outlined was "Discipline," which, unsurprisingly, he felt should form the basis of all military operations and training. Nothing new there; but then, like the author of "Battalion Command" in 1891, he laid out his second principle as being "the highest possible physical development." He stated that, although "this principle is universally recognized," there was still considerable room for improvement in the Army's methods of physical training. Again, like the author of "Battalion Command" and Major Mayne as well, he argued that gymnastics only improved the upper-body physique of the soldier and that running and frequent long-distance footmarches in addition to gymnastics were the best methods for increasing fitness and the soldier's "staying power," both crucial elements in combat effectiveness. Going further than the author of "Battalion Command," however, this "Staff Corps Captain" then went on to advocate that soldiers be required to participate in games like football and hockey, as they increased endurance as well as the "independence, resourcefulness and common sense" of the soldier:

> Therefore, this taste for games and sports ought to be encouraged in every possible way, and men who will not take part in these games ought to be kept up in their staying-powers by more marching, I do not mean mere drilling on a barrack square, but plenty of intelligent field work such as scouting, etc.[38]

This advocacy of overall fitness was not new, but the hard experience of the war made calls for change such as these more effective and more urgent. In a different article in the *United Services Magazine* published in 1904, another author urged a different kind of change to the physical training program: he argued that recruits should spend their first three months' training entirely under the control of the Gymnastic Staff. He pointed out that this method would get recruits into better condition than the then current system of one hour's gymnasium

[38] "A Staff Corps Captain," "Modern Military Training," *The United Services Magazine* Vol. 23 (1901), pp. 404–407.

work per day, and the recruit would also be better able to perform during his other training after being "shaped up" by the physical training instructors. Good points, perhaps, but clearly this idea that would radically alter the current means of training recruits must have met with serious opposition—even an editor's note after the article took strong issue with some key elements of the argument.[39]

Tacit acceptance of formal gymnastic training as an institution by soldiers throughout the Army, in spite of some dissatisfaction with the mechanics of the system, led some in the Army's leadership to question the continued need for the Gymnastic Staff as a separate entity for oversight of PT. In a move to save money following the South African War in 1903, an officer on the Army Staff forwarded a memo to the Army Council suggesting that the Gymnastic Staff be disbanded, except as a skeleton cadre to run the instructor's course at Aldershot. The memo presented the argument that gymnastic training in units could and should be managed by company and squadron officers and NCOs, and that the consequent elimination of all Staff Instructor billets in battalions would create a significant cost savings for the Army. A paper attached to the proposal briefly outlined the physical training schemes of the French, German, and Austrian armies, and showed how those schemes were run by regimental officers without a centralized system such as existed in Britain. The paper then laid out the current organization of the Gymnastic Staff, along with an estimate of the total yearly cost of the Staff: £20,970.15.[40] Not a large sum relative to the overall Army budget, but a significant one in an organization continually beset by demands for cost cutting from the Government.

Most members of the Council agreed with this argument, including Sir John French and the Adjutant General. In a note added to the memorandum, the Adjutant General strongly recommended approval of the idea, saying that the system of physical training would be better off if put into line with the systems maintained for

> musketry and other similar kinds of specialized training – units sent NCOs and officers to the Musketry School at Hythe, and once qualified as instructors they managed the training for their units.[41]

In a final minute to the proposal, and one that apparently ended the discussion, the Army's senior leader and the hero of the war, Field Marshal Lord Roberts, made an argument that not only assured the Gymnastic Staff's survival into the

---

[39]   "Chancton," "The Gymnastic Training of Recruits in the British Army," *The United Services Magazine* Vol. 29 (1904), pp. 66–71.

[40]   WO 32/7047, 1903, National Archives.

[41]   Ibid.

future, but that also acts as proof for the historian that gymnastic training and the Staff were viewed at the highest levels as absolutely essential elements in the process of preparing British soldiers for war. Roberts started his response to the minute of the Adjutant General by agreeing that, yes, having company and squadron officers supervise all of the training in their units was the ideal. He disagreed, however, with the premise that the average company officer was either capable or prepared to assume the burden of gymnastic training:

> I cannot believe that the average company officer can be expected to acquire this knowledge, and therefore I am not in favor of doing away with the present gymnastic arrangements which have effected a marvellous improvement in the Rank and File of the Army as evidenced during the recent maneuvres, when the admirable physique and marching powers of the young soldiers attracted general approbation.[42]

A more forceful endorsement of the Staff and the scheme of gymnastic training is difficult to imagine. The fact that this endorsement came from Lord Roberts himself made it a powerful argument for the system. Gymnastic training had clearly arrived as an integral part of the Army's training program.

The demands for change to the physical training program, however, could not be ignored forever. With Colonel Napier's continued advocacy at the highest levels, change did occur. In 1905 the Inspector of Gymnasia was brought under direct control of the War Office, as part of the overall Inspectorate-General at Whitehall, and in 1906 Lieutenant Lankilde of the Danish Army arrived at Aldershot to finally introduce the Ling System of physical training to the British Army. Almost immediately the new system won accolades from the Army hierarchy, medical officers and field commanders. Hated dumbbell training was eliminated, and the interiors of gymnasia were converted to accommodate the new program of overall fitness and free exercises. Lieutenant Lankilde remained at Aldershot for a full year, and his visit was deemed a great success by all concerned.[43]

In 1908 a new physical training manual was published, incorporating the Ling System along with many other new innovations such as an increased role for footmarching and Surgeon-Captain Will's insistence on anatomical and physiological information for instructors. This manual marks the reaching of maturity for the Army's physical training program, as it covered all aspects of fitness training, including, for the first time, a full integration of athletics, sports,

---

[42] Ibid., Minute 3.
[43] Starr, "War History of the British Army Gymnastic Staff," (first draft), p. 1.

and games.[44] This integration revealed a recognition by the Army's leadership that since the 1870s sport and games had become by far the most popular and frequent activities for all ranks throughout the entire Army, and that organized games, in particular, were now considered sufficiently important for the Army's effectiveness that they rated a place in the program right alongside that of gymnastics and other formal training.

---

[44]   *Manual of Physical Training* (1908).

Chapter 5

"No Better Pastime for Soldiers": The Expansion of Army and Regimental Sport

The value of active games and sports to physical training cannot be over-estimated. Games and physical training should be looked on as complementary to one another and a man's physical education can hardly be considered complete without the introduction of some form of active recreation.

Manual of Physical Training, 1908[1]

There can be no better pastime for soldiers than football, combining as it does skill, judgment, pluck, resource, activity—all soldierly qualities—and affording amusement to all, from the recruit enjoying the humble punt-about on the parade ground to the crowds of enthusiasts keenly watching a hard contested struggle for the final ties for the Army Cup.

Major General H.M. Bengough, C.B., Commanding 1st Infantry Brigade, Aldershot (1890s)[2]

In the forty years before the outbreak of the First World War one of the most remarkable social phenomena in Britain was the dramatic rise of organized sport, both amateur and, increasingly, professional. The process by which sport and competitive games became so important to Britons during this time is well documented.[3] The growing British mania for sport and games in the late Victorian and Edwardian period was important for many reasons, signaling as it did the newly acquired taste for leisure activities among the working class and the relative decline of the role of the upper class in defining the boundaries of what was acceptable in leisure time; the decline of the amateur ideal is but one example of the upper classes' loss of influence in this process.

---

[1] *Manual of Physical Training* (1908), p. 8.

[2] Phillip Warner, *Army Life in the '90's* (London: Hemlyn Publishing Group Ltd. [Country Life Books], 1975), p. 79.

[3] One of the most recent and comprehensive of these many studies is Sir Derek Birley, *Land of Sport and Glory: Sport and British Society 1887–1910* (Manchester: Manchester University Press, 1995).

Sport and competitive games became a social fixture during this time, and when one considers the truism that a society's military institutions are in many respects a close reflection of the society itself, it naturally follows that the contemporary British obsession with sport would carry over to the Army. It did, and in a way that made civilian society's passion for sport seem lukewarm in comparison. Sport and games came to dominate the lives of soldiers in this period to an enormous extent: the regimental newsletters and journals that proliferated at this time are often filled with nothing but reports of match scores, details of contests, debates over who should represent the regiment in various tournaments, and advocates of different sports making pitches for "their" game.[4]

Admittedly, space in a monthly journal is hardly sufficient cause to believe that these activities occupied such a central place in the lives of British soldiers, but when combined with articles in professional journals, an extensive photographic record, and the written memoirs of soldiers, rankers, and officers alike, a picture forms of these activities that is hard to deny. Sport even reached the poems of Rudyard Kipling: in "The 'eathen" Kipling has his budding recruit participating in physical training, and then teaching his charges to play cricket after he is promoted to Colour Sergeant.[5] During the last decades of the nineteenth century officers' traditional obsession with sport and games passed into the ranks, until by the turn of the century a commentator on the life of the soldier would say, "a really good player of one of these games [cricket/football] is almost as great a man in a regiment as he is at a public school."[6]

Just before the Second World War, the Army Sport Control Board, which had been formed in 1918 as a governing body for the growing number of various Army sports associations, published a booklet entitled *Army Sport Records 1880–1939*. As an example of the incredible proliferation of organized sport and games in the Army during the period covered by this study, that book

---

[4]   I have relied heavily in this chapter on the journals of five British Army units from this period. They are: *The Thin Red Line*, journal of the Argyll and Sutherland Highlanders; *The Thistle*, journal of the First Regiment of Foot, the Royal Scots; *St. George's Gazette*, journal of the Northumberland Fusiliers; *The Black Horse Gazette*, journal of the 7th (Princess Royal's) Dragoon Guards; and *The Journal of the Household Brigade*, *The Household Brigade Magazine*, and the *Brigade of Guards Magazine*. These last three are separate embodiments of the same journal, with periodic name changes. My reasons are many for selecting these particular journals. They represent a good cross-section of the Victorian Army—a Highland regiment, two line infantry regiments, a line cavalry regiment, and the Guards—and there are so many of these journals extant that it would be a monumental task to attempt to deal with all of them.

[5]   Rudyard Kipling, *The Barrack-Room Ballads* (Munslow: Hearthstone Publications, 1995), p. 112.

[6]   Reverend E. Hardy (Chaplain to the Forces), "Tommy Atkins at Play," *The United Services Magazine* Vol. 12 (1895–1896), p. 522.

lists fifteen major sports as being controlled by the Board, most of which have records of competitions kept at least since the 1890s, and some since the 1870s. These records cover contests in sports ranging from Athletics, Association Football, and Billiards, to Hockey, Rackets, and Water Polo. This booklet only holds records of Army, inter-service, and international (including Olympic) competitions, and when one considers that Association football alone was played at the company, battalion, regimental, installation, and major command levels, as well as the higher levels covered in the record book, a clear picture of the vast extent of sporting activities in the Army begins to take shape.[7] During the season some battalions held football matches as often as five days per week.[8]

It is an effective way to illustrate the phenomenon of late Victorian Army sport by briefly describing what were the most common and popular of the many games played by Tommy Atkins: football, cricket, and boxing. It is also useful to return to the sports day or Gymkhana; these events continued to spread during the late Victorian and Edwardian period and often included football, cricket, and boxing matches along with athletics events, gymnastics displays and competitions, and "military sports." The institution of Army sports continued beyond the Victorian period, and thrives to this day. British Army units play games, have tournaments, take rafting, skiing and mountaineering expeditions, and regularly contribute athletes to Britain's international teams.[9] Yet now these activities are routine and completely accepted as normal parts of the daily regimen. It was during the years from 1880 to 1908, however, that this activity obtained its current place in Army life.

By far the two most widespread sports in the late Victorian and Edwardian Army were cricket and Association football. These games were so popular that one often gains the impression in regimental journals that fighting was "simply an interruption." Indeed, an officer in the Royal Hampshire Regiment wrote in that unit's journal in 1903, "We mustered a punitive expedition against a sheikh at Kotaibi and returned and played football and cricket, having lost ten [casualties]."[10] The military popularity of these games is not particularly

---

7   *Army Sport Records 1880–1939*, published by the Army Sport Control Board, War Office (1939). See also *Games and Sports in the Army*, published by the Army Sport Control Board, War Office (1932–1933).

8   *The Thistle* New Series Vol. 1 No. 4 (June 10, 1904), p. 62.

9   In *Mind, Body and Spirit*, the annual journal of the Royal Army Physical Training Corps, there are reports of the Staff Instructors posted with all the various units of the Army around the world, and in these reports the instructors detail the activities of their units, some of which seem reminiscent of their Victorian forebears in the amount of sport they engage in.

10   Byron Farwell, *Mr. Kipling's Army* (New York: W.W. Norton & Co., 1981), p. 203.

surprising given that the same held true for civilian society.[11] As one might expect, the popularity of these games varied in the Army according to where a regiment was from and at least partly depending on the preferences of the officers: Scots regiments vastly favored football over all other sports, while English regiments more often preferred cricket.[12] This geographical preference generally followed the civilian world, as cricket is an English game, and in general there were fewer enthusiastic cricket fans in nineteenth-century Scotland or Wales. Nevertheless, football was the game of choice for most British soldiers:

> Among all games, football takes first place with the rank and file. In the eyes of "Tommy" it is the sport of kings. An inter-regimental match is capable of transforming the most lethargic of soldiers into an excited individual hardly responsible for his actions. Should the contest be for the Army Cup, the interest evinced by all ranks is doubled. Indeed, it is doubtful if sudden and unexpected orders to "embark for the front" would so much upset the usual tranquillity in barracks. For days before the event all other subjects of conversation are practically tabooed in the barrack-room, and the chances of victory are freely discussed. When the day fixed for the match arrives, few but those who are confined to barracks fail to witness the event, and ere the game has well begun the field is a veritable pandemonium, so loud are the cheers of the onlookers.[13]

Most units, especially those stationed in India, played cricket during the summer, and football in the winter. Summertime in India was considered too hot to play football, and the more leisurely pace of cricket lent itself to the extreme temperatures of the India summer. Some Scots regiments, however, were so enamored of football that they played year round.[14]

Many Scots regiments were almost fanatical about football. Around the turn of the century, *The Thistle*, the monthly journal of the First Regiment of Foot, the Royal Scots, and *The Thin Red Line*, journal of the Argyll and Sutherland Highlanders, contained more information about company and regimental football than about the regiments' actions on active service in India and in South Africa. A regular column, "Fitba' Blethers," appeared in *The Thistle* where discussion of who had made the regimental team, why teams wouldn't train harder in the off season, the prospects of various company teams, and other

---

[11]   See Eric Parker, *The History of Cricket* (London: Seely Service & Co. Ltd., 1950); Percy Young, *A History of British Football* (London: Stanley Paul & Co. Ltd., 1968); and James Walvin, *The People's Game* (London: Penguin Books Ltd., 1975).

[12]   Callum Beg, "The Soldier at Play," in Warner, *Army Life in the '90's*, p. 76.

[13]   Ibid., p. 76.

[14]   Ibid., p. 76.

Figure 5.1   Football match, India, c.1890s (courtesy of the Council of the National Army Museum, London)

football news and gossip would be printed. In addition to "Fitba' Blethers," editors of *The Thistle* regularly included descriptions of matches, reports of scores, and other such football information, to the extent that most issues of *The Thistle* from this period are almost entirely taken up with the topic of Football, with some room left over for other sports and athletics. Clearly this game played a major part in the life of the regiment.

In the December 1901 issue of *The Thistle*, the portion of the journal allotted to the 1st Battalion begins with an account of some recent operations of the battalion in South Africa, with a listing of where various detachments were placed on anti-guerrilla duties, and some news on officer assignments. Then follows some extensive "Football Notes" for the 1st Battalion, which begins with the lament that "Since the Battalion left Middleburg for Balmoral on 4th October the Inter-Company Competitions have been at a standstill on account of the Companies being so scattered."[15] It would seem that the fortunes of war had interrupted the beloved sporting pastime of "Pontius Pilate's Bodyguard."[16] But not so—after a quick account of where the companies all stand in the battalion league, there are two examples of how these resourceful Scotsmen managed to "play up" in spite of the war:

> While the head-quarters of the Battalion were at Balmoral a scratch team took the Burghers of the Refugee Camp in hand to initiate them into the manly game of footer, but the Burghers appeared as if they would be more at home behind a kopje. The game, which was a very pleasant one from a player's standpoint, and most amusing from a spectator's point of view, ended in a win for the "Rooineks" by 5 goals to 2 (a free issue).

This account is followed closely by a lengthy description of a game played between officers and NCOs at Gun Hill Camp, Middleburg, while the battalion was awaiting orders. It would seem as if a good time was had by all, in spite of the 109-degree heat and the fact that several players on the officers' team might have been ringers: "Please note that of those composing the Officers' team some got their commissions very quickly—for instance, Pte. McDougal, of 2nd Battalion

---

[15]   *The Thistle* Vol. VIII No. 12 (December 1901), p. 148.

[16]   The Royal Scots, or First Regiment of Foot, are the oldest line regiment in the Army—hence the numerical designation. The story, probably true, of the nickname "Pontius Pilate's Bodyguard" is that, in a recurring argument with the Coldstream Guards about age and precedence, a Coldstreamer once argued that they deserved precedence because the Coldstream Guards were Charles II's bodyguard when he returned from exile at the Restoration. The reply from the Royal Scot was, "yes, and we were Pontius Pilate's bodyguard at the crucifixion."

fame, who was previous to the kick-off an officer's servant, turns up smiling as an officer at right-back." All in good fun, no doubt.[17]

The Royal Scots were not alone in their enthusiasm for football. Other regiments were equally dedicated to the game, as an examination of other regimental journals reveals. The Northumberland Fusiliers, although perhaps more partial to cricket, played football both in India and in South Africa.[18] The various Household Brigade journals show the Guards regiments to have been avid footballers, and though the editors of the 7th Dragoon Guards' journal were perhaps more inclined to publish stories on hunting, polo, and horse-racing, they always made space for football. In 1907, *The Black Horse Gazette* congratulated the regiment's team for reaching the final of the Cavalry Cup, and vowed that next year they would win.[19] As early as 1897, the 7th had arranged with the local grammar school authorities to use their football pitch twice per week for practices and match play.[20]

Most regiments held tournaments at the company level; these were often viewed as a means of training younger players for selection to the regimental team. Company-level competition would last for the same season as inter-regimental play, and the top team would often be rewarded with a cup, shield, or other similar trophy. Company and regimental teams would normally include a mix of officers and enlisted men, for by the 1880s the practice of segregating officers and other ranks for games and athletics was primarily restricted to the occasional officers vs. sergeants match or to more exclusive sports such as polo. Teams were coached by the best players, who were often also the regiment's Gymnastic Staff physical training instructors: many photographs of football and other teams show the team members flanked by uniformed coaches, proudly wearing their Gymnastic Staff instructor's brevet over their sergeant's stripes.

The Army formally organized its myriad Association football teams and leagues into the Army Football Association in 1881, and organized an Army Cup in 1888. One of the major influences behind this organization was Major Francis Marindin of the Royal Engineers, the co-founder and president of the F.A.[21] As an indication of the dominance of football in Scots regiments, Scots regiments played in the Army Cup final ten times in the first fourteen years it was played, three of those matches were played with Scots teams on both sides, and the cup was won by Scots regiments nine times.[22] Without doubt football's

---

17   *The Thistle* Vol. VIII No. 12 (December 1901), pp. 148–50.

18   *St. George's Gazette* Vol. 21 No. 242 (1903), Vol. 31 No. 363, etc.

19   *The Black Horse Gazette* Vol. V No. 2, p. 70.

20   *The Black Horse Gazette* Vol. 2 No. 3.

21   *Games and Sports in the Army*, pp. 42–50.

22   *Army Sport Records 1880–1939*, p. 33.

TUG OF WAR TEAM 2nd BATTALION GRENADIER GUARDS

Winners of Collective weight (120 Stone) all Army Championship, Aldershot, 1894 and 1895.

Sergt. Morley (Reserve)   Private Yorke.   Private Curran.   Pioneer-Sergt. Jones, (Captain)   Pioneer Moss.   Private Bolton.   Private Bullock, (Reserve)

Private Clayton.   Private Radford.   Private Martin.   Drummer Barnes.   Private McHugh.   Private Seabourne.

Figure 5.2   2nd Battalion Grenadier Guards All-Army Tug-of-War Championship Team, 1894–1895. The team captain, Pioneer Sergeant Jones (center), has his Gymnastic Staff Instructor's brevet above the stripes on his right sleeve (courtesy of the Council of the National Army Museum, London)

popularity throughout the entire Army was unsurpassed, and the amount of time and energy spent by soldiers on football was far more than one would normally expect for a mere "leisure pastime."

The second most popular sport among soldiers was cricket. Most regiments maintained a similar establishment for cricket as that for football, with company and regimental teams, tournaments and trophies. Famous scores, like battle honors, were remembered for generations: "In the Rifle Brigade it was well known and discussed by all ranks for more than half a century that Joe Constable of the 3rd Battalion had once made a stand of 500 not out at Dinapore."[23]

Cricket was enormously popular in the Guards regiments, mainly due to its place in the rural upper-class and public-school culture of aristocratic Guards officers. Cricket occupied a similar place in the affections of the Northumberland Fusiliers as that of football in the Royal Scots. *St. George's Gazette*, the journal of the Fusiliers, always reserved a great amount of space for cricket scores and other coverage, and in the issues of the early 1880s the varied coverage of cricket and football suggests that football was far less organized and definitely less patronized than cricket: by 1882 the regiment had an organized intercompany tournament and an all-ranks integrated regimental cricket eleven, while the football games reported seem more like unorganized pick-up games.[24] The Northumberland Fusiliers also continued to play their favorite game during the war in South Africa, with reports in the April 30, 1901 issue of *St. George's Gazette* of matches at Lichtenburg between the officers and sergeants, the 5th Battalion vs. the 3rd Imperial Yeomanry, and also against Paget's Horse.[25] The Guards also played cricket in wartime, as the *Household Brigade Magazine* reported in 1901: "An interesting Cricket match was played at Springfontein, Orange River Colony, 1 December, between 1st Battalion, The Scots Guards and Lord Lovat's Scouts, who won by 16 runs."[26]

The coverage of cricket in the regimental journals differs somewhat from that of football: in the journals there are page after page of match scores, with little or no description of the matches themselves. Clearly cricket did not generate the same sort of fan involvement that football did, but it was no less popular. This fact is amply demonstrated by the fact that, in a given monthly journal issue during the season, any one of these regiments might have up to ten or fifteen match scores reported. As each cricket match might take up to a full day to play, that adds up to quite a bit of time for a military unit to spend playing cricket. This is even more remarkable when one considers that some regiments, like

---

23   Farwell, *Mr. Kipling's Army*, p. 203.

24   *St. George's Gazette* Vol. I No. 2 (February 1883), Vol. I No. 3 (March 1883).

25   *St. George's Gazette* Vol. 19 No. 220 (April 30, 1901).

26   *Household Brigade Magazine* (1901), p. 67.

the Royal Scots, held a company-level cricket season simultaneously with the football season.[27]

Unlike football, cricket did not receive a formal Army association until 1919, and had no official Army competition until 1920. There were regular Army vs. Navy matches from 1910, however, and the Army was always well represented on British international teams.[28] This lack of higher-level competition does not seem to have dampened the enthusiasm of most units for cricket, although it must have had some effect on the eventual decline of cricket's popularity in the Army after the period covered by this study.

Boxing was another enormously popular Army sport, and remains so to this day. From its beginnings as a form of physical training, boxing quickly became widespread, with tournaments and matches held year round, at all levels. In 1893 the first Army Boxing Championships were held at Aldershot under the auspices of the Gymnastic Staff,[29] and the Army Sport Control Board records championships awarded to soldiers as early as 1892.[30] These early competitions undoubtedly owed their existence in large part to men like Colonel Fox and Captain Edgeworth-Johnstone, but with the sport's growth in popularity it rapidly took on a life of its own.

Colonel Fox himself attributed the widespread military popularity of boxing to Field Marshal Lord Wolseley. In an article written in 1913 for the *Household Brigade Magazine*, Fox recalled that, in the early years of Army boxing, the sport was out of favor with the authorities, and therefore was not encouraged by most commanders around the Army. That changed, however, when the Brigade of Guards was able to convince Lord Wolseley to attend a boxing competition in 1894. After the contests were over, Lord Wolseley gave a stirring speech to the crowd, in which he said that he thought boxing was the best possible sport for soldiers, and that he hoped boxing would receive all possible encouragement. As Fox related, when the speech was published in the newspapers the next day, the acceptance and growth of Army Boxing was assured from that point on. Fox concluded his article by adding,

> I do not think there is *any* sport which equals boxing as a means of developing those qualities so essential in a soldier or a sailor. A man who is fit to box three fast rounds in the ring must be in the best possible condition for marching or for

[27]   *The Thistle* Vol. II No. 2 (May 1894).
[28]   *Army Sport Records 1880–1939*, pp. 66–69. See also *Games and Sports in the Army*, pp. 262–263.
[29]   Lieutenant Colonel E.A.L. Oldfield, *History of the Army Physical Training Corps* (Aldershot: Gale & Polden Ltd., 1955), p. 13.
[30]   *Army Sport Records 1880–1939*, pp. 45–48.

shooting, and, I may add, is as a rule entirely out of sympathy with the canteen ... the value of boxing as a sport does not merely lie in the bodily fitness it produces; it goes deeper than that ... Its manifold advantages may be briefly summed up in the motto of our physical training department, "*Mens sana in corpore sano.*"[31]

In December 1905 the *Household Brigade Magazine* reported on a boxing "entertainment" held in the gymnasium at Victoria Barracks, Windsor. The evening was sponsored by the 2nd Battalion, Grenadier Guards, but contestants were not limited to the Grenadiers: there were representatives of several Guards regiments present, and a great number of civilian spectators. The editors described this event as a great success:

> Every available inch of the hall was occupied, and it is not speaking too far to say that if the space available had been twice or three times the size it could easily have been filled.

The affair was characterized "with that military discipline and tact – a very noticeable feature of the 2nd Battalion Grenadier Guards – and which greatly added to the success of the undertaking and the enjoyment of the visitors." Although the Sergeant-Major almost had to ask for order several times, both spectators and contestants conducted themselves admirably, with the exception of Private Bowyer, who in one of the lightweight bouts gave up after being reprimanded by the referee for falling "without a blow." The highlight of the evening was the Heavyweight Championship of the Household Brigade, fought in ten rounds between Private Cashing of the 2nd Grenadier Guards and Trooper Cook of the Blues and Royals. Cashing won by points, much to the delight of his battalion.[32]

Other continuing features of Army sport were the Assault-at-Arms, military tournament, or Gymkhana. These events, which consisted of military sports, athletics competitions, and other activities, remained widespread and very popular even into the First World War: the 1919 Inter-Allied Games can be seen as nothing more than a Gymkhana on a large scale. These events ranged from simple battalion affairs to large regional competitions. There was a regular Highland Games held in India until 1912,[33] and the Mhow Gymkhana and Mandalay District Assault-At-Arms were huge events participated in by

---

[31]   Colonel Sir Malcolm Fox, "Army and Navy Boxing," *Household Brigade Magazine*, May 1913, pp. 111–112.

[32]   *Household Brigade Magazine*, December 1905, pp. 21–26.

[33]   Farwell, *Mr. Kipling's Army*, p. 204.

Figure 5.3 Boxing match, India, c.1890s (courtesy of the Council of the National Army Museum, London)

Figure 5.4   Gymnastics display at Northumberland Fusiliers Regimental
Sports, East London, South Africa, January 1, 1900 (courtesy of
the Council of the National Army Museum, London)

numerous units, including regiments from the Indian Army.[34] Because of the
disruptions to normal organized competition in football and other games
during the South African War, Gymkhana seem to have become a widely
used substitute activity. *St. George's Gazette* reports on several regimental
sports being held during the war, such as in February 1900 at the Modder
River, Cape Colony, where "In spite of the horrors of war a Gymkhana took
place early this month," consisting of tent-pegging, horse and pony races, foot
races, dancing and piping competitions, tug-of-war and a wheelbarrow race.[35]
Often these sports days focused heavily on athletics, and certainly after the
reinstitution of the Olympic Games in 1896 this event must have provided
inspiration to many unit tournament organizers. There were even unit sports
and games during lulls in the campaign to reconquer the Sudan: in spite of

---

[34]   *The Thistle* Vol. VI No. 1 (February–March 1899), p. 5, and *St. George's Gazette* Vol. 31
No. 363 (March 31, 1913).

[35]   *St. George's Gazette* Vol. 18 No. 206 (February 28, 1900).

routine temperatures over 100 degrees in the desert, soldiers played football and there was a sports day after the battle at Atbara in April 1898.[36]

The wide range of sport and games played in the Army during the late Victorian period and the pervasive nature of such activity are truly remarkable. With even a cursory overview of Victorian Army sport it is easy to see how it came to dominate so many elements of the military, from the training program of the Territorial Army[37] to the very language of military discourse. Many contemporary observers felt this dominance to be unhealthy, but in hindsight it is clear that sport had no real negative effect on the combat performance of the Army, either in South Africa or in 1914: the evidence suggests quite the contrary, especially in the enhancement of morale and unit *esprit de corps*. In fact, after the rapid growth of the late nineteenth century, Army sport settled into a routine, organized, and codified part of military life, incorporated into the *Manual of Physical Training* and governed by hierarchical bodies and associations. Between 1908 and 1914 both sport and physical training reached a level of maturity that allowed observers to focus not so much on how they had revolutionized the lives of soldiers, but on how lessons learned from the Army's success in using sport and physical training to enhance its capabilities might be applied elsewhere, both within metropolitan Britain and across Britain's Empire.

---

[36]   Edward M. Spiers, *The Victorian Soldier in Africa* (Manchester: Manchester University Press, 2004), pp. 141, 149.

[37]   Joseph Lyons, "Sports and the Territorials: How to Popularize the Force," *National Defense* Vol. 3 No. 10 (August 1909), pp. 137–139.

Chapter 6

"They Have Taken to Our Manly European Games": Military Athleticism and the Empire

... if we are to place the Native Army on an equality with European Armies apart from drill and armament, further physical culture is indispensable ... we may be quite sure that if there are men now in the Native Army, who are not fitted for the playing of games, still less are they fitted for the great game of war.

CPT F.C. Laing, 12th Bengal Native Infantry, 1900[1]

The influence of the British Army's physical culture went far beyond the ways in which formal training and recreation changed the daily life and military effectiveness of Tommy Atkins. For the British Army did not exist in a vacuum: the institutions and culture of the Army touched not only wide portions of British society but deeply influenced societies within the Empire as well. The process of cultural imperialism, or the spreading of British culture around the world, is perhaps the longest-lasting result of the British Empire, and the Army was arguably one of the most powerful agents in that process. Most native peoples had only limited personal contact with the British throughout most of the Empire, and much of what contact there was for the vast majority of the colonized was with the Army—making the Army perhaps the primary means for dissemination of British ideas, language, and other elements of culture.

Certainly there were other, very influential agents of cultural diffusion such as the educational establishment, Christian missionaries, and British merchants and businessmen. However, these agents only had contact with a relatively limited segment of the imperial population. The Army had a much broader effect: it was more visible, often more intrusive, and through native military service was able to touch vastly more individuals than any other institution. If one considers the potential effect on Indian society alone, of British cultural influence on the millions of soldiers who served in the Armies of the Raj, one

---

[1]   Captain F.C. Laing, "Physical Training in the Native Army," *Journal of the United Services Institution of India* Vol. 29 No. 140 (July 1900).

cannot fail to see the profound role of the military in the extension of British culture. The more military nature of much of the contemporary Empire in Africa would tend to put the role of the Army there into even more stark relief, and the fact that many Victorian and Edwardian imperial administrators were former or serving soldiers added additional weight to the Army's influence.

An important, and in many ways the most successfully transmitted part of British culture throughout the Empire, was the culture of sport, games, and athleticism. As stated in Chapter 3, it is quite possible that the most English of games, cricket, is more popular now in South Asia and the Caribbean than in Britain, and the worldwide cult of soccer football is, of course, the most obvious example of the proliferation of British sporting culture.[2] Given the central role of the Army as an actor in the process of cultural dissemination, it naturally would follow that the British Army's part in what historian Allen Guttmann calls "ludic diffusion,"[3] or the spread of different games and sports across cultures, was and continues to be enormous. As recently as February 2002, the British Army in Afghanistan sponsored the first soccer game to be held in Kabul Stadium since the Taliban's seizure of power in the 1990s—the game was played between a scratch team of British military personnel and the surviving players of Kabul United, before a standing-room-only crowd of jubilant Afghans. The British military team won 3–1, and presented gold medallions to the Afghan team in recognition of this momentous event.[4]

Like the application of physical training and sport within the British Army during the Victorian period and beyond, the Army deliberately and systematically used physical and recreational training to improve the combat effectiveness and leadership of its imperial troops, with the added, openly pursued goal of making native soldiers more "British." The process followed many of the same paths that it did when applied to the British Army: establishment of instructor cadre and schools, construction of facilities, debates among the leadership over methods and practices, and finally, overwhelming acceptance and success. Both formal physical training and sport had later, slower starts in the imperial military establishment than they did in the metropolis, but the final results were similar. The militaries of the "White Dominions," Canada, Australia, New

---

[2]   J.A. Mangan, *The Games Ethic and Imperialism* (New York: Viking, 1986) and ed., *The Cultural Bond: Sport, Empire, Society* (London: Frank Cass, 1991). In this second book, there is one essay of particular note for this chapter: Tony Mason's "Football on the Maidan: Cultural Imperialism in Calcutta," pp. 142–153.

[3]   Allen Guttmann, *Games and Empires: Modern Sports and Cultural Imperialism* (New York: Columbia University Press, 1994).

[4]   Scott Simon, "Soccer in Afghanistan," *National Public Radio Weekend Edition Saturday*, March 2, 2002.

Zealand, and later South Africa, were such close reflections of the British Army that it is almost redundant to discuss here the nature of their physical training establishments;[5] in a later chapter I will outline the form those armies' physical and recreational training took during the First World War. The formal imperial military establishment elsewhere in the Empire, and in particular Africa, was not developed well enough during the period covered by this study to allow for detailed examination of physical and recreational training; it was only after the First World War, for example, that the greatly expanded King's African Rifles adopted formal physical training and received a complement of Army Physical Training Staff instructors.[6]

It is in an examination of India, in the Armies of the Raj, that one can most clearly see the manner in which Victorian and Edwardian British "military muscularity" was passed on to native soldiers within the Empire, and through them to native societies as a whole. The Indian military establishment had always had, since the establishment of the East India Company's armies, a close (if not always cordial) relationship to the British Army, and when the Company was abolished and the government of the Raj established, the already close ties between the British and Indian armies became, if anything, even closer and more symbiotic.[7] To many officers and other ranks serving in British units, military service in India constituted virtually their entire careers, which of course is completely true for those British officers who served in the Indian Armies. The nature of service in India essentially defined much of the Victorian

---

5   Evidence of the formal training and sporting establishments in the dominions is available in a variety of locations. For some specifics over a range of time see "Report of the Director of Gymnastics, on the Gymnastic Instruction of the Army, for the Year 1869," *Parliamentary Papers*, 1869–1870 pp. 575–581; Major H.P.R. Inscombe, Australian Permanent Staff, "The Australian Commonwealth Forces," *Journal of the United Services Institution* Vol. 38 No. 170 (1908), p. 66, and Gavin Mortimer, *Fields of Glory: The Extraordinary Lives of 16 Warrior Sportsmen* (London: Andre Deutsch, 2001).

6   See Anthony Clayton, "Sport and African Soldiers: The Military Diffusion of Western Sport throughout Sub-Saharan Africa," in William Baker and J.A. Mangan, eds., *Sport in Africa* (New York; London: Africana Publishing Co., 1987), pp. 114–137.

7   There are a number of very good general histories of both the British Army in India and the Indian Army. See Byron Farwell, *Armies of the Raj from the Great Indian Mutiny to Independence: 1858–1947* (New York: W.W Norton & Co., 1989); T.A. Heathcote, *The Military in British India: The Development of British Land Forces in South Asia, 1600–1947* (Manchester: Manchester University Press, 1995); Daniel P. Marston and Chandar S. Sundaram, eds., *A Military History of India and South Asia, from the East India Company to the Nuclear Era* (Bloomington, IN: Indiana University Press, 2008); David Omissi, *The Sepoy and the Raj, The Indian Army, 1860–1940* (London: Macmillan Press Ltd, 1994); and Richard Holmes, *Sahib: The British Soldier in India 1750–1914* (London: Harper Press, 2005).

military experience. After the Sepoy Mutiny[8] in 1858, British battalions were routinely brigaded with Indian regiments, and many developed close, comradely associations, which in some cases still exist.[9] All of these factors, coupled with the special place held by the Raj as the "jewel" in the imperial crown, tended to make the transfer of British Army culture to Indians pronounced to the extent that it has been said that the current Indian and Pakistani armies are in many ways perhaps more traditionally "British" than the Queen's army itself.[10] Games and gymnastics were a critical part of the Indian Army's partnership role in the transfer of "Britishness" from Tommy to sepoy, and thereon to the wider culture of South Asia as a whole. The Indian, Sri Lankan, Bangladeshi, and Pakistani armies all currently maintain large physical training and sports establishments, and even a cursory view at their websites, recruiting literature, and training doctrine provides irrefutable evidence of the continued powerful influence of an essentially British military physical culture.[11]

Given the symbiotic nature of the British and Indian Armies, which readily and famously transferred to each other language, traditions, uniforms, music, and other elements of military culture, it is not surprising that the exchange of physical culture also went in both directions. The game of polo, which was quite possibly the most popular recreational activity of many British officers well into the twentieth century, is originally an Indian game. Some traditional Indian military organizations had their own well-developed physical culture; irregular *silladar* cavalry units brought with them into the service of the British a renewed interest in traditional games such as horseback wrestling.[12] Additionally, many of the field sports practiced by the British while in India, such as pigsticking,

---

8   In the Indian Army, the ordinary infantry soldier was called a sepoy, and the cavalry trooper was called a sowar.

9   Farwell, *Armies of the Raj*.

10   In 1997, I overheard a conversation between two elderly former Indian Army officers who were comparing recent visits to British regimental messes and the messes of their former units, now both part of the Pakistani Army: the conduct of the British mess, it would seem, was not as "pukka" as the messes of their old units.

11   See, for example, http://www.army.lk/sports.php, http://www.army.mil.bd/node/81, http://www.pakistanarmy.gov.pk/AWPReview/TextContent.aspx?pId=286&rnd=490, or http://indianarmy.nic.in/Site/FormTemplete/frmTempSimple.aspx?MnId=186vVOHbgS 1sAcygzDuO4w==&ParentID=6zS1jQNgsFAAoUM6utUurg==&flag=Y0UYNTCHd HYbdCZT4Hjveg==. For comparison with the British Army, see http://www.army.mod. uk/raptc/default.aspx or http://www.army.mod.uk/events/sport/default.aspx. All web pages accessed 10 June 2012.

12   Wrestling on horseback is a traditional and very ancient form of training for cavalry. It was practiced in Europe during the Middle Ages, and is still a competitive game in Central Asia. It is closely connected to games like *buzhkasi* and, of course, polo.

were derived from existing South Asian customs. This process continues even now, over sixty years after the end of the Raj. In 2007 the British Army began to formally compete at the unit level and internationally in South Asia in the traditional Indian contact game of Kabbadi, in which team members attempt to touch an opposing team member over the center line and then return to their side without being tackled. Unsurprisingly, the Royal Army Physical Training Corps, the successor organization to the Gymnastic Staff, is taking a leading role in the organization and propagation of this new pastime.[13]

Gymnastic training in the Indian Armies began soon after the establishment of the Gymnastic Staff in Britain. This training was transferred to the Raj through several means: the exchange of ideas between officers serving in British and Indian regiments, the transfer of Gymnastic Staff-trained regimental instructors to India with their units, and finally, the official implementation of a physical training scheme by the hierarchy of the Indian military. After the turn of the century, the relatively small Indian physical training establishment gradually increased, and by the First World War it had reached parity with most of the Dominion armies. In 1918 the Indian Army published its first *Manual of Physical Training*, which was in essence a close copy of the British Army's manuals of 1908 and 1914.[14] In the years following the First World War, the formal physical training system in the Indian Army was at least equal in extent and stature to those in the Dominions, if not the British Army itself.[15]

Recreational training in the form of games, sport, and athletics had an even stronger beginning in India, mirroring the establishment and growth of these activities in the British Army. Again, the impetus for instituting a system of games and recreational training came largely from British officers serving in Indian regiments, for similar reasons as their encouragement and sponsorship of games in British regiments. A difference, however, between the program of sport and games in the British and Indian Armies was that, from the beginning, British officers saw games as a means of transferring to their native soldiers capabilities of British "manliness" and a martial spirit not naturally found, in their opinion,

---

13   See http://news.bbc.co.uk/2/hi/7110012.stm (accessed April 30, 2012), among other news stories in the British press related to the game. The Army originally took an interest in the game as a potential means of attracting recruits of South Asian descent. *Mind, Body and Spirit*, the journal of the Royal Army Physical Training Corps, now includes reports on the game, which seems to have really taken hold due most likely to its simplicity and exciting nature.

14   *Manual of Physical Training for the Indian Army 1918* (Calcutta: Superintendent, Government Printing, India, 1918).

15   Lieutenant Colonel E.A.L. Oldfield, *History of the Army Physical Training Corps* (Aldershot: Gale & Polden Ltd., 1955), pp. 141–148.

Figure 6.1   Indian Army horseback wrestling (Imperial War Museum)

in the Indian population.[16] Many officers based the athletic and sports training in their native units on the fundamental prejudice that Asian soldiers were not naturally as active or militarily capable as their European counterparts, and they viewed games and sports as an essential means of bringing Indian soldiers up to the required standard of martial prowess.

The standard of desired martial prowess for Indian soldiers was based on the growing fear in the late nineteenth-century Raj about Russian expansion into Central Asia, and the perceived possibility that the Indian Army might have to defend the Northwest Frontier against European adversaries. This fear led to several developments within the Indian military establishment. Some of these were organizational reforms undertaken to ultimately eliminate the separate presidency armies and create a modern divisional structure, and the evolution of "martial race" theories that supported changes in recruiting and manpower policies. This heightened concern for improved combat capabilities also led to an erosion of the post-Mutiny concern to keep the Indian Army less well equipped

---

[16]   Instances of British officers expressing this kind of opinion are legion. See below for some especially egregious examples, especially Captain A. Masters, Central India Horse.

and less capable than the British, which explains, at least in part, the growth in support after the 1880s for modernized physical training and sport programs.[17]

The timing of the rapid growth of interest in, and therefore expansion of both formal physical training and sports programs for Indian soldiers interestingly coincides with the wider acceptance of "martial race" theory and the shift in recruiting patterns it brought. There has been much recent research into the development of theories concerning the more warlike nature and higher military aptitude especially of Sikhs, Punjabi Moslems, Gurkhas, and Pashtuns.[18] These theories gained currency and began to be energetically acted on by the Indian military establishment to a great degree after the accession in 1885 of Lord Roberts as Commander-in-Chief, India. Historians have posited many potential origins and contributors towards the development of martial race theory in the Raj; the connections between loyalty and combat performance of Sikhs, Gurkhas, Pashtuns, and Punjabis during the Great Mutiny are the most obvious. There are also powerful connections between these theories and how they evolved in the late nineteenth-century Raj and the popular perceptions surrounding the military qualities of Highlanders after the Napoleonic Wars, and even in some of the descriptions of earlier native peoples either recruited or coopted by the British in their wars of empire—for example, Iroquois people were seen during the colonial period in North America as having special talents in warfare.[19]

In spite of the probable similar genesis of martial race theory and the more powerful impetus towards improving Indian soldier capabilities that drove interest in sport and physical training, there does not seem to be any evidence in the contemporary record of the Army's leaders focusing on the physical

---

[17]   Marston and Sundaram, eds., *A Military History of India and South Asia*, pp. 46–48; Heathcote, *The Army in British India*, pp. 180–183.

[18]   Probably the most important recent study on "martial race" theory is by Heather Street, *Martial Races: The Military, Race and Masculinity in British Imperial Culture, 1857–1914* (Manchester: Manchester University Press, 2004).

[19]   See, for example, Diana Henderson, *Highland Soldier: A Social Study of the Highland Regiments 1820–1920* (Edinburgh: John Donald Publishers Ltd., 1989), p. 12; E.M. Lloyd, "The Raising of the Highland Regiments in 1757," *English Historical Review* Vol. XVII (1902), pp. 466–469; John Prebble, *Mutiny: The Highland Regiments in Revolt 1743–1804* (London: Penguin Books, 1975), p. 33. For views of the inherent martial capabilities of the Iroquois, see James Axtell, *The European and the Indian* (Oxford: Oxford University Press, 1982). There are interesting parallels between Victorian ideas and images of the connection between Scots Highland soldiers and some of the "martial races" of India as described by Heather Streets, and similar eighteenth-century connections between the same Highland soldiers and Native Americans: see Ian M. McCulloch, *Sons of the Mountains: The Highland Regiments in the French and Indian War, 1756–1767* (Fort Ticonderoga, NY: Purple Mountain Press, 2006).

improvement of native troops from any particular region, religion, or ethnicity. To the contrary, the written records of professional debate as well as the personal recollections of British soldiers do not single out any one group in the drive to impose the Army's physical culture. All Indian Army troops, regardless of their region, religion, or race, were apparently viewed as equally in need of physical training and the benefits of games. This is not surprising given the way in which Army physical culture also developed uniformly across all elements of the British Army. The complex interaction between British racial theories and recruiting, the social and governmental structures in the affected recruiting areas such as the Punjab,[20] the religious, ethnic, social, and gender identities of Indian soldiers, and how the British ethos of athleticism was used to foster loyalty to the Army and Raj is clearly a fascinating subject in need of further examination, but it lies outside the scope of this study. The purpose here is to describe the nature of physical training and sport as applied to the Indian Army as a whole, and how the process of imposing these programs in the Raj is instructive of the manner in which British physical culture was transmitted by the Army across the Empire.

As stated earlier, gymnastic training in the Indian armies was established soon after its formal founding in the British Army, for essentially the same reasons—recognition of its positive effect on combat readiness, morale, and unit cohesiveness. With the regular rotation of British battalions to postings in India, as well as the common training of officers at Sandhurst, it was inevitable that the newly established program and ideas on fitness would come to India. In this early period before the turn of the century, however, the military establishment in India moved far more slowly than its British counterpart to embrace the scheme of training and apply it to native units. In 1869 Major Hammersley, the British Army Inspector of Gymnasia, reported that "It can scarcely be said that the system of gymnastic instruction has yet commenced in India." He described a minute staff, inadequate funding for construction of facilities and procurement of equipment, and insufficient numbers of trained instructors to provide supervision of training. The last shortcoming caused him alarm: he expressed fears that lack of proper supervision might lead to accident or injury, thereby jeopardizing the status and future of the program.[21] All of these deficiencies were the result of a lack of emphasis and funding by the Army leadership in India.

In spite of this organizational inertia, at least by the mid-1870s all native recruits were being required to undergo a regimen of physical training at their

[20]   See Tan Tai Yong, *The Garrison State: The Military, Government and Society in Colonial Punjab, 1849–1947* (New Delhi: Sage Publications, 2005).

[21]   "Report of the Director of Gymnastics, 1869," pp. 579–581.

depots, but there the formal requirement for physical training ended.[22] The slow start of Indian Army gymnastic training again is connected to the reluctance, part of the hangover in the Raj from the Mutiny, of many British officers in the Indian Army to make the native soldier able to compete with the British soldier.[23] Among other results of this deliberate policy, Indian soldiers were not armed with the most modern weapons, and they were not allowed field artillery. In the realm of physical culture this reluctance was primarily directed at attempts to institute a system of games in Indian units, but it clearly applied to the foundation of physical training itself. It would not be wise, so the line of thought went, to allow Indian soldiers to compete physically with their British counterparts, and perhaps to defeat them; this possible blow to the *izzat* or prestige of the British must not be allowed to occur. As time went on, however, this reluctance was overcome, as were conservative objections to gymnastics in the British Army, by the demonstration of the scheme's effectiveness and success. Again, the connection here to late nineteenth-century fears of a Russian push against the Northwest Frontier ultimately acted as a powerful inducement to remove any possible restrictions on the fighting capabilities of the Indian soldier. This factor, related to so many important developments in the late Victorian Indian Army, cannot be overestimated as a key motivation for many British regimental officers during the 1890s and early 1900s to argue for the improvement, expansion, and modernization of the physical training of sepoy and sowar.

The initial lack of a gymnastic training program for trained soldiers across the Indian Army caused a similar debate in Indian military professional circles as the shortcomings in the home program of physical training brought about in the British Army. In an article published in the *Journal of the United Services Institution of India* in 1876, Captain R. Hennell of the Bombay Army argued, along with calls for improved pay and living conditions, that, although recruit training was a good start in getting the native soldier up to the standard of his European peers, it was not enough. He suggested that the success of some regiments in maintaining their own gymnasia should be emulated by all units, and that, by encouraging gymnasium training and exercise for all soldiers, commanders would improve both the quality of new recruits and retain more good soldiers. Hennell also strenuously argued for a formal recreation and games program—more on that subject presently.[24]

Change did not come, and mandatory gymnasium training for trained sepoys was not established; any formal physical training in native units was done

---

22   Captain R. Hennell, "Soldiers' Institutes for the Native Army of India," *Journal of the United Services Institution of India* Vol. 5 (1876), pp. 69–78.

23   Farwell, *Armies of the Raj*, p. 156.

24   Hennell, "Soldiers' Institutes for the Native Army of India."

solely on the initiative of local commanders. This kind of local initiative was supported in part by a number of privately published manuals and other books that aimed to assist the interested commander in establishing a physical training program.[25] The continued lack of higher-level support for what many officers saw as a crucial element of growing British efforts to improve the fighting capabilities of the Indian soldier and make him more like his British brother, increased the intensity of the calls for change in professional publications. The subject of the 1890 prize essay sponsored by the United Services Institution of India was "Organization, and Employment in War of Native Cavalry." Despite the rather general nature of this topic, all three prize winners focused their essays almost entirely on training, with a significant portion of each essay devoted to the subject of physical training. The Gold Medal winner, Captain C.M. Maguire of the 2nd Cavalry, Hyderabad Contingent, discussed the lack of systematic gymnastic instruction for trained soldiers, and went on to say, "It appears especially desirable that the gymnastic training of the Indian cavalry soldiers should not terminate with their instruction as recruits, as the majority of men do not lead an athletic life." This argument for gymnastics was tied to a larger call for mandatory games.[26]

The Silver Medalist, Captain A. Masters of the Central India Horse, was even more specific in his call for sustained training beyond the recruit depot:

> A course of gymnastics, comprising vaulting horse, climbing rope, wrestling, clubs, running, jumping, swimming, and wrestling on bare-backed ponies, exercised a beneficial influence in the training of recruits; it develops their strength and agility, and also tends to sharpen their wits by waking them up, in which traits the Indian valley rustic is rather deficient.

Masters went on to say that a continuation of this training was critical for continued success in maintaining combat readiness. He argued for an expansion of the tournament sports or Gymkhana, especially the annual tent-pegging competition for lancers, and for "all forms of sport that contribute to the efficiency of Native Cavalry." These sports would comprise the basis of physical training in units: in providing an element of competition, cavalry sowars would be encouraged to excel in the gym. Masters's prejudiced view of what he clearly

---

[25]   There were many of these "self help" manuals: a good example is Sergeant Major Wm. Gordon, *Physical Training Without Arms* (1890), with translations into Urdu and Nagri (British Library shelfmark 8830.a70).

[26]   Captain C.M. Maguire, "Organization and Employment in War of Native Cavalry," *Journal of the United Services Institution of India* Vol. 14 No. 81 (1890), p. 241.

saw as his soldiers' natural shortcomings did not prevent him from working to improve their fighting capacity.[27]

Finally, the third-prize essayist, Lieutenant W.W. Norman of the 2nd Punjab Cavalry, stated during his call for improvement, "Once a week in the afternoon the sowars should be put through a set of gymnastic exercises; these are necessary to make limbs supple, and to give a man confidence in himself." This confidence was central to success in war and, as a corollary, would encourage the men to participate in team games.[28]

These calls for improved, more uniformly applied training must have been partially the result of the lack of staff and resources for gymnastics training: when forced to rely on the will and resources of the regimental leadership, naturally the program would be spottily maintained and administered. In a lecture given to senior Indian Army leaders at Simla in 1893, Major the Honorable A.E. Dalzell, Inspector of Gymnasia for the Bengal Army, decried both the lack of attention given to this important training by regimental officers and the resources applied to the program by the Indian Army leadership. He started his presentation with a detailed account of ways in which soldier fitness had affected the outcome of battle throughout history, and then went on to highlight his central argument by providing a comparison of the establishments of the Gymnastic Staff in Britain and in India. At the time of his speech, there were thirty-five first-class gymnasia in the British Isles, with a large staff to support training: the Inspector of Gymnasia, the Assistant Inspector, and fourteen District Superintendents, all school-trained and drawing staff pay while seconded to the Gymnastic Staff from their regiments. In addition to the officers on the Staff, there was a Sergeant Major, two Quartermaster Sergeant Instructors, twenty-seven First Class Sergeant Instructors, and twenty-eight Second Class Sergeant Instructors, all exclusive of the school-trained regimental instructors. Each first-class gym had a staff instructor permanently attached to supervise the regimental instructors, and the entire Staff was provided a yearly budget of £6,000.[29]

In contrast to this establishment, in all of India there were only two Gymnastic Staff officers drawing staff pay, four first-class gyms with assigned Superintendents (unpaid and unseconded), and only twelve NCO Staff Instructors. The yearly budget allotment for this tiny staff was half that of its metropolitan counterpart. Given that during any given year prior to the First

---

27   Captain A. Masters, "Organization and Employment in War of Native Cavalry," *Journal of the United Services Institution of India* Vol. 14 No. 81 (1890), p. 273.

28   Lieutenant W.W. Norman, "Organization and Employment in War of Native Cavalry," *Journal of the United Services Institution of India* Vol. 14 No. 81 (1890), p. 299.

29   Major the Hon. A.E. Dalzell, "Special Lecture Transcript," *Journal of the United Services Institution of India* Vol. 22 No. 107 (1893), pp. 362–385.

World War the Indian Army was vastly larger than the home-based British Army, the complaints of Indian Army officers over the lack of attention given to physical training by the leadership were certainly justified. Major Dalzell finished his lecture by giving an impassioned plea for a renewed commitment to gymnastic training in units, describing the extraordinary "keenness" of native soldiers for gymnastics—his small staff trained an average of forty native regimental instructors each year.[30] This fact, coupled with other descriptions of the eagerness of sepoy and sowar for physical training,[31] suggests that the culture of athleticism, so much a part of the British military ethos and a major pillar of the concept of military gymnastics, was by the 1890s becoming a feature of the Indian Army as well.

After the rough start up to the 1890s, the slow acceptance of gymnastic training by the Indian Army leadership broadened—and just as in the British Army, the consequences of the South African War for physical training were to be of great importance. Gymnastics, footmarching, and swimming all received an intense review in India, and ultimately became just as accepted as elements of training in India as they were in Britain. In two articles written in 1897 and 1900, Captain F.C. Laing of the 12th Bengal Native Infantry discussed the current system of physical training for both recruits and trained soldiers, analyzing its strengths and weaknesses with an eye to making improvements. His first article advocated the institution of swordsmanship training, managed and supervised by the Gymnastic Staff, in much the same manner as was then being done in Britain by Colonel Fox.[32] In his second article, written in 1900, Laing clearly demonstrated the deliberate British imposition of athleticism on Indian soldiers. He added to his argument suggestions that included compulsory games for recruits, an update of the gymnastic training scheme in order to reduce the expensive requirement for facilities and apparatus, and intensified training and compulsory games for trained soldiers as well:

> In addition to the recruits' ordinary training, he should be made to play hockey, football, or some similar game at least twice a week instead of afternoon drill; it is a pleasant change from routine; he doesn't lose much as a soldier, and he may gain an appreciation for a manly game which otherwise would never appeal to him.

---

[30]   Ibid.

[31]   For example, in addition to the other articles cited here, see Major Nigel Woodyatt, 3rd Gurkhas, "Notes on Hill Training," *Journal of the United Services Institution of India* Vol. 36 No. 166 (1907), pp. 155–157.

[32]   Lieutenant F.C. Laing, "The Encouragement of Fencing," *Journal of the United Services Institution of India* Vol. 26 No. 127 (1897), pp. 137–139.

Laing likened the native regiment to a public school, arguing that a rigorous program of physical training and mandatory games would have the same beneficial effects in character building for sepoys as it did for British schoolboys (see the quote at the start of this chapter).[33] It is difficult to see the transfer to the Indian Army of British ideas concerning sport and character as anything but inevitable; as British officers became more concerned with modernizing the native army, it was entirely natural that they use the techniques proven to be successful in Britain. Grafting cultural mores onto the Indian soldier was clearly a deliberately undertaken part of this process.

In 1901, the United Services Institution of India's prize essay contest topic was "The Practical Training of British and Native Troops in India with Reference to the Lessons of the War in South Africa." All three prizewinners strongly emphasized gymnastics as a central component of improved training. The Gold Medal winner, Lieutenant Colonel G.P. Ranken of the 46th Punjab Infantry, strongly objected to the contemporary practice, then in vogue both in Britain and India, of rote and slavish attention to the mechanics of "physical drill" in mass formations. His emphasis on focusing training on the individual soldier was pointed:

> The object of our physical training is according to the drill book "not display but the setting up of the soldier and the strengthening and rendering supple of his muscles," and yet, in nine cases out of ten, the physical training of regiments is tested at the annual inspection by making the whole regiment perform the exercise in perfect time to the band. Would not the real results of the training be more practically tested by the inspecting officer selecting, say, half a company and making the men perform the exercises stripped to the waist?[34]

Emphasizing the individual in training, improving independent thought and action, quickening reflexes, all were goals of the gymnastic training program. These goals became more important when viewed in the light of the Army's performance in South Africa, and along with the previously discussed fears of Russian expansion, were also instrumental in breaking down objections to bringing the Indian soldier up to par with the British. After the turn of the century, officers in India began to distinguish less and less between British and Indian soldiers in the nature and practice of training, making intensive preparation for modern war an imperative that had not been seen in the Raj

---

[33]   Captain F.C. Laing, "Physical Training in the Native Army."

[34]   Lieutenant Colonel G.P. Ranken, "The Practical Training of British and Native Troops with Reference to the Lessons of the War in South Africa," *Journal of the United Services Institution of India* Vol. 30 No. 144 (1901), pp. 153–180.

since before the Mutiny—a superb example of this breakdown in distinction is the topic of the 1901 Prize Essay itself, and most articles on training published during this time in the Indian Army made no distinctions between British and Indian soldiers.[35]

The 1901 Silver Medal essay, by Captain W.B. James of the 2nd Bengal Lancers, demanded just the kind of heightened intensity called for by this dissolution of British–Indian distinction:

> The present system [of physical training] can hardly be improved. It is, however, important to emphasize the necessity for the training to be constant. Muscles become soft and wind short when training is neglected or performed in a desultory manner. There is a certain class of men, both in the British and Native Armies, who tries to avoid exercise and bodily exertion as much as possible. Particular attention should be paid to those who do not take part in games.[36]

Two years later, Major F.V. Whittall of the 1st Infantry, Hyderabad Contingent, called for still more updates and intensification of physical training in the native army. He said that, in addition to the normal course of instruction, soldiers should perform "field gymnastics," or negotiate assault or obstacle courses, just as soldiers were then beginning to do in Britain:

> Leap-frog, follow my leader, football, hockey, tug-of-war are all aids to the development of lungs, muscles, sinews, and alacrity of brain. I would include all of these in the gymnastic training, or, indeed, training of the soldier.[37]

All of these calls for refinement of physical training parallel the movement in the British Army for a modern, diverse military physical culture. Writing in his 1903 report, the first annual report of its kind, Lieutenant Colonel E. Cleary Hill, the Inspector of Gymnasia for India wrote: "The value of gymnastic training is now fully recognized by all ranks. His physical culture and well being yearly appeal more to the British Soldier in India." As for the Indian soldiers, including

---

[35]   Again, see Major Nigel Woodyatt, 3rd Gurkhas, "Notes on Hill Training" and "G.A.T." (Major G.A. Trent, Indian Army Inspector of Physical Training), "Physical Training of the Infantry Soldier in India," *Journal of the United Services Institution of India* Vol. 38 No. 174 (1909), pp. 201–211.

[36]   Captain W.B. James, "The Practical Training of British and Native Troops with Reference to the Lessons of the War in South Africa," *Journal of the United Services Institution of India* Vol. 30 No. 144 (1901), pp. 186–212.

[37]   Major F.V. Whittall, "The Training of the Native Infantry Recruit," *Journal of the United Services Institution of India* Vol. 32 No. 152 (1903), pp. 267–271.

the 105 NCOs and soldiers trained as regimental instructors by the Staff that year, "They are full of work, keen, and anxious to improve." Hill also noted with approval the growing number of sporting competitions occurring in the Indian Army, stating that they "have a most beneficial effect."[38]

Even with acceptance and continued improvements, however, the Indian Army continued to be hampered in its training by lack of uniformity in enforcing standards, and lack of funding. Swordsmanship and bayonet training were particularly affected by shortage of funds, and the very limited construction of facilities and apparatus restricted Indian units from being able to conduct training in the ways demanded by regulation.[39] The leadership of Indian units, especially in the cavalry, clearly had not yet begun to place formal physical training for their soldiers at the same level of importance as their counterparts in British units. The reports of the Inspector of Gymnasia in India during these years are full of comments regarding the lack of uniform training across units, and the exhortations to the Indian units are, for reports of this kind, quite vehement. In 1907, Lieutenant Colonel H.J.S. Landon commented:

> This branch of soldiers' training [bayonet fighting] I cannot report well of. The supply of spring bayonets and equipment (6 to a battalion) is utterly inadequate for anything like the thorough training of a complete unit ... I venture to express the opinion that the time has come to place the physical training of the soldiers in the Indian Army on an improved footing. Much is expected ... In the Cavalry there are still regiments who have not adopted the course in spite of the instructions contained in Adjutant-General in India's letter no. 623-G, dated 20th June 1906.[40]

Attached to Landon's report was a memorandum from the Adjutant General of the Indian Army, stating unequivocally, "Physical Training is a matter of great importance and requires very systematic attention. The object or spirit of the orders should not be lost sight of."[41] These instructions had an effect. Within a year of this report the Inspector of Gymnasia was able to report great improvements, including widespread use of the newest training programs brought over from Britain. The Indian Army even sent a cadre of its Gymnastic Staff instructors to the school in Aldershot so they could be trained in the newest techniques of free gymnastics, and bring that knowledge back to the subcontinent. By 1909 the

---

[38]   "Annual Reports of Inspector General of Gymnasia in India 1903–1916," *India Office Records (IOR)* British Library (L/MIL/7/17086), 1903 report, paragraphs 12, 19.

[39]   Ibid., 1905 report, paragraph 12.

[40]   Ibid., 1907 report.

[41]   Ibid.

Inspector of Gymnasia could report that in general Indian units' performance was much the same as their British counterparts, to such an extent that from that time on formal reports did not distinguish between British and Indian units, only between the branches of Infantry, Cavalry, and Artillery.[42]

When the British Army published its first manual of physical training in 1908, it was adopted by the Indian Army soon afterwards.[43] Moreover, just as in Britain, when the new manual included the full integration of games and athletics within the training program, it was a recognition of the central place in Indian Army life long held by organized games and recreational training: games and sports in the Indian Army had almost reached the same level of significance as they had in Britain, and were certainly more important in the life and training of soldiers than gymnastics.

By the late nineteenth century, the British in India had begun to see powerful incentives to make their native soldiers equal to the challenge of combat against European adversaries. A critical part of this imperative was to instill in them the same attributes that games would impart to British other ranks: fitness, physical courage, mental agility, teamwork, and a superior moral character. The "games ethic" was always the primary factor in motivating the British to develop sports and athletics in native regiments, although many officers saw games as a superb way to encourage bonds of good feeling between sepoy and British officer, and between the various ethnic and religious groups found within native battalions. What better way to encourage regimental *esprit de corps* in a "class company battalion" comprising separate companies of Sikhs, Punjabi Moslems, and Rajputs, than to field unified regimental teams that could win on the cricket or football pitch?

In some cases, British officers coupled sports with other activities designed not only to demonstrate British concern for the various religious and ethnic identities found within Indian units but also to foster a sense of organizational loyalty and unity in spite of those sometime competing identities:

> After the Id in 1917, one Muslim trooper recalled how "all the Mahomedans of the Division had their prayers together. About 1500 men assembled and prayers were offered for the victory of our King. After that we had sports and such a display of joy that I cannot describe it. All the Sahibs thanked us for what we had done and now at midnight full of happiness I am sitting down to write this letter."[44]

---

[42]   Ibid., 1908, 1909 reports.
[43]   "G.A.T.," "Physical Training of the Infantry Soldier in India."
[44]   Omissi, *The Sepoy and the Raj*, p. 101.

The introduction of British games in the Indian Army by the leadership had always been far more successful than the implementation of gymnastics training. Repeatedly, officers emphasized how native soldiers took to games with enthusiasm, in spite of their lack of knowledge or practice; it was a commander's responsibility to make his soldiers play games in order to be better fitted for war. In this respect, Captain Hennell's previously cited 1876 article in the *Journal of the United Services Institution of India*, is worth quoting at some length:

> A supply of outdoor games should be kept up for the use of the regiment. No one can have travelled much of late years in India, without having noticed how wonderfully the natives have taken to our manly European games. In native regiments, both Cavalry and Infantry, this progress is even more noticeable; and I have played both with and against elevens composed of native soldiers, who would gain applause from the public at Lords or the Oval.
>
> Young native soldiers I have known, who have excelled their teachers— University men—in our national game of cricket—and to play with whom it was a real pleasure. I have frequently seen young sepoys after a few weeks training stand up before the wickets against swift bowling, and that without pads or gloves, in a style which would have done the heart of any old English *pater familias* good to have seen. In the hottest stations of India, I have played football with native soldiers and enjoyed their evident eagerness after the game, which is supposed to be so entirely suited to a cold climate. But who were the prime movers in these cases—who were the promoters of this social intercourse? Why, the commanding officers of the regiments of course.[45]

A more cogent description of the process of cultural imperialism performed by the British military is difficult to imagine—British officers teaching and coaching their native soldiers to play British games in order to make them conform to British ideals of soldierly qualities. Hennell clearly, if unconsciously, articulated here the real reasons behind British efforts to introduce their games to native soldiers: if a young sepoy could stand up at the wickets against "swift bowling" and not flinch, he had passed the acid test of true manliness insofar as the Victorian military was concerned, and was ready to enter combat on the same level as his European counterpart.

Games and recreational training in Victorian and Edwardian Indian Army regiments held virtually the same pride of place as they did in British regiments. The rhythm of the training day was often governed by scheduled sport or games. Always, the recreational training of units was directed and led by the British

---

45   Hennell, "Soldiers' Institutes for the Native Army of India."

officers. They acted as teachers, coaches, and members of teams, and encouraged soldiers to excel, in spite of the difficulties sometimes attendant on teaching men to follow the precepts of British sportsmanship, which were perhaps somewhat alien to them:

> The sahibs, as the sepoys call their officers, endeavour to teach their men such games as hockey, football and cricket; for such is the nature of these queer Englishmen that they cannot sit still ... It is not always an easy task ... Although good soldiers, the young recruits were little use at hockey. Yet the officers thought the task not so hopeless as it seemed, for the men were keen to play, if not to learn. Breaches of rules were so frequent, that if the play had been stopped each time, there would have been no game at all ... As it can be imagined, it is no light matter to enter into such a contest. As one man put it when describing a game to me, "Some got hit in the face, some on the top of the head; but all got hit."[46]

As in the British Army, regiments in the Indian Army often specialized in a favorite game or pastime—following the example of their close comrades the Scots, Gurkha battalions often were partial to football.[47] Of course, Indian cavalry regiments played polo, and were sometimes hard to beat.[48] By the turn of the century, it was not uncommon to see native teams playing in polo tournaments against the British, and in the regular gymkhana held around the Raj, Indian units routinely competed against British units in sports such as tent-pegging. In the March 1914 issue of the *Black Horse Gazette*, the descriptions of the 7th Dragoon Guards regimental sports of February 20 include references to Indian Army units competing in section tent-pegging, foot and horse races, and polo. The same number gives an account of the January 1914 Laver Cup Hockey Competition, in which several Indian Army units took part.[49] Other Gymkhana mainstays like gymnastics and athletic competitions were still very often kept segregated; again, fears about potential damage to prestige would not allow for formal competition between the races (although mixed informal

---

[46]   A.G. Thomson, "Hockey with Rajputs," *The United Services Magazine* Vol. 17 (1898), pp. 556–558.

[47]   Charles Allen, *Plain Tales from the Raj* (London: Abacus, 1994), p. 130.

[48]   In the journal of the 17th Indian Cavalry, *The Star and Crescent, A Quarterly Record of Sport and Soldiering*, there are long articles and numerous references to the unit's polo playing prowess. Lists of team members always include native officers, NCOs, and the occasional soldier, and the journal is printed in both English and Urdu, so as not to leave anyone out of the discussion of the unit's favorite pastime.

[49]   *The Black Horse Gazette, Journal of the 7th (Princess Royal's) Dragoon Guards* Vol. XII No. 1 (Secunderabad, March 1914), pp. 5–8, 9–12, 23–24.

games occurred at many stations). This unwritten policy lasted at least up to the First World War, but under the strains of mutual service at the front these restrictions were soon relaxed.[50]

An exception to the restriction against interracial games was the routine inclusion of British officers on Indian soldier teams. Officers played on teams with other ranks right from the beginning of the institution of games in the Indian Army, partly for the reasons of teaching sepoys to play, but there was another imperative: just as the military philosophy of athleticism demanded that officers show an example of sportsmanship to British enlisted soldiers, it demanded that British officers participate in games with Indian soldiers in order to reduce barriers between the races so that British officers might be more effective leaders. Healthy competition and team building would create understanding between soldier and sahib, so that when the game of war was played, the spirit of the pitch would carry on to the battlefield.

This idea was expressed over and over again in the professional literature. As put by Captain W.C. Walton, 4th Bombay Rifles, in 1901:

> It is very difficult for British Officers to keep thoroughly in touch with the native soldiers under them, but any officer will find that there is no nearer way to win the trust and confidence of his men, and learn to appreciate their virtues and their failings from a just standpoint, than by playing games with them, and giving up his spare time to them. Any games which will foster the spirit of comradeship, and the power of working together, are useful practical training.[51]

This concept of promoting racial harmony was not only applied to team games but eventually to field sports. As discussed in Chapter 1, India was a mecca for the military sportsman. As with games, it was virtually inevitable that British officers would apply their philosophy of sport and war to the development of their Indian officers, NCOs, and even soldiers. Major R.G. Burton, that prolific spokesman for *shikar*[52] who advocated tiger hunting as valuable training for British junior officers, echoed his contemporary, Baden-Powell, in urging Indian officers to train their soldiers in scouting techniques by taking them hunting.[53] He also, in one of his many hunting articles, described how he brought his

---

[50] See Farwell, *Armies of the Raj*, chapter 11.

[51] Captain W.C. Walton, "The Practical Training of British and Native Troops with Reference to the Lessons of the War in South Africa," *Journal of the United Services Institution of India* Vol. 30 No. 144 (1901), pp. 261–295.

[52] *Shikar* is the Urdu word meaning sport, or, more precisely, hunting.

[53] Captain R.G. Burton, 1st Infantry, Hyderabad Contingent, "Shikar as Training for Scouts," *Journal of the United Services Institution of India* Vol. 28 No. 134 (1899), pp. 88–90.

Figure 6.2   45th Sikhs Tug-of-War, sports day, 1918 (Imperial War Museum)

native officers and NCOs on hunting trips not only in order to train them for war but to help increase cooperation and understanding between the races.[54]

These practices may have helped to overcome some of the racial prejudices held by the British in their dealings with Indian soldiers, but clearly those prejudices remained strong right up to independence in 1947. In spite of the admiration routinely expressed by officers for the soldiers of the "martial races," and in spite of the superb combat performance of Indian Army units throughout not only the period of this study but beyond, there persisted in some quarters of the military establishment (and even more so in the civilian establishment) disparaging beliefs about their military abilities and their general inferiority to Europeans. The author of an article entitled "Reflections on the Training of British and Indian Troops," appearing in the *Journal of the United Services Institution of India* in 1910, was a lone voice in his call for fully integrated training and games between Tommy and sepoy. He said that, although other ranks of the two armies were discouraged from playing against each other, policy needed to be rethought, in order to encourage better understanding.[55] That this full measure of integration never occurred is a tragedy for the history of British–Indian relations; if the phenomenal success of the British transfer of the "games ethic" to India is any indication, it may have been that fully integrated games among British and Indian soldiers would have reduced the racial tensions and prejudice that contributed to the acrimony surrounding the last years of the Raj.

Both formal gymnastic training and recreation within the Indian Army were tools used by British military leaders to accomplish two primary goals: first, to make the Indian soldier more fit, and to increase his fighting capacity; second, to make the sepoy a better man—one who matched the British conceptions of character, morale, and martial aptitude. That the first goal was accomplished is not in doubt—even a cursory examination of the Indian soldier's fighting record in the First and Second World Wars will bear out that conclusion.[56] The nebulous nature of the second goal makes it less easy to determine success or failure. Nevertheless, it is indisputable that a perhaps unintended consequence of the Indian military establishment's use of sport and gymnastics to accomplish its training ends was the wholesale transfer of the British culture of athleticism

---

54   Major R.G. Burton, 94th Russell's Infantry, "The Image of War," *Journal of the United Services Institution of India* Vol. 37 No. 171 (1908), p. 221.

55   "A.L.B.," "Reflection on the Training of British and Indian Troops," *Journal of the United Services Institution of India* Vol. 39 No. 178 (1910), pp. 129–130.

56   See Farwell, *Armies of the Raj*, Field Marshal the Viscount Slim, *Defeat into Victory* (London: Cassell & Co., Ltd., 1956), and Lyn MacDonald, *1915: The Death of Innocence* (Baltimore, MD: Johns Hopkins University Press, 1993).

and games to the larger Indian society. It is too bad that the British in the Empire, both within the Army and without, were unable or unwilling to follow their philosophy of sportsmanship to its logical conclusion—racial equality and integration for all.

PART III
"Training For Sport is Training For War": 1908–1914

Chapter 7
Physical Training and National Preparedness

In nearly every unit physical training is receiving careful attention. Cross-country running is practised in most battalions, and the men are frequently put over the obstacle course. Undoubtedly the men are far more active and alert than they were a few years ago.

Memorandum on Army Training, 1912–13[1]

Recent reports on the deterioration of our race ought to act as a warning to be taken in time before it goes too far. One cause which contributed to the downfall of the Roman Empire was the fact that the soldiers fell away from the standard of their forefathers in bodily strength ... The training of Boy Scouts would therefore be incomplete if it did not endeavor to help in remedying these evils ... Since most of these causes of physical decay are preventable, they open to instructors a field for doing a work of national value.

Lieutenant General R.S.S. Baden-Powell, 1908[2]

The years between the release of the first *Manual of Physical Training* and the outbreak of the First World War were marked by a consolidation of the efforts at reform and modernization that characterized the previous half century. After the institution of the Haldane reforms in the first decade of the twentieth century, the great Army reform movement of the Victorian and Edwardian era was to a great degree completed.[3] Efforts at making training programs and equipment more capable of producing victory on a modern battlefield also

---

[1] *Memorandum on Army Training, During the Individual Training Period 1912–1913*, WO 279/553, National Archives.

[2] Lieutenant General R.S.S. Baden-Powell, *Scouting for Boys, Part IV* (London: Horace Cox, 1908), pp. 208–209.

[3] The major elements of the Haldane reforms were the creation of a General Staff and an Expeditionary Force designed for a continental war, and the amalgamation of the Yeomanry, Militia, and Volunteers into a first-class Army Reserve and the Territorial Army. See Edward Spiers, *Haldane: An Army Reformer* (Edinburgh: Edinburgh University Press, 1980).

seemed to have reached the point of completion, as most of the lessons learned in South Africa had been internalized and acted upon. The years leading to the outbreak of war in 1914 were used to refine new doctrine and institutions while ensuring that the Army was prepared for the continental war that most soldiers expected. Everything from infantry and cavalry tactics, to artillery equipment and the soldier's uniform had been upgraded based on hard experience and the perceived necessities of modern war.

The area of musketry training, which was to have such an incredible influence on the outcome of the battles of 1914, deserves particular mention. In the years before 1914 the average British infantry soldier was required to fire a minimum of 500 rounds per year on the rifle range. By comparison, current rifle qualification standards for the U.S. Army require approximately 100 rounds per soldier. The pre-First World War British infantryman qualified by firing fifteen rounds per minute with his bolt-action rifle, while prone, at moving, khaki-colored targets at ranges of up to 500 yards. This demanding training program derived from hard experience in South Africa was what resulted in the extraordinarily high rates of accurate rifle fire generated by the British Expeditionary Force in 1914. Using these techniques the BEF caused enormous German casualties, and many German commanders stoutly maintained, even after the war, that they had been faced with large numbers of entrenched British machine guns in the opening battles of the war. In fact, in 1914 each British infantry battalion was equipped with only two machine guns, and roughly 1,200 highly trained marksmen.[4]

Military physical training seems also to have reached this point of professional maturity. Once the new manual was published in 1908, and the new system fully in place throughout the Army, the leadership of the Army Gymnastic Staff focused its efforts primarily on the oversight of the new physical training (now referred to in most correspondence as "PT") program, making only minimal modifications in organization and administration, while adding a few nuances to the training scheme such as a new emphasis on "field PT." Despite the pace of change slowing down, this period before the war saw the spread of the Army's system in various forms to many schools and universities in Britain, as civilian authorities saw the benefits the program provided to the Army and became increasingly desirous of a fitter and consequently more militarily capable populace.[5]

By the start of hostilities in August 1914, physical training and sport were totally integrated into the doctrine and traditions of the Army. The extent to

---

[4]   See Lyn Macdonald, *1914* (New York: Atheneum, 1988), pp. 97–99, for a first-person account of the Army's pre-war musketry training program, along with a detailed description of its results at Mons in August 1914.

[5]   Lieutenant Colonel E.A.L. Oldfield, *History of the Army Physical Training Corps* (Aldershot: Gale & Polden Ltd., 1955), pp. 18–20.

which these once-revolutionary institutions had become part of the fabric of the Army is most fully shown by how well they survived, in fact thrived, despite the almost complete destruction of the pre-war Regular Army in 1914–1915.[6] Military physical culture reached this level of development between 1908 and 1914, in time to allow soldiers to prepare their bodies for the arduous campaign that would result in their preventing a quick German victory at the cost of their own annihilation.

As outlined in Chapter 4, the Swedish or Ling system of physical training was officially adopted by the British Army in 1907, after its introduction to the Gymnastic Staff the previous year by Lieutenant Lankilde of the Danish Army. The then Inspector of Gymnasia, Colonel (later Brigadier General) S.P. Rolt of the York and Lancaster Regiment, detailed his Assistant Inspector, Major Charles Moore, to work with Lieutenant Lankilde to write a comprehensive physical training manual for the Army. This manual was to include all elements of the Ling system, along with instructions regarding the use of footmarching, games, sport, and many other elements long requested by units in the field. The end product was the landmark *Manual of Physical Training* that was finally published in 1908 and was used, with few updates, until the massive influx of recruits in 1914 necessitated changes to the standard methods of training.[7] In recognition of its tan-colored cover, the new book was known Army-wide, affectionately or otherwise (doubtless depending on a soldier's position as instructor or trainee), as the "Yellow Peril."[8]

After the adoption of the new physical training system and the publication of the *Manual*, very few changes or developments occurred in the realm of organization and administration of gymnastics training before the start of the First World War. Those changes that did take place were relatively minor, such as the addition of an officer to the instructor staff of the School of Physical Training at Aldershot, and the establishment of the position on the Staff of Master at Arms, an officer responsible for oversight of fencing and bayonet fighting instruction. The first officer appointed to this position was Lieutenant J.L. Betts, a former Gymnastic Staff Sergeant Major who was the first man from the Staff to receive a commission from the ranks, and who would play a central role in the Staff's expansion and operations during the First World War.[9]

---

6   For a brief description of the sports and morale programs in the British and Imperial forces during the First World War, see J.G. Fuller, *Troop Morale and Popular Culture in the British and Dominion Armies 1914–1918* (Oxford: Clarendon Press, 1990), chapter 8.

7   Captain F.J. Starr, "War History of the British Army Gymnastic Staff," (first draft) unpublished manuscript, Army Physical Training Corps Museum File #1664, p. 1.

8   Oldfield, *History of the Army Physical Training Corps*, p. 18.

9   Ibid., pp. 18–20.

One of the few innovations in the conduct of military physical training in the years immediately before 1914 was known as "field PT," which amounted to attempts to create situations in which units could perform physical training under conditions approximating a combat environment – thereby giving commanders one more tool to evaluate the readiness of their units. Ultimately these efforts coalesced into the development of the "assault course," or what is more commonly known today as an obstacle or confidence course. The assault course was a series of obstacles such as walls, fences, ditches, and tunnels, spread out over various distances. Soldiers would negotiate the course either individually or as a unit for time. It was hoped by the leaders of the Gymnastic Staff that by running soldiers through these courses they would increase their overall level of fitness, while simultaneously improving unit teamwork and morale.[10] An added, side benefit to units negotiating the course would have been an opportunity for junior NCOs to develop critical leadership skills by moving squads in an organized fashion through the course. That these goals were being met in the years just prior to the start of the World War was confirmed by the Inspector General:

> In nearly every unit physical training is receiving careful attention. Cross-country running is practised in most battalions, and the men are frequently put over the obstacle course. Undoubtedly the men are far more active and alert than they were a few years ago.[11]

An example of the assault course being used as a competitive event during training occurred in 1910, at the conclusion of the Aldershot Command Maneuvers. The "Connaught Shield," the award for an assault course competition for battalion teams, was to be presented to the winners of a difficult course run at the conclusion of the unit sports (by this time, virtually all major training exercises, including the annual two-week Territorial Army training camps, included a sports day or gymkhana as the final event). The competition was administered by the Inspector of Gymnasia on the grounds near the Headquarters Gym at Aldershot, and had as the first prize a silver shield, presented by the Duke of Connaught. Second- and third-place teams received awards of 15 and 9 pounds sterling, respectively—handsome prizes for what was clearly the crowning event of the training year. The teams from each battalion were to consist of 106 men

---

10   "G.A.T." (Major G.A. Trent, Indian Army Inspector of Physical Training), "Physical Training of the Infantry Soldier in India," *Journal of the United Services Institution of India* Vol. 38 No. 174 (1909), pp. 201–211, and David Lomas, *Mons 1914: The BEF's Tactical Triumph* (London: Osprey, 1997), p. 13.

11   *Memorandum on Army Training, During the Individual Training Period 1912–1913.*

each, replicating a rifle company, with the course to be run as "a fighting unit from start to finish."[12]

The philosophy behind the implementation of this kind of training is easily understood through a reading of the directions for the competition, some of which are worth quoting here in full:

> 18. The conditions of the competition have been drawn up with a view to encouraging the training of a large number of men to traverse a piece of ground intersected with various obstacles at a foot pace and in a really practical manner, without allowing it to develop into a mere time test which would possibly give rise to straining the men (especially in the case of the younger soldiers) rather than training them.

> 19. It is not intended that there should be any display, fancy or barrack square drill methods of approaching or surmounting the obstacles. The methods employed should be those of *maneuver* rather than *drill* and should represent the practical way which a company of infantry in the field, composed of highly trained, active men, would actually surmount the various obstacles, walls, posts and rails, etc., the whole company being the while under practical control as a fighting unit ready for any emergency [author's italics].[13]

These guidelines clearly show the Army's continued interest in comprehensive training, physical and otherwise, as a synchronized and practical method of ensuring the combat readiness of soldiers and units. Again, competitions such as these clearly were not developed and run by disinterested amateurs, but rather by thoroughly modern military professionals; the British Regular Army officer corps had by this time largely completed its transformation begun in the years following the Crimean War and pursued throughout the period of this study. An innovation like "field PT" is but one piece of the considerable body of evidence that by 1910 the days of the gentleman amateur were long past.

Another permutation to the assault course was that it was sometimes used as a means of updating the Army's method of bayonet training to make it more closely conform to actual fighting conditions, by placing straw-filled dummies at key points along the course and having soldiers "attack" the dummies while moving through the obstacles.[14] This method of training was not widely practiced

---

[12]   "Orders for Conduct of the 'Connaught Shield' Obstacle Course for Battalion Teams" (papers of General Sir Ivor Maxse, 69/53/1 File 3, Imperial War Museum Archives).

[13]   Ibid.

[14]   Oldfield, *History of the Army Physical Training Corps*, pp. 18–20.

before the war, and was only implemented by the Gymnastic Staff Army wide after 1915.[15]

Clearly the system in place after 1908 was seen by soldiers throughout the Army to be so satisfactory that it required no serious adjustments: the six-year period between 1908 and 1914 was the longest in the brief history of the Gymnastic Staff with no major changes to the training program. Evidence of the Army's satisfaction with the new program lies in the fact that, in the major Army professional journals, only one article appeared in those years advocating a change to the physical training program.[16] When contrasted with the number of similar articles appearing in the previous ten years, this fact seems almost miraculous.

Satisfaction with the program did not result in complacency on the part of the Army's leadership, however. Inspection teams carefully monitored unit implementation of required physical training and constantly admonished units that were not reaching the desired standard. Sections devoted to evaluating the physical fitness and training levels of each type of unit in the Army—infantry, artillery, engineers, etc.—were included in the annual *Memoranda on Army Training*, the reports published by the Inspectorate General following the Individual and Collective Training periods each year. An example of the kind of favorable report commanders would like to have received is quoted at the start of this chapter. While this kind of favorable comment was not rare, it was certainly less common than reports such as this:

> **Artillery:** <u>Physical Training and Marching Drill</u> – Some brigades do a great deal of physical training, but others do very little. This form of training should be universal. Running is a valuable form of physical exercise. It is not generally realized how physically fit an artilleryman must be in order to carry out his duties to the best advantage.[17]

The Territorial Army also received reports on its training status, and perhaps unsurprisingly, given that the inspectors were from the Regular Army, the Territorials often were not given very high marks for physical stamina: the Inspector General strongly advocated in the 1910 report, for example, that all Territorial Army units practice routine physical training "such as the regular soldier is given," with more practice in footmarching. The concern about the capacity of part-time Territorial units to conduct long marches was perhaps a

---

[15]   Starr, "War History of the British Army Gymnastic Staff" (first draft), p. 4.

[16]   Lieutenant Colonel H. de B. Hovell, D.S.O., "Physical Training in the Army and Navy: Why the Systems Fail in their Object," *The United Service Magazine* Vol. XLVII (1913), pp. 79–83.

[17]   *Memorandum on Army Training, During the Individual Training Period 1912–1913.*

little misplaced—the inspector noted that during the maneuvers most units routinely conducted movements of up to 34 miles without undue hardship![18]

Even given the concerns of inspectors, the viability of the new system was evident to all who were familiar with it, and within a few years of its implementation it was earning praise from observers both in the Army and outside it. Advocates of conscription, in particular the National Service League whose journal *National Defense* consistently argued the need for military preparedness, urged adoption of a national program of physical training based on the Army's. The new Boy Scout organization, founded and led by the former Inspector General of Cavalry, Lord Baden-Powell, urged members in its publications to follow the example of soldiers in keeping fit,[19] and educational organizations and institutions sought to initiate physical training programs to instill discipline and encourage the "sound mind in a sound body" concept first advocated by adherents of public-school athleticism. Many former and serving soldiers became a part of this movement and published a large number of books with such titles as *National Physical Training: An Open Debate*, *Physical Training for Boy Scouts*, and *Military Training for our Schoolboys*,[20] all of which were designed to spread the Army's experience of physical culture and wartime readiness to the larger civilian population of Britain and the Empire.

The appointment of Colonel Fox to the position of Inspector of Physical Training for the Board of Education is just one example, albeit a significant one, of the cooption of former soldiers by educators to manage and conduct fitness programs in the schools.[21] Another salient example of the Army's role in school fitness programs can be found in the 1903 Report of the Royal Commission on Physical Training (Scotland): on behalf of the Education Department Captain Armitage, Superintendent of Military Gymnasia for Scotland, inspected the Teacher Training Colleges' physical training programs, and according to the Commissioners, "we expect that similar inspections will be continued."[22] Small wonder that civilian agencies would rely on the Army, as the practical experts,

---

[18]   "Report on Physical Capacity of Territorial Forces Troops to Carry Out the Work and Endure the Hardships which were Incidental to the Maneuvers of 1910," WO 279/48 p. 8, National Archives.

[19]   Tim Jeal, *The Boy-Man: The Life of Lord Baden-Powell* (New York: Wm. Morrow & Co., 1990), pp. 357–362.

[20]   John B. Atkins, *National Physical Training: An Open Debate* (British Library Acc. # 7404.d.21); Alfred Bradley, *Physical Training for Boy Scouts* (Glasgow: J. Brown & Son, 1916); Thos. Brodribb, *Military Training for our Schoolboys* (Melbourne, 1909).

[21]   *Mind, Body and Spirit: The Annual Journal of the Army Physical Training Corps* No. 79 (1995/96), p. 123.

[22]   "Report of Royal Commission on Physical Training (Scotland)," *Parliamentary Papers* Vol. I (1903), Cd. 1507 xxx. 1., p. 10.

Figure 7.1   Gymnastic Staff Instructors gymnastic display, *c.*1895 (author's collection)

to provide advice and assistance in organizing and conducting fitness programs throughout the country.

The potential connection between military physical training and the civilian population was an important one to advocates of national military preparedness. With the prospect of war on the Continent growing increasingly greater, the realization that Britain's small expeditionary force would be overwhelmed by the huge conscript armies of Europe resulted in calls by many people, civilian and military, for more military preparedness among the general population. Articles published in contemporary periodicals such as *The Nineteenth Century and Beyond* and *Blackwood's* reflect these ideas, many of them focusing heavily on the supposedly degenerating state of physical fitness in the British population.

Unsurprisingly, the most strident of this type of article appeared in *National Defense*, where regular calls to the public for preparedness often took on the topic of physical training. In 1908 *National Defense* published a paper by Sir Lander Brunton entitled "Physical Education and Training in Relation to National Defense," in which the author advocated compulsory physical training in all schools and for the Territorial Army. Brunton argued that this mandatory program should be implemented and supervised by the Army, based on their extensive and highly successful experience of physical training.[23] In the same issue of *National Defense* an article by R. Munro Ferguson entitled "Physical Training and Drill in Relation to Compulsory Continuation Classes" argued the same type of program, with the addition of military drill.[24] Other articles published in this magazine during this period argued that encouraging sports and fitness programs in both the Territorial Army and the Regular Army would attract more athletic young men to the colors.[25] Calls for integrating gymnastic instruction into civilian programs, to increase both readiness and the popularity of the programs, were not unique to metropolitan Britain; in 1913 physical training was substituted for drill for boys under fourteen in the New Zealand Cadet Force.[26]

As the head of the National Service League and former Commander-in-Chief of the British Army, Lord Roberts's ideas on applying the military's experience to civilian physical training were especially influential. He, like

---

[23] Sir Lander Brunton, "Physical Education and Training in Relation to National Defense," *National Defense* Vols. 1–2 (1908), pp. 503–511.

[24] R. Munro Ferguson, "Physical Training and Drill in Relation to Compulsory Continuation Classes," *National Defense* Vols. 1–2 (1908), pp. 511–520.

[25] See Eugene Sandow, "Physical Exercise in the Services," *National Defense* Vol. 4 (1910), pp. 295–297, and Joseph Lyons, "Sports and the Territorials: How to Popularize the Force," *National Defense* Vol. 3 No. 10 (August 1909), pp. 137–139.

[26] "Report on Defense Forces of New Zealand for the period from 28 June 1912 to 20 June 1913," p. 6 (papers of General Sir Ivor Maxse, 69/53/1 File 5/9, Imperial War Museum Archives).

many others in the League, had strong ideas about the importance of fitness to national preparedness. In February 1909, Lord Roberts sponsored a speech by National Service League member Judge Hans Hamilton, during which the judge advocated the creation of a "National Sports Association" to organize athletics, sports, and games on the military model, whose proceeds would be applied to support schemes of National Service.[27] This association was never formed, but it is perhaps not coincidental that, just a few years after this proposal was made, there was a strong movement within the Army to create an encompassing body to govern all military sports, games, and athletics. Before the Great War there was resistance to a military sports association, and it, too, was not created until 1918 when the Army Sport Control Board was formed.

The debate around the formation of a governing body for military sport came as a consequence of the continued importance of recreational training, as it was now beginning to be called, as an integral element in the Army's overall physical training system. Additionally, there was a growing awareness within the Army's leadership of how the institutionalized nature of Army sport could be used to capitalize on British society's interest in physical culture: an improvement of the Army's image among and connection to civilians might improve the perennial shortage of manpower in the service, while continuing to promote readiness in the nation at large.

These debates surrounding soldier and civilian fitness are only remarkable when considering that, in the years prior to 1908, military gymnastic training was in such an evolutionary state: the fitness system had not matured to the point where a debate on larger issues concerning the Army and society was possible. After 1908, the formal gymnastic training of soldiers, and the fitness philosophy connected to that training, were woven so deeply into Army life that they had become almost transparent. It took a shock to the Army's training systems such as that administered by the mobilization in August 1914 to once again demonstrate to the Army's leaders just how vital a part of the soldier's training gymnastics had become. As the more visible element of the fitness training scheme, the role of sport in the military's culture was more easily defined than gymnastics, despite the entirely symbiotic relationship between the two. The 1908 "Yellow Peril" *Manual of Physical Training* codified that relationship for the first time, and in the years leading up to the start of hostilities in 1914 the final maturity of Army sport signaled by that codification was sealed.

---

[27]   Papers of Lord Roberts of Kandahar, WO 105/45, National Archives.

Chapter 8

Maturity: The Institutionalization of Army Sport

War being simply sport on a grand scale, and the individual qualities exercised in both being to some extent synonymous, any attempt to justify sport's appropriateness for soldiers should be superfluous ... Training for sport is training for war.

An "Ex-Non-Com," 1910[1]

Between 1908 and the outbreak of the First World War in 1914, British Army units continued to participate in sport and games at the same level as they had in the decades before the turn of the century. Embedded in the military culture as firmly as any other tradition, sport and games in the Army continued the process of institutionalization that had begun in 1881 with the foundation of the Army Football Association. Army leaders established many new championships and governing bodies to oversee the wide range of games and sport participated in by British soldiers, and the leadership of the Army Gymnastic Staff and others initiated a serious effort to gain approval for the creation of an umbrella organization for military sport that, although unsuccessful in 1914, would come to fruition as the Army Sport Control Board after the war. Between 1903 and 1914 the Army created institutions to govern sports from rugby, golf, and rackets, to billiards and hockey,[2] and Territorial Army battalions, Regular regiments, and divisions continued to institutionalize their sports days to act as the official culminating event of the yearly training period.[3] All of these efforts and accomplishments point

---

[1] "Ex-Non-Com," "The Soldier in Relation to Regimental Sport," *The United Services Magazine* Vol. XL (1909–1910), p. 35.

[2] *Games and Sports in the Army, 1932–33*, published by the Army Sport Control Board, War Office (1932–1933).

[3] Lyn Macdonald, *1914* (New York: Atheneum, 1988), pp. 12–13. The regimental journals from this time almost all reflect this practice, with sports days often taking up more text space than the training conducted. For example, see *The Thin Red Line* (November 1912, Fort George), pp. 20–22 – the article briefly outlines the summer training camp of the Territorial battalions of the regiment, and then describes in detail the Brigade sports day, held at Troon on July 22. This comprehensive event consisted of piping, a 1-mile race, a quarter-mile and 100-yard sprint, a team marathon race, tug-of-war (light and heavyweight), hammer throw, shot-put, high jump, a "band and piper's race," and highland dancing.

to the fact that, by 1914, Army sport had reached a point of maturity such that, as described by one officer after the First World War, the Edwardian period was the "golden age" of British Army sport.[4] The story of Army sport between 1860 and 1914 provides a superb example, in microcosm, of historian Allen Guttmann's model of sports evolution—codification and institutionalization indicate the modernization of these activities in the British military.[5]

Many strides were made by soldiers during the period before the Great War toward regularizing the Army's sports programs. One of the more important advances was the Army Council's adoption of a grand scheme to provide a sufficient number of standard playing fields at each garrison in the British Home Commands. This scheme was conceived and initially put into operation by an obscure company commander in the 1st Battalion, Royal Irish Fusiliers, who along with his battalion had just arrived at the Aldershot garrison in the spring of 1908. Captain Reginald Kentish was assigned, as an additional duty, as the officer in charge of managing his battalion's football programs—inter-company as well as inter-regimental and higher-level competition. He was dismayed to find when his unit arrived in Aldershot that, although the military post there was the largest in Britain, housing the majority of the troops that were to make up the Expeditionary Force, there was a totally inadequate number of playing fields for units to continue playing football at all the levels to which they had become accustomed. In addition to the lack of facilities, the existing playing fields had been constructed many years before and had not been maintained properly. This distressing state of affairs, as Kentish described in his memoirs (unpublished), was a major contributing factor to the increased levels of drunkenness, crime, and venereal disease in the Aldershot Command.[6]

The reasons for this unfortunate level of dissipation are unsurprising: there were only enough playing fields at Aldershot for each battalion-level football team to play just six games per month during the season, which must have created a near-crisis situation for most units. If that restriction on higher-level play were not enough, the lack of space made holding inter-company and platoon matches completely out of the question. The resultant lack of playing opportunity prevented the vast majority of soldiers from being able to participate in any games at all. Because of the now-systematic practice of units spending afternoons at sport, during the Individual Training Period in the winter months there was

---

[4]　*Household Brigade Magazine* (November 20, 1920), "Household Brigade Cricket Club," pp. 54–55.

[5]　Allen Guttmann, *From Ritual to Record: The Nature of Modern Sport* (New York: Columbia University Press, 1978).

[6]　Papers of Brigadier General Reginald Kentish, Imperial War Museum Archives, "The Army and its Recreation Grounds," pp. 3–4.

Figure 8.1   Cricket match, 14th (King's) Hussars NCOs vs. 7th Dragoon Guards NCOs, Canterbury, May 9, 1906 (courtesy of the Council of the National Army Museum, London)

nothing for soldiers to do in the afternoon but, as Kentish put it, go "into the town to the Public Houses to drink and to look for women, and the latter didn't take much looking for."[7] He further stated in his memoir that, when his battalion arrived at Aldershot, a consequence of this lack of opportunity for games was a dramatic rise in the incidence of venereal disease among the soldiers. As it was his responsibility to look after the unit's games program, he took it upon himself to develop an idea that would rectify this "appalling" situation.[8]

Kentish proposed to his Brigade Commander, Major General Colin Mackenzie, that each unit in the Aldershot Command set up a detail of soldiers, each of which would work under the supervision of a Royal Engineer officer to construct standard cricket and football pitches on waste ground around the post. The end result would be that, in a matter of two to three years, each battalion at Aldershot would have its own dedicated playing fields for platoon, company, and battalion matches. Major General Mackenzie enthusiastically supported the scheme, and asked Captain Kentish to present his ideas to the General Officer Commanding, Aldershot Command, Sir Horace Smith-Dorrien. This he did, and after receiving the entire approbation of General Smith-Dorrien, Kentish convened a committee to organize and put into practice his scheme.[9] According to Kentish, work was carried on quickly and with relish by the officers and soldiers, and within three years Aldershot had its new playing fields. Kentish produced no evidence in his memoir that the incidences of drinking, crime, and venereal disease were reduced after the fields were built, but clearly there had to have been some positive results after the restoration of the beloved company- and platoon-level games.[10]

After being assigned as the Brigade Major of the London Brigade, along with assuming duties as the voluntary Secretary of the Army Football Association, Kentish decided in 1913 that his experience at Aldershot should be extended to all the military installations in Britain. Accordingly, he obtained an interview with the Permanent Undersecretary of State for War, Sir Edward Ward, in order to present his expanded idea. Ward was also very supportive, and brought the matter up before the Army Council for consideration. The idea was approved, and in the winter of 1913–1914 Kentish was assigned the task of chairing a committee responsible for organizing the construction of playing fields Army

---

7   Ibid., p. 3.

8   Ibid., p. 4.

9   General Sir C.H. Harington in *Games and Sports in the Army, 1932–33*, preface, p. 21.

10   Kentish, "The Army and its Recreation Grounds," pp. 4–8.

wide. Work had scarcely begun on this expanded project when war broke out, and, as put so well by Kentish, the troops had "to go and dig elsewhere."[11]

Ultimately this scheme was continued after the war, still supervised by Kentish (now a Brigadier General) and under the aegis of the newly formed Army Sport Control Board. The scheme was eventually broadened to include all Army garrisons world wide, with the Indian Army adopting it wholesale as well.[12] Kentish's scheme, in its unhesitating adoption by the most senior leadership of the Army and its rapid spread around the Army's worldwide stations, is a vivid illustration of the fundamental place of sport and games in the culture of the pre-war British Army. The resources and man-hours applied to the construction of these playing fields clearly had to be quite substantial, and only a project of extreme importance could warrant such a commitment. This commitment demonstrates that military sport was fully institutionalized by 1914: not only was it included as a regular part of the training regimen, but by the start of the war in 1914 most Army installations had a gymnasium, along with standard games and athletics fields as well, built mostly by the soldiers themselves. These fields gave the Army more visibility and credibility in civilian sporting circles, as they greatly facilitated more standardized and orderly conduct of regular games in the Army. An additional feature of the new playing fields was that many of these recreational grounds were used during the vast expansion of the Army after 1914 to drill new soldiers in their stocking feet because sufficient quantities of boots were as yet unavailable.[13]

Standardization of playing fields was only part of the modernization of Army sport in the early years of the last century. By 1908 the Army had long sponsored football with an association and the Army Championship. There were also regular Army polo and boxing championships, but the remainder of sport and games participated in by soldiers was largely unregulated outside of the local unit level. Between roughly 1903 and 1914 this situation was to change dramatically.

In 1903 the first Army Singles Championships were held in the sport of rackets (racquetball), while a doubles championship had been held since 1892 for unit teams. These events would continue until the Second World War, with

---

[11]   Ibid., p. 8. For a secondary narrative version of these events, see Basil Kentish, *This Foul Thing Called War: The Life of Brigadier-General Reginald Kentish, CMG, DSO (1876–1956)* (Sussex: The Book Guild, 1997). An interesting aside about Kentish: he was imprisoned with Winston Churchill in the same Boer prisoner-of-war camp in Pretoria during the South African War in 1899.

[12]   Harrington in *Games and Sports in the Army, 1932–33*, preface, p. 22.

[13]   Brigadier-General Reginald Kentish, Letter to the Editor, *Aldershot News and Military Gazette* (February 23, 1945). Many thanks to Miss Sylvia Nash for providing me with this information.

an unavoidable hiatus in the years 1914–1919. They were managed by the Army Rackets Committee, which consisted of two officers and an Honorary Secretary. From 1903 the number of such organizations grew: for golf, a Unit Challenge Cup was established in 1904 and an Army Championship in 1911, and in 1906 the Army Rugby Union was formed with an Army Challenge Cup competition continuing from that year on. In 1908 the Army Billiards Championship was established, and the Army Hockey Association was formed in 1909 and began an inter-unit tournament that year as well as a regular Army vs. Navy competition. In 1910 a committee was formed to establish and govern an Army Lawn Tennis Tournament, and that same year an annual Army vs. Navy Cricket match began as an annual First Class match and was played at Lords over a three-day period. Finally, in the spring of 1914 a committee met to establish the Army Athletics (track and field) Association, but because of the outbreak of the war that summer the effort to start the Association was abandoned and not resurrected until 1919.[14]

A fascinating spin-off of the efforts to create an Army Athletics Association was the debate surrounding possible establishment of an Army-wide governing body for all sports. In the end, this drive was to be unsuccessful in 1914, but the discourse among the Army's senior leadership surrounding the idea is highly illuminating. It demonstrates not only how the critical importance of sport for soldiers was completely accepted at the highest levels of the military, but how once again physical training and sport provide an intriguing window into how the Army, in this case the Army Council, set priorities. When this debate was at its most intense, the Army was being convulsed by the events that would later be known as "The Curragh Incident," in which a large part of the Army officers in Ireland threatened to resign over the prospect of Irish Home Rule, resulting in the resignation of the Chief of the Imperial General Staff, Field Marshal Sir John French.[15] Military games must have been important indeed to take up the time of the Army Council when what looked like a major mutiny seemed so close at hand.

In the late summer of 1913 the Inspector of Gymnasia, Colonel V.A. Couper of the Rifle Brigade, wrote to the Army Council proposing that an Army Athletics Association be formed, to "encourage and control cross-country running and athletics generally throughout the Army." At the time, the Army Athletic Committee (AAC) organized and conducted the annual Army Athletic Meeting at Aldershot. On July 24, 1913 the AAC had held a meeting with

---

[14]   *Games and Sports in the Army, 1932–33.* This volume contains a brief history of each of the committees and associations administered by the Army Sport Control Board, related at the start of each section of the book.

[15]   For a comprehensive treatment of the Curragh "mutiny," see *The Curragh Incident,* by Sir James Fergusson (London: Faber and Faber, 1964).

Figure 8.2 7th Dragoon Guards Association Football Team, 1907 (courtesy of the Council of the National Army Museum, London)

representatives from thirty-six units of the Home Army, and thirty-four of the representatives voted in favor of forming an Army Athletics Association. They also passed a "resolution to the effect that the A.C. [Army Council] should be asked to approve all forms of Army games and recreation being brought under one committee, with one common fund, and that an officer should be specially detailed whose sole work should be to look after the fund and presumably to act as Secretary of Army Games." The letter was signed jointly by Colonel Couper, his Assistant Major Wright, and the two men who were to have possibly the greatest influence on Army sport and physical training over the next ten years, Captain Reginald Kentish and Captain Ronald Bruce Campbell.[16]

The permanent Undersecretary of State, Sir Edward Ward, who had already demonstrated his support for Army recreation by agreeing to Kentish's project, added to the original letter from Colonel Couper this note of support, clearly intended to sway the more doubtful members of the Council:

> It is not, I think, fully understood how complicated are the questions which arise in connection with the various games played by soldiers. The difficulties and complications arise not so much as regards the soldiers themselves but from the watchful action of the various Associations which now rule over Athletics in this country. Hardly a match of any importance takes place without some question arising which has to be settled by authority, and on the manner in which these frequently difficult questions are decided rests a great deal of the reputation of the Army among the civil population for fairness in sports. At present we have officers, one especially, Captain Kentish, who gives up all his spare time to the Honorary Secretaryship of the Football Association, but he is a unique example, and yet in addition to Football, there are Boxing, Hockey, and other sports.
>
> I suggest on account of the advantages gained in recruiting alone from a proper conduct of our athletics that an additional Instructor be given to the Headquarters Gymnasium Aldershot, whose work should be entirely that of supervising the athletics of all the Army outside the regulation items. I am informed that the Football Association can pay for any clerical help required.[17]

As the successful precedent of establishing similar organizations made the adoption of this measure almost moot, debate within the Army Council on the formation of an Army Athletics Association was non-existent. The Army Athletic Association was approved by the Council in November 1913, with a decision on funding for the Association to be delayed until spring 1914.[18] From

---

16 Letter, WO 32/5492, National Archives.
17 Ibid., Minute #23.
18 Ibid.

this point on, the discussion centered entirely around the far more controversial and, from the viewpoint of an historical examination of the evolution of Army sport, far more interesting issue of the formation of a governing body for Army games and recreation.

Judging from the minutes and notations in the War Office files, most members of the Army Council disagreed with the idea, with the notable exception of the influential Sir Edward Ward—the Permanent Undersecretary was doubtless influenced in this matter by his acquaintance, Captain Kentish. Disagreement from the Council was not on the fundamentals of the idea; minutes from other members said such things as, "This is rather a new departure ... There is no doubt a great deal to what the P.U.S. [Permanent Undersecretary] says."[19] Disagreement, rather, predictably coalesced around the issue of expense. Sir John French dealt with the question by directing a minute to the Adjutant General, Lieutenant General Sir J.S. Ewart, KCB: "I agree in principle with all P.U.S. says in his minute. The difficult questions which arise are within all our experiences. But the expenses involved would only be justified if we may expect an appreciable effect upon recruiting and you are the best judge of that."[20] The Adjutant General responded, "F.M. [Field Marshal] I do not think this is a justifiable expenditure of public money, or one that we should recommend to the Treasury. If this secretary were started, the next thing would be a demand for clerical assistance and a heavy traveling bill."[21]

Not giving up on his idea in the face of this opposition from his superiors, the Inspector of Gymnasia suggested the abolition of the post of Superintendent of Gymnasia in South Africa and the transfer of the Gymnastic Staff officer thus made available to Aldershot, where he could be assigned to supervise Army Games. He justified this transfer given the fact that at the time the garrison in South Africa was being successively reduced as the new Union took over responsibility for its own defense. Colonel Couper stated, "at the present moment the proper management of the games and sports of the Army is of greater importance than the Superintendence of the physical training of the units in 'South Africa.'" He also remarked, in reference to an earlier suggestion from the Council, that there were no funds in his budget to pay a retired officer to fulfill the duties of Secretary of Army Sport. Finally, as a means of further strengthening his argument, Couper informed the Council that, in the absence of an officer detailed to perform the job, all of his Superintendents would be required to give up their honorary appointments to run the various Army sports

---

19   Ibid., Minute #24.
20   Ibid., Minute #25.
21   Ibid., note dated November 6, 1913.

associations because they no longer had the time for both those responsibilities and their growing physical training duties.[22]

This threat was not idle. Captain Kentish, who was not even a Gymnastic Staff officer, was assigned as the Brigade Major of the London Brigade, was Honorary Secretary of the Army Football Association, and was responsible for supervision of the construction of playing fields on Army installations all over Britain. He had to have been overstretched. Colonel Couper's concern that his own officers were spending too much time on their voluntary duties was clearly not misplaced, even in light of the importance the members of the Gymnastic Staff placed on the proper conduct of games for all soldiers.

Sir John French did agree with Couper's idea of reassigning the Superintendent from South Africa to Aldershot, but the Adjutant General disagreed yet again with this proposal on monetary grounds. It was also his opinion that a post of Games Secretary was not a fit one for a serving officer. In the middle of March 1914, French and Ewart agreed to bring the matter up before the Army Council for a final decision. Ewart wrote to French, "It is difficult for me to estimate the value to recruiting of a proper and systematized organization of Army games, but I am quite sure as to its value to the physical training and fitness of the Army generally."[23] Accordingly, the Army Council considered the idea, and on May 1, 1914 finally decided that not only would there be no public funds designated to support the formation of the previously approved Athletics Association, but that there would be no officer added to the Gymnastic Staff at Aldershot to supervise Army games.[24]

Colonel Couper made one final attempt to see the idea through. On May 14, he proposed to the Council that a grant be made from the "South African Canteen Fund" to pay a retired officer to run the Athletics Association. He justified this proposal on the grounds that the progressive withdrawal of troops from South Africa obviated the need for the Canteen Fund, and he argued that the money could be better used to support the nascent Association. We can probably assume that he also thought this retired officer could take on the additional task of Secretary of Games for the Army. In his memorandum he again emphasized the issue of his subordinates' time:

> The future of the Army Athletic Association is a serious one. The Staff of the Head Quarter [*sic*] Gymnasium can no longer cope with the work in conjunction

---

[22]   Ibid.
[23]   Ibid., notes dated March 13 and 16, 1914.
[24]   Ibid.

with their proper duties, and with their resignation it seems inevitable that the recreation of the soldier will be seriously prejudiced.[25]

In response to this final appeal, the Army Council established a committee to examine the proposal, and this committee decided that in order to make a proper decision they would have to first get the finances of the Canteen Fund in order and under the control of the Adjutant General's office. Only then could they come to a conclusion about disbursement for specific purposes. Unfortunately, before these actions could occur, the war intervened and the Army had to wait until the return of peace to form the organization that would oversee all the military games and sporting associations established up to 1914.[26]

After the war, when the Army Sport Control Board was finally established to regulate all of these disparate organizations, still more sports and games—cricket, swimming, and squash, to name but a few—came under the control of committees and associations.[27] This trend, however, began in the period before the war, and this series of events, along with the establishment of standardized grounds, signals the achievement of maturity for Army sport. From haphazard pick-up games inspired by public-schoolboy officers, to the formation of Army-wide committees and associations that published rules and regulated competitions, the fifty years of Army sport between 1860 and 1914 are a superb example in microcosm of the evolution of leisure pastimes throughout British and indeed all of Western society during that same period. During this time, sport began to become such a part of the fabric of society in the Europeanized world that its influence is now manifest in virtually every aspect of that culture. Although this trend continues to touch us in ways not unique to the military, as in so many things, an examination of the military experience with sport can be illuminating with regard to the rest of society.

One of the more fascinating developments concerning sport in the late Victorian and Edwardian Army is the entrance of sporting jargon into military language, and vice versa. Some examples of this language transfer would be "kicking off" an offensive, and a football team launching a "spirited attack." So many instances of this phenomenon still exist, both in the British Army and elsewhere, that this language exchange has become virtually transparent, but its first manifestations appear in the late nineteenth century; by the start of the First World War it had become commonplace. The intrusion of sporting language into military discourse has many possible causes: officers carrying over public-school parlance into the Army, and sporting slang from the working classes entering

---

25 WO 32/5493, letter dated May 14, 1914, National Archives.
26 WO 32/5493, National Archives.
27 Ibid.

the Army with recruits, to name just two. Clearly a mixture of these causes is most likely, with the prevalence of military sport providing a reinforcement. The symbiosis between sport and war suggested by this etymological relationship has an ancient history. We have long recognized the close connection between many sporting pastimes, such as hunting, horse racing, and fencing, and warfare, and even games such as lacrosse have martial roots. Some historians even argue that ancient Greek games and sports such as wrestling form the origin of much of the manner of Western warfare: the desire to close with the enemy and seek a decisive outcome through hand-to-hand struggle stems from violent Greek athletic contests.[28]

This relation between sport and war was clearly recognized by Victorian soldiers, and as we have seen it was a major justification for the creation of the Army's sport and physical training programs. It would seem only natural, then, that, as sport for these men was training for war, war would be the ultimate form of sport. This view is amply demonstrated in contemporary literature. Lord Baden-Powell repeatedly referred to sport in his manual for Army scouts, and even described scouting in combat as "the best sport in the world,"[29] and in an article published in the *United Services Magazine* in 1910 an "Ex-Non-Com" flatly stated, "War [is] simply sport on a grand scale."[30] The political and military maneuverings between the British, Afghans, and Russians were referred to as "the Great Game," and countless examples exist of combat being described by contemporary British soldiers as "sport," a "scrimmage," a "contest," and other athletic terms.[31] Perhaps the most famous literary instance of this linkage between sport and war is, again, in the Henry Newbolt poem "Vitaï Lampada."

A classic non-literary example of sporting terminology being applied to war occurred in the South African War, when at the Siege of Mafeking Sarel Eloff arrived as the new Boer commander for a final attempt to reduce the town. One of Eloff's first acts was to send a message to the British commander of the town's garrison, then Colonel Baden-Powell, suggesting that he should bring in a cricket team to play the town eleven. Baden-Powell's reply was typical:

---

[28]   John Keegan, *A History of Warfare* (New York: Vintage Books, 1993), pp. 244–254.

[29]   Colonel R.S.S. Baden-Powell, *Aids to Scouting to NCOs & Men (Reprint of the Original Edition of 1899)* (Houston: The Journal of Scouting History, 1994), and "Ex-Non-Com," "The Soldier in Relation to Regimental Sport," p. 35.

[30]   "Ex-Non-Com," "The Soldier in Relation to Regimental Sport," p. 35.

[31]   For examples of this kind of language see Winston S. Churchill, *The Boer War: London to Ladysmith via Pretoria, Ian Hamilton's March* (New York: Dorset Press, 1991); Byron Farwell, *Queen Victoria's Little Wars* (New York: W.W. Norton & Co., 1972); and Byron Farwell, *Eminent Victorian Soldiers* (New York: W.W. Norton & Co., 1985).

Mafeking, in the game it is playing at present, is 180 [the number of days the siege had then lasted] not out against the bowling of Cronje, Snyman and Eloff. Don't you think you had better change the bowling?[32]

It is, perhaps, reasonable for men whose time was spent almost entirely on the pursuit of two things—sport and war—that the two would come to resemble each other in the minds of soldiers. Military terminology entered the language of sport: attack, defense, defeat, victory, and many other terms of armed aggression are common in sport and games. British soldiers equally admired "pluck," "manliness," and team spirit on the games field and in battle. And there lies, at least partially, the explanation for occurrences such as that when Lieutenant Colonel John Campbell, VC, of the Coldstream Guards (pre-war Master of the Tanet-Side Harriers), rallied his men to a counter-attack during the battle of the Somme by sounding his hunting horn. It was the use of this horn that inspired his men to follow him after suffering severe losses, and the success of that counter-attack won Campbell his Victoria Cross and the everlasting admiration of military sportsmen.[33]

The close relation between sport and the Army was at times a source of humor. In 1901 *The Thin Red Line* published, under the heading "Army Orders and Regulations," the following:

FOR THE DIRECTION OF MILITARY CRICKET MATCHES.

I. - Batsmen must go to the wickets in order of seniority under the regulations issued in 1868.

II. - Patterns of the uniform to be worn can be obtained from the Army Clothing Department, Pimlico.

III. - Any batsman wishing to make a stroke must state his reasons for doing so in writing.

IV. - The ball must be non-explosive, as laid down in the terms of the Geneva Convention. Soft-nosed or explosive balls are strictly prohibited.

---

[32] Reginald Hargreaves, *The Enemy at the Gate* (London: Macdonald & Co., Ltd. [no date]), p. 252, footnote #1. Thanks again to Miss Nash.

[33] Lionel Dawson, *Sport in War* (London: Collins, 1936), pp. 13–16. Another example of this kind of leadership occurs in the motion picture "A Bridge Too Far" (Joseph E. Levine Productions, 1977), where Lieutenant Colonel John Frost of the 2nd Battalion, The Parachute Regiment, is portrayed as rallying his men with his hunting horn during the fight at Arnhem, Holland, 1944.

V. - The disposition of the fieldsmen, hereinafter called the "outposts," shall be in the hands of the commander of the company, who is responsible to his commanding officer, who is responsible to the brigade-major, who is responsible to the brigadier-general.

VI. - If one of the outposts misses a catch he must report the matter to the non-commissioned officer in charge of the picket, who must report it to the officer commanding the company, who must report it to the colonel.

VII. - No alteration of the disposition of the outposts can be made without the sanction of the officer commanding troops.

VIII. - Permission to change the bowler can only be obtained through the brigadier-general, who will forward the application to the general officer in command of the division, who will forward it to the chief of staff, who will acquaint the field-marshal of the same.

IX. - The umpires will be considered neutral, in accordance with the customs of war as laid down by the Geneva Convention (*vide* Mil. Law, sec. xiv.).

X. - Anyone disputing the decision of the umpires will be liable to be tried by a field general court-martial, and undergo the extreme penalty of the law (*vide* Mil. Law, R. 117.).

XI. - A player receiving injury in the field can only retire on sick leave on the recommendation of a medical board, who will forward his application to the A.A.G., War Office.

XII. - A suspension of hostilities on any pretext whatever can only be obtained by the officers directing the operations coming to terms. Negotiations to be conducted under a white flag. - "The King."[34]

Clearly this list of rules was printed in good fun; regiments that engaged in sport to the extent that the Argyll and Sutherland Highlanders did would definitely never deny the value of sport and games in training for war. The engagement of units in sport continued until the outbreak of war, and sometimes units were playing games almost right up to the moment of their embarkation for the front: the 6th Battalion (Territorial Army), Northumberland Fusiliers, held a battalion sports day at the end of their summer training camp on September 1, 1914, and the battalion was mobilized for war on 4 September.[35]

When the European powers went to war in 1914 the British Army eagerly went to the front with the others, well trained, physically fit, and, although naive, perhaps better prepared for the coming ordeal than the other combatants. The highly professional nature of the British Expeditionary Force (BEF) and the

---

[34]   *The Thin Red Line* Vol. 7 (1901), p. 159.

[35]   *St. George's Gazette, Journal of the Northumberland Fusiliers* (September 30, 1914), p. 122.

FOOTBALL AT MHOW.   OFFICERS V. SERGEANTS.
(Photo by Lieutenant Powell).

Figure 8.3 Northumberland Fusiliers Officers vs. Sergeants football, Mhow, India, 1913 (courtesy of the Council of the National Army Museum, London)

extensive combat experience of its officers and men would stand it in good stead. The fact that this small force endured the privations and extreme exertions of the campaigns of 1914, and was so successful, is not only a testament to the qualities of those soldiers as individual men but was also the clear result of the modern and effective training program instituted over the previous fifty years. Physical training and sport was an important part of that program. There can be no doubt that the *esprit de corps* and stamina engendered by the Army's sports programs were major factors in the fighting qualities of the BEF, along with the physical training program that made men capable of expending the extraordinary efforts required of them in 1914.[36] These institutionalized elements of the Army's training were, in fact, deemed such an integral part of training doctrine and so essential to success in combat that they long outlasted the original BEF. Sport and gymnastics remained essential ingredients in the training program of the New Armies and primary elements of the Army's morale programs throughout the war.[37]

---

[36] For descriptions of the savage fighting that effectively destroyed the BEF in 1914, see Correlli Barnett, *The Swordbearers* (Bloomington, IN: University of Indiana Press, 1963); John Keegan, *Opening Moves: August, 1914* (New York: Ballantine Books, 1971); John Terraine, *Mons, the Retreat to Victory* (London: B.T. Batsford, Ltd., 1960); Barbara Tuchman, *The Guns of August* (New York: Macmillan Publishing Co., 1962); and Macdonald, *1914.* See also the war memoirs of the BEF commander, Field Marshal Viscount French of Ypres, *1914* (London: Constable & Co., Ltd., 1919).

[37] J.G. Fuller, *Troop Morale and Popular Culture in the British and Dominion Armies 1914–1918* (Oxford: Clarendon Press, 1990), chapter 8.

Chapter 9

The War Game: Mobilization and "The Death of an Army"[1]

At the time of writing news has just been received that war has been declared. We wish the 1st Battalion the best of luck, and that we could be with them. Very little has happened during the past month in the way of games owing to the rain, which has made the ground unplayable.

St. George's Gazette, Journal of the Northumberland Fusiliers,
August 5, 1914, Sabathu, India[2]

The gallant old "Contemptibles"! There isn't much remains of them,
So full of fun and fitness, and a-singing in their pride;
For some are cold as clabber and the corby picks the brains of them,
And some are back in Blighty, and a-wishing they had died.

Robert Service, "Tipperary Days"[3]

What happened to the Army Gymnastic Staff in 1914, and the sports and physical training systems that were such a critical part of the pre-war Army's training regime and, indeed, the basis of so much of the Army's culture? Did these structures and programs survive the virtual annihilation of the original BEF in the opening six months of the war? The answer is, of course, yes. The physical culture of the pre-war Army survived and was, if anything, expanded upon during the war. The survival of the Gymnastic Staff and its programs was deemed so important that, within days of the Mobilization Order being issued, a plan was being developed by the War Office that would ensure that gymnastic training and sport would be just as much a part of the training of the new enlistees who were then flocking to the colors as it was part of the lives of the Regulars who were fighting in France and Belgium.

---

[1]   Anthony Farrar-Hockley, *The Death of an Army* (New York: Wm. Morrow & Co., 1968). This book is a seminal work on the opening battles of the First World War, with emphasis on the First Ypres Campaign in November 1914.

[2]   *St. George's Gazette* Vol. 32 (August 31, 1914), Second Battalion Notes, p. 106.

[3]   Quoted in Lyn Macdonald, *1914* (New York: Atheneum, 1988), p. 423.

The sports and recreation programs of the pre-war period were, unavoidably, largely put into abeyance in the Regular Army during the first months of the war—clearly the fluid and very bloody nature of the Mons, Marne, Aisne, and First Ypres Campaigns did not allow for any organized games or sporting activities. But the Army still managed to get in some fun, in spite of these conditions. When out of the line, it was said that British soldiers never went anywhere without a football,[4] even in the earliest phases of the war. The deeply ingrained games and sporting traditions of the Army survived and did resurface, often in some unexpected ways. Their ultimate retention and even expansion came as these traditions were passed on to the New Armies by older "Dug-out" officers and NCOs who, along with cadres from the Regulars, formed the nucleus of Kitchener's volunteer forces.

Upon the Army's receipt of the order to mobilize, to prepare for movement across the English Channel to support the French Army in the execution of its War Plan 17, the Army Gymnastic Staff was effectively dissolved. This dissolution came as the result of the organizational quirk that all members of the Staff were only seconded from their respective regiments—that is to say, still assigned to the parent regiment, and only "on loan" to the Staff for a nominally temporary assignment as an enlisted Staff Instructor or as a Superintendent of Gymnasia.[5] Not only did the Staff lose its limbs and sinews as the Superintendents and Staff Instructors returned to their units and embarked for the front, but it lost its head as well: Colonel Couper left the position of Inspector of Gymnasia and was assigned to the command of an infantry brigade.[6] Within days of the mobilization order, the pre-war Gymnastic Staff of 172 officers and other ranks was reduced to the fifteen enlisted Staff Instructors assigned to the Royal Military College, Sandhurst, and the Royal Military Academy, Woolwich. There was no longer any organization to accomplish the vital tasks of physical training for the entire Regular Army, the training of regimental PT instructors, fencing and bayonet training, and the informal (mostly volunteer) but very important role of games organization. The only really positive aspect of this dismal situation was that Colonel Couper's pre-war Assistant Inspector, Major Walter Wright, was retained on the Staff and within a few weeks was promoted to Inspector.[7]

---

4   Sir Douglas Haig in Stanley Weintraub, *Silent Night: The Story of the World War I Christmas Truce* (New York: Penguin Putnam Inc., 2001), pp. 96–98.

5   Captain F.J. Starr, "War History of the British Army Gymnastic Staff," (first draft) unpublished manuscript, Army Physical Training Corps Museum File # 1664, p. 2.

6   Lieutenant Colonel E.A.L. Oldfield, *History of the Army Physical Training Corps* (Aldershot: Gale & Polden Ltd., 1955), p. 21.

7   Ibid., p. 21.

The critical decisions surrounding mobilization of units and individuals that affected the Army's peacetime training establishment, including the Gymnastic Staff, were made in a series of Army Council and Cabinet meetings that occurred in the several days following the Declaration of War. Historians have discussed these meetings mostly in the context of the decision first to send the Expeditionary Force to France at all, and then the discussions surrounding the ultimate decision to retain two of the BEF's originally planned six divisions in the home islands to defend against a potential German seaborne invasion.[8] The plan was to release these divisions to the BEF once the Territorial Army was fully mobilized and prepared to assume its statutory role of Home Defence.[9] The decisions taken at these meetings relating to the structure of the Army remaining in Britain as a nucleus for reception, integration, and training of the Territorial formations and Kitchener's New Armies have not been as widely discussed by historians as those concerning the size and concentration areas of the deploying BEF. However, these decisions dramatically affected the future military capabilities of Britain to the extent that they were perhaps ultimately more important than many others made in that time.

Sir Douglas Haig portrays in his memoirs the special Cabinet meeting to which he was summoned on August 5, 1914, the day following the Declaration of War. He described the discussions taking place at the meeting as centering on the correct size, mission, and concentration areas of the BEF. In his account of the meeting, Haig takes credit for an assertion widely attributed to Lord Kitchener: that the country needed to prepare for a long war by creating an army of at least one million soldiers. He further states that, in order to make the creation of such a force possible, he urged the necessity of leaving behind a large cadre of officers and NCOs from the BEF, to become the trainers and the nucleus of the new Army. Haig states that he was mostly overridden in this particular desire, with the commander of the BEF, Sir John French, only acquiescing to the retention of three officers per battalion in regimental depots at home.[10]

Regardless of whether the suggestion to mobilize a mass army was made by Haig or by Kitchener, Field Marshal French's decision to leave only three officers per battalion in Britain was to have dramatic consequences for the future formation and training of what became Kitchener's Armies. Because of this

---

[8]   For some classic examples, see Philip Magnus, *Kitchener, Portrait of an Imperialist* (New York: E.P. Dutton & Co., 1959), pp. 278–280, or Captain Basil H. Liddell Hart, *The Real War 1914–1918* (Boston: Little, Brown & Co., 1930), pp. 50–51.

[9]   Field Marshal Viscount French of Ypres, *1914* (London: Constable & Co., 1919), p. 4.

[10]   Robert Blake, ed., *The Private Papers of Douglas Haig, 1914–1919* (London: Eyre & Spottiswoode, 1952), pp. 68–69.

paucity of trained and experienced leaders at home, the creation from nothing of such a large force was to take far longer than originally hoped and would take Herculean efforts to prepare for modern war. By the end of August 1914, the War Office was faced with a shortage of trained leaders at all levels for the Kitchener battalions that was reaching crisis proportions: almost 150,000 new volunteers were arriving at depots around the country, and there was effectively no apparatus to organize and begin training them to fight.[11] That required combat training, of course, had gymnastics at its foundation. Unfortunately, by the end of August the Gymnastic Staff had for all intents and purposes ceased to exist, and none of the officers designated by Sir John French to remain in Britain was from the Staff.[12]

When on August 23 the newly appointed Inspector of Gymnasia, Major Wright, was summoned to the War Office to discuss the necessity for physical training in the New Armies, he was faced with the dramatic consequences of the decisions that had gutted the Staff, along with the rest of Britain's military training establishment. He was asked to develop a scheme to restart the instructor's training course at the Headquarters Gymnasium in Aldershot, provide adequate numbers of qualified NCOs to conduct physical training for the New Armies, and develop a shortened course of exercises to get the new enlistees ready for combat within a six-month period.[13]

These were daunting tasks, given alone the shortage of trained Gymnastic Staff personnel available. But Major, soon to be Colonel Wright was resourceful and energetic, exactly the kind of officer who rose to the occasion in so many arenas during this critical time. Working with the War Office, he developed two potential courses of action to get gymnastic training back on a footing that would meet the needs of the Army. His first course of action involved a return to his control of all qualified Gymnastic Staff Instructors and Superintendents still remaining with their units in Britain, most of whom would have been assigned to units in the two divisions initially kept back from France. Along with the return of those NCOs and officers, Wright also suggested that the War Office issue an appeal to any retired Staff Instructors or Superintendents to return to the service to assist with the emergency, and to university and public-school Officer Training Corps (OTC) programs to release qualified instructors as well. Along with the call to OTCs would be a solicitation for any other qualified physical training instructors from schools around the nation[14]—many of these

---

[11]   See Peter Simkins, *Kitchener's Army: The Raising of the New Armies, 1914–1916* (Manchester: Manchester University Press, 1988), chapters 2, 6, 7.

[12]   Starr, "War History" (first draft), p. 2.

[13]   Oldfield, *History of the Army Physical Training Corps*, p. 22.

[14]   Starr, "War History" (first draft), pp. 2–3.

instructors would have been former Gymnastic Staff soldiers who had left the Army for civilian employment.[15]

The second course of action suggested by Wright was essentially the same as the first, only it allowed for the Army to retain all qualified Gymnastic Staff personnel with their regiments for service overseas and to fill the needs of the Staff from retired soldiers, OTC, and other school instructors. This was the course of action that was ultimately approved by the War Office. None of the serving infantrymen or cavalrymen who were qualified instructors was released from their units, and only six artillerymen were allowed to return to the Staff. Nevertheless, in spite of this difficulty, by September 1 Major Wright was able to put together a staff of eighty instructors made up from soldiers recalled to the service, released OTC instructors, and the fifteen remaining NCOs who had been assigned to Woolwich and Sandhurst.[16] In this group of eighty, he had two officers that he could use as Superintendents: Lieutenant Betts, who had been commissioned from the ranks in 1907, and who held the pre-war position of Master-of-Arms for the Gymnastic Staff, and the late Officer Instructor at the Headquarters Gymnasium, Aldershot (a position officially authorized in 1907),[17] who had been declared medically unfit for service overseas. These officers were immediately assigned as Superintendents at Grantham and Dublin respectively.[18]

In addition to working to cobble together the shell of a staff to run the Instructor's Course at the Headquarters Gymnasium, and to provide gymnastic training to the Kitchener battalions, Major Wright had to develop the course of instruction for the new volunteers that was to be significantly shortened from the pre-war recruit training scheme. The pre-war physical training tables mandated that each recruit attend a total of 110 hour-long sessions at the gymnasium.[19] Clearly this standard was unrealistic for the emergency the Army found itself in. Not only were there not enough qualified instructors for each new battalion, there weren't enough gymnasia or the equipment and various apparatus called for by the training tables. Wright, in concert with his newly formed staff, developed a physical training system that overcame most of these obstacles. It cut the amount of required training almost in half, and called for a progressive series of free exercises that "aim[ed] chiefly at procuring the utmost activity of brain and limb which it is possible to obtain in recruits taken in large

---

[15]   See Chapter 7, p. 109.

[16]   Starr, "War History" (first draft), p. 3.

[17]   Oldfield, *History of the Army Physical Training Corps*, pp. 19–20.

[18]   Starr, "War History" (first draft), p. 2.

[19]   Major J.R.M. Taylor, "Scheme of Training New British Armies, 1911," *Infantry Journal* (US) Vol. XI No. 5 (Mar.–Apr. 1915), pp. 704–715, and Starr, "War History" (first draft), p. 3.

classes and without proper clothing and apparatus."[20] Regular route marching was to be a staple of this program as well.[21]

These new training tables were published in small pamphlets, accompanied by simple drawings and diagrams that would enable "any intelligent non-commissioned officer" to understand them and begin training his soldiers.[22] These pamphlets, only periodically updated, remained in use throughout the war.[23] By September 10, the newly reconstituted Army Gymnastic Staff was sent out to the new battalions to begin physical training at the units, and on September 15, the first wartime Instructor's Course was begun at the Headquarters Gymnasium at Aldershot.[24] The rapidity with which the large obstacles faced by the Staff were overcome, and the ultimate success of those efforts, is albeit a small part, but a crucial part nonetheless, of the dramatic overall story of the Army's response to the extraordinary conditions of the summer of 1914.

The sporting instincts and morale fostered by unit games in the pre-war Army were evident in numerous instances at the outset of the war. It is remarkable that, in the absence of any significant time "out of the line" for the vast majority of the BEF during the fall and early winter of 1914, and in the face of nearly constant brutal combat resulting in the destruction of entire units, it would seem that Tommy and his officers still had the desire to "play up" in any way they could. Major General Nicholson noted in his wartime diary that his battalion came out of the line and moved to Divisional rest billets at Pont Riqueil on November 23, 1914. Nicholson recorded his unit's recreational training:

> The country round the billets was highly cultivated and very wet with the result that facilities for training and recreation were practically non-existent. Both were carried out to a small extent in the orchards and grass fields close to the farm houses.[25]

Despite the sporadic opportunities to participate in games, often the sporting impulse, without pitches, bats, balls, or the time to use them, came out in the form of the older, more traditional form of field sports.

---

[20]   "Special Tables, Physical Training 1916," National Army Museum Class. 355.545 acc.# 27161, overleaf.

[21]   Taylor, "Scheme of Training New British Armies, 1911," pp. 704–715.

[22]   "Special Tables, Physical Training 1916," overleaf, and Starr, "War History" (first draft), p. 3.

[23]   See, for example, "Special Tables, Physical Training 1916," or "Supplementary Tables, Physical Training 1916, reprinted with amendments, March, 1917 and Games, Issued by the General Staff, 1917," National Army Museum Class. 355.545.

[24]   Starr, "War History" (first draft), p. 3.

[25]   "Diary of Major General Sir (Cecil) Lothian Nicholson KCB CMG," unpublished manuscript, entry dated November 23–25, 1914, Imperial War Museum Archives 01/14/1.

Figure 9.1   9th Battalion, the London Regiment Recruit PT, December 1914 (Imperial War Museum)

When the 4th Guards Brigade occupied positions in Polygon Wood during the First Battle of Ypres in October 1914, the irrepressible sporting instinct of the pre-war British soldier came out in full force. At the center of the wood was the racecourse and training ground of the Belgian Army Cavalry School. The entire area was an "elliptical-shaped" clearing cut out from the firs in the center of the wood (thus the name "Polygon"), and was filled with the apparatus of horse training—bars, fences, walls—all still in place after the rapid departure of the Cavalry School staff and students for the front two months previously. Later, Colonel R.D. Whigham recalled:

> The sight of these fences was too much for some of our young officers, and in spite of the fact that there was a good deal of shelling going on and quite a number of shells were dropping into Polygon itself, a dozen or so of our young bloods were soon careering round the school and over the fences until they were sternly ordered by the Brigadier to stop.[26]

Troops in the wood had to be reprimanded during the battle, and the Brigade Commander, the Earl of Cavan, put out a general order prohibiting wastage of ammunition on shooting hares, as this was a potentially dangerous practice. Although the extra rations were desirable, "bullets were intended for the slaughter of Germans and under no circumstances for the slaughter of game." One soldier, however, managed to evade this proscription by hiding himself along one of the paths of the wood. Within half an hour he shot four pheasants and seven Germans as they attempted to cross the road. After he presented two of the pheasants to the Battalion Headquarters, he was praised for his "accidental" game shooting; eleven hits on moving targets at a range of 200 yards wasn't bad.[27]

By far the most famous sporting incidents that occurred in the opening months of the war were the spontaneous football games that started up between British and German soldiers during the "Christmas Truce" of 1914. There are many stories of these games on Christmas 1914, some apocryphal and many quite real. These games occurred both inside the British lines as soldiers took advantage of the quiet afforded by informal truces to relax with a familiar pastime, and in "No Man's Land" between British and German units. Virtually all of the accounts of football games between British and Germans that day have a similar ring; generally the day of truce began with parties of soldiers from both sides moving out into the areas between the lines to bury dead and recover personal effects. Once the dead were buried, and the land was reasonably clear,

---

26   Macdonald, *1914*, pp. 372–373.
27   Ibid., pp. 373–374.

a variety of activities then occurred. A representative example of these events is related in the war diary of the 133rd Saxon Regiment, which described "Tommy und Fritz" chasing hares together in a cabbage field. This innocuous activity soon evolved into kicking around a football furnished by, who else, a Scottish soldier. As the war diary relates, "This developed into a regulation football match with caps casually laid out as goals. The frozen ground was no great matter." According to the diary, after a spirited match the Saxons came out as winners, three goals to two.[28] Perhaps the unknown British unit recorded the match score in a more flattering manner. Either way, events like these were repeated all along the front where "Tommy und Fritz" faced each other.

British soldiers reported fraternizing with Germans who had worked in Britain before the war, who eagerly asked them about the performance and prospects of their favorite Football Association teams—some Germans even claimed to have played professional football in Britain.[29] Most of the games reported during the truce seem to have been unorganized "punt-abouts" using makeshift balls, often sandbags filled with rags. Sometimes the games were reported to have occurred in parts of the line where the truce was not being widely adhered to. Corporal William Hunt of the Nottingham and Derbyshire Regiment (Sherwood Foresters) wrote on Christmas afternoon that "not the slightest notice" was taken of shelling "when a football match is on the go."[30]

These games were apparently unique to those areas of the front where the British and Germans faced each other; the French were perhaps not fond enough of "footer" to let it get in the way of their war to rid France of the invader. Several Tommies reported home that they were involved in football games in sectors bordering French units, and that fighting went on not more than 800 yards away from the games. The French also reported on some of these games—another opportunity to shake their heads at the curious English.[31]

Were these manifestations of the games ethic an example of the unmilitary British not taking their position seriously or even not understanding the nature of modern war? Clearly they were not, nor were they an act of incipient rebellion against the authorities of the Army who were managing the slaughter in France and Belgium. Games as morale events during a sporadic and unofficial truce were effectively no different from games and sports engaged in for morale and *esprit* before the war—an opportunity to relieve stress and boredom, and here to recall a time and place where imminent disaster meant the loss of a match, not death or

---

[28]   "9. Königlich Sächsisches Infanterie-Regiment Nr. 133 im Weltkrieg 1914–18," cited in Weintraub, *Silent Night*, p. 104.

[29]   Ibid., p. 102.

[30]   Ibid., p. 106.

[31]   Ibid., p. 107.

dismemberment. The fact that the BEF did engage in such widely reported games at this point in the war suggests rather that the morale of units was still high after the terrific bloodletting of the fall, and the games point to soldiers holding onto a kernel of humanity in the face of unimaginable horror. The pre-war games ethic was at least partially responsible not only for keeping morale at a reasonably high level, but for fostering the spirit of sportsmanship that would allow for friendly games between deadly wartime adversaries. Another manifestation of the British military games ethic, one more hidden but certainly more important than sportsmanship between the lines at Christmas, was in the superb combat performance of the Regular Army in the opening months of the war.

On the morning of August 22, 1914, a week after arriving in France, C Squadron of the 4th Dragoon Guards was conducting a reconnaissance patrol along the Mons–Brussels road, near the village of Soignies in Belgium. While the squadron was halted to water their horses, dismounted pickets alerted the squadron commander, Major Sir Thomas Bridges, that four German lancers, or Uhlans, were approaching on the road from Soignies. Bridges was elated; if he could ambush these Germans, not only would his squadron be able to take prisoners that would provide the Army valuable intelligence as to the location, strength, and intentions of the enemy, but they would also have the honor of being the first British unit to see combat during the war. Bridges quickly ordered two of his four troops to dismount and prepare to engage the Uhlans; dismounted fighting had been standard practice for British cavalry since the South African War. Just as Bridges gave his order, the four advancing Uhlans halted, perhaps alerted by the sound of Bridges's men moving into position. The Germans began to move back up the road to join up with their main body just now coming over the horizon from Soignies, about two hundred yards from the British. The Dragoons let out a groan of disappointment.

Bridges, however, still had two troops in the saddle, and when Captain Hornby, commanding 1st Troop, begged, "Let us go after them, Sir!" Bridges gave the order to pursue. In an instant the two troops were on the road, riding hell bent for leather after the Uhlans, swords drawn and Captain Hornby in the lead, hallooing "Chaaaarge!" They galloped flat out, racing to see who could get to the Germans first. Bridges quickly mounted his other two troops and went after Hornby, ready to rapidly dismount and provide covering fire if necessary.

Meanwhile, Hornby's men had caught the retiring Uhlans inside the village. Horseshoes rang sparks from the cobblestones, men growled and shouted, and swords flashed as the Dragoons of 1st Troop scattered the Uhlans, who were unable to effectively defend themselves with their unwieldy lances. After a brief mounted skirmish, the Dragoons withdrew under supporting fire from the dismounted troopers of 4th Troop, with five prisoners in tow. Captain Hornby rode all the way back to the regiment that day with his sword drawn, held at the position of Attention. It was covered with the blood of a slain German, and he wanted it to stay that way until he could show it off to his fellow officers, his trophy of the first German killed by the British Army in the Great War. The Dragoons were satisfied that in dying by the sword that German had died like a gentleman. Hornby was awarded the Distinguished Service Order for his exploit.[32] "There was no hatred of the Germans," Major Bridges later remarked. "We were quite ready to fight anybody ... and would equally readily have fought the French. Our motto was, 'We'll do it. What is it?'"[33]

Just seven days later, the BEF was in the midst of the long retreat from Mons that would eventually end with the Battle of the Marne. The First and Second Corps were separated by a dangerous gap of roughly ten miles, and the troops were exhausted, having marched almost sixty miles in the past three days while continuously fighting sharp rearguard actions. With little or no food and an average of only eight or ten hours of sleep during that time, the men of the BEF desperately needed a chance to rest and regroup. On August 29, the French Fifth Army counterattacked at Guise to allow the BEF that chance. The 2nd Battalion, Royal Sussex Regiment made the most of it. They slept all night and into the day, had a hot meal, and did what they could to clean their equipment and themselves. Late that afternoon their commander, Colonel Montresor, paraded the battalion on a village green:

> He stood the men at ease and spoke a very few words, reminding them that B Company had won the Regimental Cricket Cup in the course of the summer. The Cup had naturally been left at home for safety, but the silver medallions had been mailed to the battalion and had miraculously caught up with them. One by one each member of the cricket team was called out to receive his inscribed medallion and a handshake from the Colonel.[34]

The following day the retreat resumed.

These two incidents would appear to be completely unrelated. One is a stirring example of dash, bravery, and cavalry *élan*, while the other is a mundane formation to hand out what would seem to be totally irrelevant medallions to exhausted soldiers during a retreat. But they *are* connected. These two incidents truly typify sport and its role in the late Victorian and Edwardian British Army. The charge of the 4th Dragoon Guards has all the hallmarks of a foxhunt or

---

[32]   MacDonald, *1914*, pp. 84–88.
[33]   Barbara W. Tuchman, *The Guns of August* (New York: The Macmillan Co., 1962), p. 312.
[34]   Macdonald, *1914*, pp. 237–238.

pigsticking meet: men without malice racing to "come to grips" with their quarry, vying to see who will be first to get the trophy. The galloping horses, the leaders "hallooing," and the danger and excitement of the chase—this incident highlights why the combat-experienced officers of the Victorian Army encouraged their young officers, and later their soldiers, to hunt. When Captain Hornby gleefully showed his bloody sword to his friends, he might just as well have been showing off a fox brush or the head of a wild Indian boar.

Hornby's charge and Bridges's handling of his squadron that day were tactically sound and highly successful. They not only captured the required prisoners, but they did so with an aggressive and well-executed maneuver. This "sporting" action and others like it in the early days of the war clearly established for the British a moral ascendancy over their adversaries. As a result, the Germans would be tentative and quick to back down in all of their subsequent meetings with the British in 1914, a fact that perhaps saved the BEF during the retreat from Mons and in the First Battle of Ypres.[35]

When Colonel Montresor called his battalion to a formation in order to present the B Company cricket team their medals, he did so in the certain knowledge that the tournament meant more to his men than the medallions; it was an event that inspired unit *esprit de corps*, built morale, and reinforced connections to home. For soldiers who had been forced to make a demoralizing "strategic retirement," fighting all the way without ever suffering a tactical defeat, a formation for this purpose would only remind them of their traditions, their close comradeship, and their belief in a moral and cultural superiority represented by their games and sporting ethic. This reminder could only serve to boost their morale, one of the major stated purposes of British Army sport before the war. These two incidents highlight what was best about sport in the pre-war British Army. It inspired teamwork, camaraderie, and aggressiveness, building morale and unit traditions of excellence on what General Douglas MacArthur would later call "these fields of friendly strife." The Army's leaders who encouraged sport knew of these potential outcomes, and consciously set up their sports programs with the intent of achieving them in the interest of enhancing the Army's effectiveness.

The same was true of the establishment of the Army's physical training program. Closely related to sport and the philosophy of athleticism, physical training in the late Victorian and Edwardian British Army was adopted and

---

[35]   There are many examples of hesitation and reluctance to push home attacks on the part of the Germans during the first months of the war. The British Second Corps was allowed to escape from Le Cateau in spite of being virtually surrounded; at Landrecies a handful of Guardsmen held off a vastly superior force, largely because of German hesitation, and at First Ypres the Germans could have broken through the decimated BEF on several occasions but failed to follow up penetrations.

vigorously pursued as a training method with the improvement of the Army's fighting capabilities as the desired end result. The BEF's long forced marches with little food and even less rest during the opening months of the war in 1914 are not in themselves remarkable; soldiers throughout history have performed similar or even more strenuous feats. What is remarkable about these marches (and later the bitter fighting of the Aisne and Ypres campaigns of 1914) is that the BEF executed them almost immediately after disembarking in France, without any period of time to get acclimated to the environment of war or to get into shape. Moreover, they conducted these movements in conjunction with violent and sustained combat action, with no reserves or possibility of relief. These factors set the BEF apart from its European counterparts in 1914. When these conditions are considered along with the fact that, unlike the French and German armies in 1914, the overwhelming majority of the soldiers of the BEF came from an urban environment, it becomes clear that, without the comprehensive physical training program begun in 1860 and administered by the Army Gymnastic Staff, the BEF would not have been able to fight in the way it did in 1914.

Sport and physical training in the late Victorian and Edwardian British Army are only a part of the fascinating saga of the radical transformation of that organization between 1860 and 1914. Nonetheless, the lessons that can be gleaned from studying the role that sport and physical training played in that transformation illuminate many aspects of the Army's training and tactical doctrine, organization and institutional methods, and the connections between the British Army and its parent society. The British Army in 1914 was a highly professional, well-trained, and thoroughly modern force. Instead of detracting from its competence, the Army's sport and physical training systems were major contributors to its level of excellence. Additionally, the links between the revolution in the Army's training and doctrine and Victorian social change have not been fully explored. Many historians, for example, have tended to see the widespread incidence of sport in the Army during the First World War as an example of civilian society's influence on the hidebound, conservative military through the wartime influx of citizen soldiers.[36] Knowledge of pre-war Army sport and physical training, however, reveals this phenomenon as a mere continuation and expansion of existing systems. Just how these systems that embodied the Army's physical culture before the war were kept alive and grew after the destruction of the old Regular Army in 1914, is intimately bound up with the way in which the members of the regenerated Gymnastic Staff and others built and trained Kitchener's volunteers to replace the "Old Contemptibles."

---

36   See J.G. Fuller, *Troop Morale and Popular Culture in the British and Dominion Armies 1914–1918* (Oxford: Clarendon Press, 1990).

PART IV
"The Greater Game": Army Physical Culture in Wartime

Chapter 10

Civilians to Soldiers: Sport and Fitness in Kitchener's New Armies

In the meantime more recruits had arrived and when the drivers were sorted out from the gunners ... we gunners went back to drill and PT ... I thought I was very fit before I joined up, but I discovered a lot of muscles I never knew I had, and they all ached at first.

R.W. Brierley, 1915[1]

Our battalion is now "rigged out" with proper football kit, and if they manage to play half as well as they look, they will have more than a sporting chance even with the United.

St. George's Gazette, Journal of the Northumberland Fusiliers, January 1915[2]

"Your King and Country need you." "Women of Britain Say, 'Go!'" These calls to young British men brought enormous numbers into regimental depots during the last months of 1914 and well into 1915: 33,204 men enlisted on September 3, 1914 alone.[3] Volunteers continued to join Kitchener's New Armies in smaller yet still sufficient numbers throughout 1915 so that Britain did not have to institute a draft until 1916. The introductory military experience of most of these men was chaotic, until the War Office was able to put systems in place to accommodate this unprecedented military expansion. At first, billeting was haphazard, food was sparse, and uniforms and equipment were, for most, non-existent. One experience, however, was constant. Initial training of Lord Kitchener's volunteers consisted largely of close order drill and physical training. These two elemental building blocks of the process of transforming civilians into soldiers remained constant for the duration of the war, and indeed served as an

---

[1]   "War Memoirs of R.W. Brierley," unpublished manuscript, Imperial War Museum Archives P191.

[2]   *St. George's Gazette* Vol. 33 (March 31, 1915), 12th (Service) Battalion Notes, p. 47.

[3]   Peter Simkins, *Kitchener's Army: The Raising of the New Armies, 1914–16* (Manchester: Manchester University Press, 1988), p. 66. This book is perhaps the most exhaustively complete treatment in print of the creation of the New Armies.

important bridge between the Old Army and the New-. Through the media of drill and physical training, the Army's cultural attitudes about discipline and fitness were passed on to new volunteers by the Regular cadres and "dug out" retired officers and NCOs who trained "Kitchener's Mob."

As the new battalions progressed in their training, physical training continued to be an important part of soldier and unit development. The pre-war germination of ideas that would put the conduct of fitness training more into the context of maneuver or tactical exercises—assault courses, for example— evolved in the wartime period of austere facilities into a reliance on footmarching and other operations-based activities to maintain strength and harden soldiers' bodies for combat. Trench-digging practice, for example, served as a way to both teach tactical lessons and ensure men were fit. Through a combination of formal gymnastics, and then field-oriented fitness training, the Army's leaders hoped to turn raw civilians into disciplined, fit soldiers who could fight effectively in the many environments of the war.

Fitness training for British soldiers, of course, went beyond formal gymnastic training, and had to include sport and games. Any commander who neglected this second of the twin pillars of Army physical culture would have been seen not only as jeopardizing the health and welfare of his troops but as failing to look after the morale of his men and the *esprit de corps* of his unit. As soon as they were formed, the new battalions began playing games. At first these units followed, in microcosm, the pattern of Army sport development seen during the last years of the nineteenth century—unorganized pick-up games evolving into more elaborate intra- and inter-unit systems of play. In the New Armies, the most common game by far was football, which was a function not only of the ease of organizing and supplying the equipment for the game but also of the overwhelming popularity of football among the vast majority of Britons. Men entering the Army as volunteers brought the national game with them. Although wholesale adoption by these new units of traditional Army sporting practices was clearly at least partially due to the popularity of games among the "citizen soldiers" comprising the units, there was another key to this process. The continuity of formal Army sports between the Regulars and the Kitchener battalions was again, like the conduct of physical training, provided by the cadres of Regulars and recalled soldiers who acted as the initial backbone of the new units.

Sport, games, and physical training were fundamental elements of the Army's morale and training programs before the First World War, and they remained as such throughout the war. The influx of civilians into the Army that began with Kitchener's call for volunteers in August 1914 brought with it middle- and working-class Britain's love of sport, which fit perfectly with and complemented the Regular Army's traditions. Sport, games, and physical training acted as an important means of facilitating the transition of civilians into military life and built unit *esprit de corps*, as well as providing an invaluable service in sustaining morale and soldier fitness through the grinding misery and horror of the war experience. The link between the Old Army and the New- provided by Regular and recalled trainers and leaders meant that, as in the years before the war, Army sport and physical training during the First World War would continue to be vital to the wellbeing and military effectiveness of the British soldier.

Despite the efforts of the newly reconstituted Gymnastic Staff at Aldershot, gymnastic and physical training of recruits in the New Armies got off to an unsteady start. During the fall and early winter of 1914 the situation would improve, but at the outset there were problems. Anecdotal evidence from soldier letters and diaries, along with columns contributed to the few regimental journals that stayed in print during the war,[4] point to what would seem to be an uneven application of the program set out in August 1914 by Colonel Wright and the new members of the Staff. One can cite numerous causes for this less-than-complete adherence to the new scheme. For example, many new units were immediately faced with severe billeting shortages that forced them to disperse soldiers around wide areas to stay with local residents until adequate camps could be built to house them.[5]

This kind of situation challenged commanders in maintaining any kind of coherent training program, as the travel time alone for soldiers to move from billets to training areas severely constrained what could be realistically scheduled. Another reason for units initially not adhering strictly to the recommended physical training outline was that, until the restarted instructor's course could generate adequate numbers of trained NCOs and officers to run unit exercise programs, commanders had to rely on soldiers with some pre-war experience, or they had to improvise. All types of unit training were similarly affected by this shortage of trained officers and NCOs as well as shortages in billets and

---

[4]   Most regimental journals were suspended for the duration of the war but began publication again soon after the Armistice in 1918 or early in 1919. There were a few that continued to appear throughout, and I have relied heavily on some of these in this part of the chapter: *St. George's Gazette*, *The XI Hussar Journal*, *The Green Howards Gazette*, *The Light Bob Gazette*, and *The Highland Light Infantry Chronicle*. The 1914 volumes of these journals, with the exception of *St. George's Gazette*, were mostly taken up with detailed accounts of operations in France; of course, these accounts ceased as soon as the Army established its censorship system.

[5]   Simkins, *Kitchener's Army*, chapters 6, 7, 9. See also Malcolm Brown, *Tommy Goes to War* (London: J.M. Dent & Sons Ltd., 1978), pp. 26–29.

equipment. Not until the end of 1914 and into early 1915 could the War Office report that training in the New Armies was meeting all expectations.[6]

At first, formal physical training for some units consisted primarily of marching to training areas from billets. For others, units that were fortunate enough to have either recalled NCOs and officers or a complement of Regulars acting as a cadre, getting in shape took on a different complexion. R.W. Brierley recorded in his diary that, when he first arrived at his unit, all the recruits conducted some rudimentary exercises under the control of NCOs at the depot, but when he moved to the 46th (North Midland) Divisional Training Battery, Royal Field Artillery, and began training in earnest, his squad sergeant had his own approach. This old army NCO started teaching his charges close-order drill, and made them run wind sprints when they made mistakes. This practice continued through their more specialized training as gunners. Once his basic training was finished and his unit was waiting to ship out for France, Brierley recorded, "All we had to do now was keep fit with endless PT [physical training] and drill ... Days went by and we were kept active and fit by long sessions of PT and a route march or two and a Sports meeting."[7] Brierley and his comrades may not have agreed, but they were luckier than many in having an experienced NCO to improvise techniques, pass on his knowledge to them, and get them ready for their coming trials.

Territorial Army battalions were among the units that benefited from having some leaders trained by the pre-war Staff. The Territorials had long internalized the Army's practices of fitness training, and after mobilization they conducted vigorous PT programs to get themselves up to the standard required for deployment. Like their predecessors during the South African War, some Territorials continued to pursue their fitness training on shipboard while bound for imperial garrisons to free up Regulars for the war in France. Sergeant J.W. Whatley recorded in his diary in October 1914 that his Territorial unit conducted PT every day while on board ship bound for India. They also conducted a bayonet fighting and tug-of-war competition on the ship at Port Suez, while waiting to pass through the canal.[8] Major the Honorable R.E.S. Barrington of the Scottish Horse wrote home to say that, while on the troop ship bound for the Gallipoli Campaign in August 1915, his Territorial unit's physical fitness benefited enormously from the assignment of Lieutenant Jones,

---

[6]   Letter from Sir Archibald Murray, Deputy Chief of the Imperial General Staff, to Sir John French, 3 April 1915, French papers, Imperial War Museum Archives 75/46/13. See Simkins, *Kitchener's Army*, p. 318.

[7]   R.W. Brierley, Imperial War Museum Archives P191.

[8]   "Diary of J.W. Whatley," unpublished manuscript, Imperial War Museum Archives 96/48/1.

formerly a PT instructor in The Blues and Royals. Barrington wrote that he took physical training twice per day, and was "quite fit."[9]

During the fall of 1914, the new instructor's course at Aldershot began to turn out numbers of trained officers and NCOs that began to make a difference in sharpening up the physical training of the volunteer battalions. The 7th (Reserve) Battalion, Northumberland Fusiliers regimental journal column for October 31, 1914 noted that the battalion was conducting PT every morning and footmarches on alternate days.[10] Again, steady improvement in physical training was comparable to developments in the other types of training needed to get units ready to move to the front. To meet the enormous and pressing demand for trained Staff Instructors, the new Inspector of Gymnasia, Colonel Walter Wright, retained at Aldershot ten of his initial complement of eighty NCOs to set up and run the new instructor's course. Colonel Wright and his staff made the decision that, in spite of the soldiers coming to the new course being practically raw recruits, most of them without uniforms and even some without service numbers yet assigned, "the incentive of war and their superior intelligence" were such that the pre-war instructor's course of almost six months' duration could be shortened in the crisis to a course of twenty-one working days.[11] The first course, which started on September 15, 1914, had 180 students, and after the new twenty-one-day program these men went back to their units to assist the seventy original Staff Instructors in putting their battalions through the Physical Training Tables each day.[12] In a report written for the War Office later in the war, the Staff recorded that:

> Each month [since September 1914] an Instructional Course of 21 days has been held, the numbers attending quickly increasing up to 500 in order to meet the growing demand for Instructors, which, even with an Army Gymnastic Staff of 1,000 Instructors, and after having put through some 12,000 N.C.Os., is far from satisfied, and for every vacancy there are still two applications to attend a course.[13]

This huge increase in the size of the course added to the already heavily burdened facilities at Aldershot—the pre-war Instructor's Course had averaged

---

9   "War letters of Major the Honorable R.E.S. Barrington," unpublished microfilm file, Imperial War Museum Archives PP/MCR/55.

10   *St. George's Gazette* Vol. 32 (October 31, 1914), 7th (Reserve) Battalion notes, p. 138.

11   "Report of the Army Physical and Bayonet Training Staff, 1916," unpublished manuscript, Army Physical Training Corps Museum file #1664, p. 2.

12   Ibid., p. 3.

13   Ibid., p. 3.

only 350 students per year.[14] At first, new students had to be housed right in the Headquarters Gym, but later two more gyms were built and with tents and newly constructed barracks by the summer of 1915 the situation had improved.[15] In addition to the Staff's main school at Aldershot, and the later schools set up at Borden and Portsmouth, by 1916 each Home Command in Britain had a School of Physical and Bayonet Training, run by the Command's Superintendent and his staff of instructors.[16]

With the increase in trained officers and NCOs produced by the Instructor's Course, physical training continued to progress and become more regularized for the new units. Corporal Ralph Clark of the 4th (TA) Battalion, The Lincolnshire Regiment, wrote in his diary that his battalion held physical training parades from 6 to 7 o'clock virtually every day before breakfast, and on the days when they did not, they were often on a route march of from 8 to 15 miles duration. Parades this early for PT were generally in violation of what was then accepted practice, but Clark was still glad to say that he was fitter than he had ever been.[17]

Long and arduous route marches were a signal feature of the training in new units, and virtually every volunteer recalled these marches with a mixture of pride in accomplishment and relief that they were over. Route marches started slow and short, and when the men had gotten into shape and their feet were tough enough, became progressively longer. By the time units were ready to move to the front, they were fairly routinely conducting marches of over twenty miles. An unintended consequence of these arduous events was that sometimes

---

[14]   Lieutenant Colonel E.A.L. Oldfield, *History of the Army Physical Training Corps* (Aldershot: Gale and Polden Ltd., 1955), p. 24.

[15]   "Report of the Army Physical and Bayonet Training Staff, 1916," p. 3. By 1917 the school at Aldershot, renamed the Army School of Physical and Bayonet Training, had vastly expanded its operations. See *Training at Home*, issued by the General Staff, 1917 (papers of General Sir Ivor Maxse, File 58, Imperial War Museum Archives), p. 21: "Army School of Physical and Bayonet Training, Aldershot. (a) Object – To train and supply officer and NCO instructors in physical and bayonet training for the Army. Duration – 21 days. (b) Numbers under instruction – 50 officers, 700 NCOs, and in addition to the above, 70–100 candidates for the Army Gymnastic Staff undergo a probationary course. Special training in remedial exercises is also given to AGSI and past instructors, the course lasting four to six weeks. (c) Syllabus includes – Physical Training, bayonet training, class taking and instruction in physical training games. Lectures are also given on the above and on anatomy."

[16]   Colonel Walter Wright, draft letter dated December 3, 1917, Army Physical Training Corps Museum file #1664.

[17]   "Diary of Corporal Ralph Clark 4th (Territorial Army) Battalion, The Lincolnshire Regiment 27 July 1914–27 July 1915," unpublished manuscript, National Army Museum Archives acc. #7606-45.

soldiers were overcome by heat or fatigue. Percy Croney of the 12th Battalion, The Essex Regiment recalled a march in 1915 after which seventy-three soldiers were hospitalized and three died of heat exhaustion. He added, however, that he and his mates were "filled with pride" after an old Regular who had enlisted in the battalion told them, "You Kitchener's men did tidy well!"[18]

Commanders noted vast improvements in the fitness and health of soldiers, and were pleased to note that Kitchener's citizen soldiers had begun to look and act like Regulars. Major General Sir Ivor Maxse had left his combat command of the 1st Guards Brigade in late 1914, and was promoted to command of the new 18th Division then training in Britain. Maxse regularly wrote for dissemination to the War Office and other commanders his "Notes on the New Armies by a Divisional Commander," in which he laid out lessons learned, practical ideas on training and leadership, and assessments of unit progress. Both of his first two "Notes" referred to physical fitness as a key requisite for combat readiness, and in them he strongly stated that he was very pleased with the progress in fitness in his subordinate units.[19]

Just as Corporal Clark wrote in his diary, the new soldiers themselves noted the improvement in their physique and abilities, and recorded deep satisfaction with their accomplishments. An example of one of these statements appeared in the February 27, 1915 issue of *St. George's Gazette*:

> Each day sees this Battalion becoming more and more fitted for whatever lies before it in the future, and we feel sure that the careful and systematic training which we are undergoing cannot but bear its fruit in due season. Perhaps the most important innovation during the past month has been the inauguration of early morning parades at which the officers and men are engaged in physical exercises. There can be no doubt whatever that the physique of the men has increased to such an extent that they are now able to make light of the strenuousness of their training ... That part which athletics ought to play in the course of training has been fully appreciated, and every possible encouragement is given to the various sports with which men occupy their spare time. The rugger and soccer teams are now quite an institution and every Saturday afternoon sees an inter-Company match or a match with some local battalion.[20]

---

[18]   Percy Croney, cited in Simkins, *Kitchener's Army*, p. 303.

[19]   "Notes on the New Armies by a Divisional Commander," nos. 1, 2 (Maxse papers, 69/53/1 File 11/1, Imperial War Museum archives).

[20]   *St. George's Gazette* Vol. 33 (February 27, 1915), 16th (Service) Battalion notes, p. 31.

Tying together sport and gymnastics as twin elements of physical preparation for combat, this author demonstrates that the Army's traditions of physical culture had indeed been passed on to the new volunteers. Right from the start of hostilities, the imperative of unit leaders to promote, manage, and conduct sports and games was at least as important as the mission to conduct standard physical training. From the very first days of the creation of Kitchener's Armies, Britain's new citizen soldiers indulged in sports and games.

Like other regimental journals, the 1914 and 1915 issues of *St. George's Gazette* reported not only on the combat action of the two Regular battalions of the regiment in France but also on the formation and training of the new Kitchener battalions of the regiment in Britain. The contrast in these 1914 journals between the Regulars and the New Armies is striking. On the pages devoted to the Regulars there is a sad and extensive series of obituaries of young officers, senior NCOs, and other ranks killed in France, with such eulogies as "Distinguished soldier, all-round sportsman." This kind of tragic news is related while on the new battalion pages there are cheery accounts of training exercises and football matches, much the same as the reporting in most regimental journals before the war. The death of the Victorian Army is juxtaposed in these journals against the description of its resurrection, through the continuity of its traditions among the New Armies.[21]

Some units began playing games almost as soon as the soldiers reported into the depots. On October 31, 1914, one battalion reported in its regimental journal column that it was already engaged in a full schedule of inter-company and inter-battalion football matches,[22] and its sister unit passed on the information that they had received a full issue of "footballs, quoits, etc.," in spite of the fact that they still had not gotten military uniforms or equipment, and were without sufficient quarters.[23] Corporal Clark of the Lincolnshire Regiment left an interesting record in his diary of the manner in which the Army's scheme of operating sports programs was passed on to the new arrivals. He described some unorganized pick-up football games that occurred in his unit – some section versus section games in his company in October, 1914, and then again in November. In that month he had been selected for promotion to Corporal, and as one of the junior leaders in the battalion, was informed that there was to be a meeting on December 5, chaired by the battalion commander, where the unit was to set up a football program.[24]

---

[21] *St. George's Gazette* Vols. 32, 33.
[22] *St. George's Gazette* Vol. 32 (October 31, 1914), 10th (Service) Battalion notes, p. 142.
[23] *St. George's Gazette* Vol. 32 (October 31, 1914), 11th (Service) Battalion notes, p. 143.
[24] Ralph Clark, October 20–December 5, 1914.

Figure 10.1 1st Battalion, the Wiltshire Regiment football after coming out of the line, 1916 (Imperial War Museum)

Prior to the meeting that day the battalion held a football match between "old hands" and recruits—a way of inaugurating the formal program. Later, at the meeting, the battalion commander spoke to the NCOs about the need to have a battalion team to compete with other units in the area: it was essential for the unit's pride and morale that they make and accept sporting challenges. The leaders then selected a battalion team from among the best company players, and voted to set up a committee to manage the team's schedule. Regular games began later that month.[25] This is a clear description of the way in which Regular officers throughout the new units, like Clark's battalion commander, taught their men the proper way to play. By bringing in the NCOs of the unit and allowing them to participate in the set up and management of the battalion's system, Clark's battalion commander was also giving them a training opportunity in organization and leadership that could only serve to enhance the effectiveness of his command.

Although one unit reported that "Football is considered <u>the</u> pastime here,"[26] soccer was not the only game Britain's new warriors engaged in. Boxing, athletics meets, cross-country races, and the traditional events of the unit sports days were all played.[27] Sport was also used by the Army at this time to bring men into the new units. Recruiting sergeants from the depot of the Northumberland Fusiliers went to football grounds to distribute leaflets: "At the cup tie on Newcastle United's ground today a few thousand forms will be issued at the turnstile to those who appear likely to come up to the required standard."[28]

The War Office even worked to enlist entire "sportsmen's battalions," an experiment repeated by the government in Australia.[29] In September 1914 the entire Northern Foxes Football Team of Leeds enlisted in the Leeds Pals Battalion (15th Battalion West Yorkshire Regiment).[30] The 12th Battalion East Yorkshire Regiment was recruited as the "Hull Sportsmen and Athletes," and the 17th and 23rd Battalions of the Middlesex Regiment were called the 1st and 2nd "Football Battalions."[31] These sporting Pals Battalions were units recruited from local lads who played on a team, were supporters, or just wanted to have the association. A famous recruiting poster from October 1914 that was originally

---

[25]   Ibid.

[26]   *St. George's Gazette* Vol. 33 (January 30, 1915), 12th (Service) Battalion notes, p. 15.

[27]   See, for example, *The XI Hussar Journal* Vol. VI (October 1915), 12th Reserve Cavalry Regiment notes, and *The Green Howards Gazette* Vol. 22.

[28]   *St. George's Gazette* Vol. 33 (January 30, 1915), Depot Battalion notes, p. 7.

[29]   Murray G. Phillips, "Sport, War, and Gender Images: The Australian Sportsmen's Battalions and the First World War," *The International Journal of the History of Sport* Vol. 14, No. 1 (April 1997), pp. 78–96.

[30]   Brown, *Tommy Goes to War*, p. 23.

[31]   Simkins, *Kitchener's Army*, pp. 88, 123.

a *Punch* cartoon showed Mr. Punch saying to a professional football player, "No doubt you can make money in this field, my friend, but there's only one field today where you can get honor."[32]

In Australia the "sportsmen's battalions," only resorted to as a recruiting technique in 1917, had relatively less success in attracting men to the colors. Because of differences between the way British and Australian units were maintained (Australia never authorized a draft, for example), the sportsmen's units recruited for the Australian Imperial Force (AIF) were never sent to fight as stand-alone battalions. Rather, they were fed piecemeal to the AIF as replacements for extant units. Despite organizational differences, however, the motivation behind and techniques used by the Australian government for establishing sportsmen's units were very much the same as in Britain. The Australians used slogans such as, "We're getting together a team to thrash the German Hun. WILL YOU MAKE ONE?," "The greatest sport of all—Hun-hunting," "Be a real man and join the Sport's Unit," and finally, "Be a man, play a man's part. Don't sit at home and let your pal do your bit. Enlist in the Sportsmen's Unit. You will feel all the better afterwards for having done so." All of these appeals to antipodean masculinity were deliberately constructed to take advantage of the Australian male self-image as a better than average athlete and sportsman, one who in recent years had begun to more than hold his own against the best metropolitan Britain could produce. Regardless of the relative success of the Australian sports recruiting campaign, the campaign itself is highly illuminating when one considers its implications for the role of sport and images of masculinity in Australian society.[33]

Physical training was a central part of the process of making Kitchener's volunteers into soldiers. As in the years before the war, gymnastics and field PT served to get soldiers from industrial and urban areas fit and healthy enough to withstand not only the rigors of their combat training but also the trials of actual combat. Soldiers felt pride in themselves and their units after shaping up and accomplishing feats they had not imagined possible—men felt that they were warriors. Whether they were or not is immaterial. What was important is that they *felt* they were, and engendering that feeling, along with the physical conditioning of soldiers, had always been dual goals of the Army's physical training and sports programs. In making a man feel like a soldier, physical training was a critical element of a volunteer's transition into the Army.

The other pillar of military physical culture was sport. Sport, too, acted as a key part of the transition of civilian volunteers into the Army. Working-

32   Stanley Weintraub, *Silent Night: The Story of the World War I Christmas Truce* (New York: Penguin Putnam Inc., 2001), p. 96.

33   See Phillips, "Sport, War and Gender Images," pp. 78–96.

and middle-class Britain's love of games fit well with the Army's pre-existing traditions of formal and informal sport. New soldiers brought their games into the Army with them, and then their leaders showed them the Army's way to organize and conduct those games. The Army also put those games to use, in precisely the same manner as before the war, to build unit pride and traditions of excellence, enhance teamwork and leadership skills, and complement formal physical training in getting soldiers fit. The continued validity of these uses of sport and PT ensured that British soldiers continued to play games and conduct PT throughout the duration of the war. The Army Gymnastic Staff, and its incarnation as part of the BEF, the Physical and Bayonet Training Staff, was responsible for management and promotion of these activities. From the hectic and somewhat disorganized situation in which it found itself in late 1914, the Staff rebounded to such an extent that by 1918 it had grown to over 100 times its pre-war size and was managing the physical, bayonet, and recreational training of British and Commonwealth soldiers in operational theaters around the globe.

Chapter 11

"Make Them Tigers": The Army Physical and Bayonet Training Staff

To sum up, Physical Training should be regarded as the foundation of all training.

"Supplementary Tables, Physical Training 1916," reissued
by the General Staff, 1917.[1]

Get the bayonet into the hands of despondent troops and you can make them tigers
within hours.

Lieutenant Colonel Ronald B. Campbell, Superintendent
of Physical and Bayonet Training, BEF, 1916–1918[2]

As the war ground on into 1915, the chaotic nature of the transition for the Army's training establishment from peacetime to total war evolved into a more regular and ordered system, where the pre-war institutions were expanded and adapted to the needs of a mass army. Existing schools increased in size, and new facilities were built to handle the exponential growth in numbers needing to be trained in combat and leadership skills. Brand new schools and courses of instruction were established to cater to the need for soldiers to become versed in the new technologies and machines of modern war. Gas, machine gun, and wireless signaling schools, flying schools and courses of instruction for engineers and gunners in the art and science of trench construction and destruction, were all novelties begun in reaction to the realities of fighting in Flanders and elsewhere. Moreover, for the first time in its history, the British Army exported its training and administrative apparatus overseas. Wherever the Army went, its trainers, instructors, and schools went also. Commands established mechanisms, sometimes within sight and sound of the front lines, to provide refresher training, basic instruction in new techniques and equipment, and staff and leadership courses for newly promoted soldiers.

---

[1]   "Supplementary Tables, Physical Training 1916, reprinted with amendments, March, 1917 and Games, Issued by the General Staff, 1917," National Army Museum Class. 355.545, p. 2.

[2]   John G. Gray, *Prophet in Plimsoles: An Account of the Life of Colonel Ronald B. Campbell* (Edinburgh: Edina Press, 1977), p. 28.

The Army Gymnastic Staff was part of this dynamic. From its pre-war size of 172 officers and enlisted men, it had expanded by 1918 to 2,299 all ranks. The Staff's School of Physical Training at Aldershot, which before the war had averaged no more than 350 students per year, had grown by 1918 to the point where branch schools had been established at Borden and Portsmouth, and between them these schools graduated an average of over 6,000 regimental officers and NCOs per year. The Staff had also established several schools overseas, in virtually every major theater of the war. After the Armistice the Staff estimated that it had trained over 2,000 officers and 22,500 NCOs as Assistant PT Instructors and Superintendents in its training centers.[3] At its schools overseas, the Staff trained British, Commonwealth, American, and other Allied soldiers in its techniques for physical and bayonet training. The Staff itself underwent numerous changes: its name changed first from the Army Gymnastic Staff to the Army Physical and Bayonet Training Staff, then to the Army Physical and Recreational Training Staff, and finally to the Army Physical Training Staff. The mission of the Staff evolved concurrently with its name, and with these evolutions it became as an institution even more ingrained in the fabric of the Army than any of its staunchest supporters could have imagined in 1914.

An offshoot of this process of expansion and evolution was the creation of formal physical training establishments in the armies of Canada, Australia, and New Zealand. These imperial organizations were mirror images of their metropolitan model, and in 1917 the British Staff began to hold regular meetings with their Commonwealth counterparts to share ideas and ensure uniformity of practice. By the end of the war these meetings often included Americans as well—the U.S. Army's current methods of bayonet training, right down to many of the commands and specific drills, are virtual carbon copies of the British techniques passed on starting in 1917.[4] By January 1919, the Army Physical Training Staff was one of the most well-known and respected organizations in the British Army. This prestige came directly as the result of efforts made during the period between 1916 and 1918 to improve the fitness, morale, and close-quarters combat skills of British, Commonwealth, and Allied soldiers—approximately one fourth of the training of the British infantryman was the responsibility of the Staff.[5] The Army recognized the enhanced position

---

[3]   Captain F.J. Starr, "War History of the Army Gymnastic Staff," (second draft) unpublished manuscript, Army Physical Training Corps Museum file #1664, p. 13.

[4]   See U.S. Army Field Manual 21-150, *Combatives*. A comparison of the training outlined in this manual with that described by British soldiers during the First World War reveals remarkable similarities.

[5]   Lieutenant Colonel E.A.L. Oldfield, *History of the Army Physical Training Corps* (Aldershot: Gale & Polden Ltd., 1955), p. 26.

of its PT corps by using its image after the war to improve recruiting and to further the goals of its newest offspring, the Army Sport Control Board.

A review of the story of the Army Gymnastic Staff's involvement in the First World War and the manner in which the Army's PT programs evolved during that time is important in many ways. First, the Staff's progress through the war mirrors that of many of the Army's other training systems and institutions—once again, an examination of the Staff provides a clear picture of the manner in which the British Army continued its process of modernization through the war years. Second, such an examination serves once again to emphasize the powerful influence exerted by the Army's physical culture on all aspects of its training and warfighting doctrine. Third, the story of the Staff during the war clearly demonstrates how the Army continued to act as an agent of cultural proselytization among Britain's imperial partners, as well as her allies. Finally, the story of the Gymnastic Staff in the war is one of completion. By the end of the war the task begun in 1860 by Major Frederick Hammersley and the "Twelve Apostles" had achieved its ultimate end: formal PT was so imbedded in all of the Army's systems and practices as to make it possible for the BEF's Directorate of Training to issue a publication in 1917 that flatly stated, "Physical Training should be regarded as the foundation of all training."[6]

By the middle of 1915, the new Kitchener divisions were steadily passing their evaluations and being sent overseas to complete their final training and in some cases to go directly into combat. In addition to the New Army divisions, replacement drafts for Regular and Territorial units poured into France to replenish battalions decimated in the fighting at Ypres, Neuve Chapelle, and elsewhere. The originally small establishment of the BEF had to rapidly grow to accommodate the large numbers of arriving soldiers and to cope with the increasingly industrial nature of the war. Huge depots were eventually set up at the major ports of disembarkation, where men would briefly stay until they could be sorted out by unit and shipped to the front lines. These depots consisted mostly of tent cities, often exposed on the dunes by the seashore, where soldiers' time was occupied mainly with work details, gambling, and seeking ways to elude restrictions placed on movement out of camp, often in order to pursue more salacious activities. The largest and most notorious of these camps was at Etaples, a huge base that could accommodate up to 100,000 men.[7]

---

6   "Supplementary Tables," p. 2.

7   Etaples is perhaps the most-mentioned replacement depot throughout the manuscript, diary, and published record of soldiers' memories of the war. See, for example, Malcolm Brown, *Tommy Goes to War* (London: J.M. Dent & Sons Ltd., 1978), pp. 43–46. Another source that illustrates the vast numbers of soldiers that passed through Etaples is the "War Diaries of Commandant, Étaples 1917–1919," WO 32/4027, National Archives.

Besides the depots, an enormous system of rear-area activities had to be set up to manage the logistical tail of the BEF: lines of communication, medical units and convalescence depots, repair depots and supply dumps, and camps for units rotating in and out of the trenches. In tandem with the military systems, civilian organizations like the YMCA and the Red Cross created rest camps, hospitals, and kitchens.

By the end of 1915 the leadership both of the BEF and in the Imperial General Staff had concluded that, with the static nature of fighting, more needed to be done to regularize the apparatus set up for rest periods and to provide for formal training in France. Until 1916, soldiers would typically arrive in France, stay for a period at a depot, board a train for the front, arrive at an Army, Corps, or Division-level replacement center, and then eventually join their unit. This process might take up to several weeks, and during that time the soldier might participate in little or no training other than some desultory classes or some other less-than-valuable exercises, and perhaps an occasional working party.[8] In addition to the replacements, soldiers in units rotating out of the front lines might engage in some level of training with their units, but there it generally ended. There existed no formal structure beyond that which the more energetic local commanders had created to ensure a soldier's skills were sharpened and his health and morale were restored, and that newly promoted officers and NCOs had the knowledge required to successfully perform in their increasingly complex jobs.[9] There was a need to train soldiers in evolving techniques, tactics and procedures in signaling, trench emplacement and construction, wiring, artillery employment, field sanitation, and the use of machine guns, to name just a handful of areas.

In response to these needs, Brigade, Division, Corps, and Army-level commanders began to establish schools and training centers in their areas to train new officers and soldiers, and to retrain soldiers coming out of the lines. In many

---

There are many photographs of this place, a dreary, windswept city of canvas tents set up among the dunes on the Channel coast near Boulogne. In late 1918 soldiers there rioted over what they perceived as poor living conditions and the unfairness of the restrictions and rigorous training regimen imposed on them.

8   Brown, *Tommy goes to War*, pp. 51–61. See also John William Lynch, *Princess Patricia's Canadian Light Infantry, 1917–1919* (Hicksville, NY: Expedition Press, 1976).

9   See Maxse Papers and Kentish Papers, Imperial War Museum Archives. These two energetic officers, who both had perhaps a more avid interest in training than many others, often noted the lack of quality courses available for training their subordinates. Both men developed courses for their commands, Maxse for his division and corps, and Kentish for his battalion and brigade. It was Kentish's success in independently developing training courses for his soldiers that led General Allenby to select him to set up the 3rd Army School at Flixécourt in 1916.

cases commanders established procedures to use the latest information from the front lines to continually update methods taught in training courses. It was in the context of this process that the leaders of the Army Gymnastic Staff began to discuss the possibility of sending a team of instructors to France, to explore ways in which their skills could be employed to assist commanders in improving fitness, morale, and bayonet training in the BEF. The lead in this enterprise was taken by Major Ronald Bruce Campbell. Campbell had begun his service with the Gymnastic Staff prior to the war and was one of the signatories to the 1913 letter requesting that a Secretariat of Army Games be established. Like so many other Gymnastic Staff officers, however, he had returned to his regiment, the Gordon Highlanders, upon mobilization in 1914. After service in the First Ypres Campaign, where he was wounded and awarded the Distinguished Service Order (DSO) for his performance under fire, he returned to Aldershot and took up duties as the Assistant Inspector of Gymnasia and the Staff's resident expert in bayonet fighting[10]—the Staff had been teaching soldiers to use bayonets at least since the days of Colonel Fox in the 1890s, but was only formally given the mandate to manage all such instruction Army wide in 1915.[11]

Major Campbell, who was to become one of the most influential of all Gymnastic Staff officers, quickly became known as the Army's greatest exponent of close-quarters combat instruction. He wrote the Army's bayonet fighting manual, titled "The Spirit of the Bayonet," and made himself famous (or infamous) by his bloodthirsty exhortations to soldiers while they were training. It was this enthusiasm for physical and bayonet training, along with his leadership abilities and proven battlefield record, that led Colonel Wright to appoint Campbell as the officer in charge of a team from the Gymnastic Staff that was to visit France.[12] The team was to stay for two months and attempt to convince the leaders of the BEF to establish schools of bayonet and physical training in theater.[13] Accordingly, on March 2, 1916, Major Campbell led a contingent of fifty-one Staff Instructors to France. Twenty of the instructors were detailed to set up demonstration PT and bayonet training courses at the major depots in Etaples, Rouen, and Le Havre.[14]

The remaining thirty-one instructors, led by Major Campbell, went to the Third Army School at Flixécourt, the first such institution to be set up by a major subordinate command of the BEF. Major Campbell and his team had been

---

[10] Gray, *Prophet in Plimsoles*, p. 19.

[11] Starr, "War History of the Army Gymnastic Staff" (second draft), p. 5.

[12] Gray, *Prophet in Plimsoles*, pp. 19–21. See also Oldfield, *History of the Army Physical Training Corps*, p. 24.

[13] Ibid., p. 27.

[14] Starr, "War History of the Army Gymnastic Staff," (first draft), p. 2.

invited to establish themselves at Flixécourt by the school's new Commandant, none other than that indefatigable champion of Army sport and fitness, the newly promoted Brigadier General Reginald Kentish.[15] Kentish was to remain a fixture in the Army's training and educational structure through the remainder of the war, and was widely recognized by leaders such as Lieutenant General Sir Ivor Maxse, by 1918 the BEF's Inspector General of Training, as one of the most effective instructors in the Army.

At each of the locations where the Gymnastic Staff cadre were established, they quickly constructed some rudimentary physical training facilities and, more importantly, a bayonet assault course. These courses were, at first, relatively simple affairs, with obstacles, trenches, and some straw-filled bags suspended from cross-bars to act as the "enemy." Campbell and his men sent out invitations to local commanders and to the BEF's higher-level leadership, to observe demonstrations of PT and bayonet training at the new facilities. The commander of the Third Army, General Allenby, later conqueror of Jerusalem and Damascus, observed one of the demonstrations put on by Major Campbell at Flixécourt, and was impressed enough to ask that another be put on for Field Marshals Foch and Haig, along with several other dignitaries. The success of this demonstration virtually assured the Gymnastic Staff its permanent place in the organization of the BEF. Foch was to say of this demonstration, "this training will have a great tactical value."[16]

After the initial successes of the Gymnastic Staff cadre in impressing upon the BEF's chain of command the usefulness of their program, Field Marshal Haig provisionally accepted formal gymnastic and bayonet instruction in the field armies and depots. Approval being given, Campbell quickly sent most of the Third Army School's initial cadre of thirty-one Staff Instructors out to provide training and demonstrations to units in the line.[17] The cadre at each of the depots remained, and they began to expand the scope of their training. By war's end, the training conducted at the replacement depots was extensive. Soldiers' accounts of PT conducted in "the Bullring" at Etaples describe rigorous sessions in all weather, administered by instructors who were alternately feared, hated, and respected.[18]

The remainder of the cadre left at Flixécourt formed a small school that began to provide a six-day course to selected regimental NCOs and officers in PT and bayonet fighting instruction.[19] By May 1916, Campbell and his

---

[15]   Ibid., p. 2.
[16]   Ibid., p. 3.
[17]   Ibid., pp. 3–4.
[18]   See Brown, *Tommy Goes to War*, pp. 43–46.
[19]   Starr, "War History of the Army Gymnastic Staff" (first draft), p. 4.

instructors had relocated with the Third Army School to Auxi-le-Château.[20] In early 1917, after the Staff was formally directed to become part of the BEF's permanent establishment, the school was finally moved to St. Pol, where they would stay for most of the remainder of the war.[21] While at that location the school underwent many changes, with construction of billets, new and updated facilities for training, new curricula, and new personnel rotating in and out of the cadre. Fundamentally, however, the mission of the school remained the same—preparing unit-level officer and NCO leaders to properly instruct their soldiers in physical training and bayonet fighting, in environments ranging from frontline trenches to rear area Royal Flying Corps aerodromes.[22]

From the beginning of the time that the Staff remained in France, Campbell established what was to be one of the most salient reasons for the success of his unit and the ideas they presented. He undertook regular tours of frontline units and positions, often participating in combat actions with the units he visited. He used these visits both to "sell" his training program and to ensure that the Staff were using the most updated information from the front to provide viable instruction. Campbell also made it a point to visit rear-area units and convalescent depots, where he could learn about the training needs of soldiers in those environments as well. As a consequence of "Bloody" (as he came to be known) Campbell's tours, and the fact that he insisted his instructors make visits to the front as well, the Staff gained a reputation as *bona fide* practitioners of what they taught[23] and also brought honors to themselves through being decorated or mentioned in dispatches for their performance in combat.[24] Campbell made sure that his instructors would be recognized by commanders and troops at the front by directing that they wear their distinctive instructor's uniforms, even

---

[20]   Oldfield, *History of the Army Physical Training Corps*, p. 27.

[21]   Starr, "War History of the Army Gymnastic Staff" (first draft), p. 5. See also Maxse Papers, Imperial War Museum Archives, file #58.

[22]   The schools overseas were mirrored by counterparts in the Home commands in Britain, which had been set up in late 1916. See *Training at Home*, issued by the General Staff, 1917 (papers of General Sir Ivor Maxse, File 58, Imperial War Museum Archives), p. 25: "Command Schools of Physical and Bayonet Training (a) Object – (1) To train an adequate number of officers and NCOs as platoon bayonet training instructors and in the trained soldiers' physical training tables. (2) To hold preliminary courses for officers and NCOs whom it is proposed to send to the Army school. (3) Refresher courses for instructors for whom no accommodation can be found at the Army school. Duration – 11 days."

[23]   Gray, *Prophet in Plimsoles*, p. 22.

[24]   See "War Diary of Physical and Bayonet Training Staff," WO 95/55, National Archives. In this operations journal, Captain Starr recorded each time a member of the Staff was mentioned in dispatches or decorated—14 soldiers in April 1918 alone.

while under fire.[25] This determination to be close to the front and some of its results were outlined in the Staff's 1916 report:

> Training "in the field" is carried out in difficult circumstances; for the most part it takes place in a shelled area and classes under instruction have sometimes been reduced by casualties; but the men are keen and thoroughly believe in the efficacy of the present method of Bayonet training, which they often practice immediately after leaving the trenches.[26]

The credibility thus gained by the Staff in France went a very long way toward ensuring that they continued to receive recognition and resources from the Headquarters of the BEF. A high degree of credibility also guaranteed the Staff that there was, throughout the rest of the war, a constant demand for their services that they would never be able to wholly meet with the number of soldiers they had assigned. With the establishment and expansion of the Staff overseas, many of the officers and NCOs who had been assigned before the war returned to their duties as Staff Instructors and Superintendents, and many new officers and soldiers joined as well. One example of a transfer of this kind is the assignment to Campbell's staff, on December 30, 1916, of 2nd Lieutenant (later Captain) Frank J. Starr, a pre-war sportswriter with an interest in Army sport, who in addition to his official duties as Recreational Training officer acted as the Staff's chronicler (he maintained the unit's Operations Journal, wrote all of the unit's wartime reports, and was the author of the unit's official, and unpublished, War History).[27] Another example is the assignment of Captain W. Delany of the Durham Light Infantry, who on October 10, 1916 was sent to the Third Army as the Acting Superintendent of Physical Training—Delany was transferred to the Staff by General Couper, pre-war Inspector of Gymnasia, who by 1916 was commanding the 14th Division.[28]

By the end of 1916, then, the Staff had become a permanent part of the BEF establishment and thus regularized its infrastructure so that it could perform its growing duties uniformly throughout France.[29] Campbell was eventually

---

[25]   Gray, *Prophet in Plimsoles*, p. 23.

[26]   "Report of the Army Physical and Bayonet Training Staff, 1916," unpublished manuscript, Army Physical Training Corps Museum file #1664, p. 5.

[27]   Tony Mason and Eliza Riedi, *Sport and the Military: The British Armed Forces 1880–1960* (Cambridge: Cambridge University Press, 2010), p. 103, and Starr, "War History of the Army Gymnastic Staff" (first draft), p. 8.

[28]   Ibid., p. 5.

[29]   When the probationary period of the Staff's tenure in France expired, GHQ, British Expeditionary Force, requested that the Staff be made a permanent part of the BEF

promoted to Lieutenant Colonel and was formally assigned as Superintendent of Physical and Bayonet Training, BEF.[30] Each field army in the BEF was assigned a Superintendent of Physical and Bayonet Training, who reported to Campbell, and each division was to be assigned an officer as well—divisional officers were somewhat less commonly assigned, due to the chronic shortage of officers not only on the Staff but throughout the Army.[31] The school operated continuously, training regimental officers and NCOs to manage their own units' training. Courses consisted of bayonet fighting instruction, both of simple exercises, and the use of the increasingly complex and realistic assault course. Additionally, soldiers were taught how to conduct PT for their units. This instruction continued to evolve along with bayonet training, and the Army published regular updates to the training tables.[32] In these updates, commanders and NCOs were given basic theories underlying the Army's PT programs and were presented with fundamental "dos and don'ts" regarding unit PT.

One of these fundamentals that was to be a recurring source of contention was the admonishment, "No form of Physical Training or Running Training should be done in the early morning (unless the men have had something substantial to eat before parade) or until half an hour after breakfast and dinner."[33] In spite of this clear statement, commanders must have persisted in making soldiers conduct PT in the early morning before breakfast, because that very vocal supporter of fitness, Brigadier Kentish, gave this subject his attention in more than one recorded instance during the war. Late in the war he wrote to Lieutenant General Maxse a polemic on the subject, which because of its value in showing Kentish's philosophy of leadership as well as fitness, I will quote at length:

> I know of units in which the men when coming out of the trenches to rest and train for a week are on parade before breakfast doing "monkey tricks" on an empty stomach, what time their officers are sleeping peacefully in their beds. In my brigade I discourage such nonsense before breakfast, and if a commanding officer desires to have his battalion out and carrying out this form of torture –

---

establishment. By the end of July 1916, this change had been accomplished along with approval of an increase in the Staff's authorized strength. See ibid., p. 5.

[30]   Ibid., p. 13.

[31]   See "Report of the Army Physical and Bayonet Training Staff, 1916," personnel table.

[32]   See Colonel Walter Wright, draft letter dated December 3, 1917, Army Physical Training Corps Museum file #1664, and "Report of the Army Physical and Bayonet Training Staff," p. 2.

[33]   "Special Tables, Physical Training 1916," National Army Museum Class. 355.545 acc.# 27161, overleaf.

and it is, I submit, torture to men, who are by way of resting after a hard time in
the trenches to be pulled out in this manner – then I insist on every officer from
the Commanding Officer downwards coming out to parade and going through
the same "Monkey Tricks" as their men. And I do so because I take it that these
exercises are supposed to be for the benefit of the body, and the bodies of the
officers require just as much attention in this respect as those of their men.[34]

It is clear that Kentish's strong feelings about physical training were tempered by
his concern for soldier welfare and proper leadership: in spite of the value he must
have assigned "Monkey Tricks," it is also equally obvious that he accorded them
less importance than his first real love, Sport. On the subject of leadership the
Army's other contemporary fitness champion apparently agreed with Kentish—
"Bloody" Campbell's biographer described his attitude thus: "'Leadership,'
Campbell said, "must be by example.'"[35] In his unpublished memoir, Kentish
described another way he used to reinforce this principle, with regard to early
morning PT. At the end of the war, he had been assigned to set up a training
course for senior leaders, in order to prepare them for command. He related how
he had them awakened before dawn on the first day of the course and paraded
for PT before breakfast. After hearing their complaints, he told them that, if
they didn't like being treated in that way, they should remember that when they
wanted to do the same to their troops after coming out of the line.[36]

Early on during its time in France, the Staff had taken on the responsibility of
conducting physical training programs in convalescent depots and hospitals, in
order to assist in rebuilding the bodies and morale of wounded men. This mission
was seen by Lieutenant Colonel Campbell as one of his staff's most important,
and he consistently maintained instructors at the major depots and hospitals for
this purpose.[37] The Staff's efforts at a depot in Rouen were described by Major
General Sir Wilmot Herringham in his memoirs:

On one side of the road were the dormitory huts, the mess rooms, kitchens,
parade ground, and gymnasium. The morning was given up to spells of various
training exercises, these included dancing, for which there was band, and several
of the games which have taken the place of the Swedish physical exercises, and
are a great improvement on them. In the afternoons there were cricket or football

---

[34]   Brigadier Reginald Kentish, unpublished letter (Maxse papers, File #60, Imperial
War Museum Archives).

[35]   Gray, *Prophet in Plimsoles*, p. 23.

[36]   Brigadier Reginald Kentish, unpublished memoir, Kentish Papers, Imperial War
Museum Archives.

[37]   "Report of the Army Physical and Bayonet Training Staff, 1916," p. 11.

matches and cross-country runs. In the evenings concerts, plays, lectures, and boxing competitions ....[38]

In January 1917, the Staff was recognized by the King's personal physician, Sir Bertrand Dawson, for the work done in the area of physical therapy and convalescent recovery;[39] the present-day Royal Army Physical Training Corps still maintains instructors at British Army medical facilities to perform the same function.[40]

The other, and frankly more visible, responsibility of the Staff in France was bayonet training. It was to bayonet and close-quarters combat training that Lieutenant Colonel Campbell gave most of his attention, and it was that training which gave him his reputation. He saw hand-to-hand combat training as critical to maintaining the morale and aggressiveness of soldiers who could easily become demoralized by the awful conditions at the front. He later admitted that he recognized that the bayonet as a major weapon was obsolete on the modern battlefield, but he saw in his training methods a way to instill or re-energize the fighting instinct in soldiers.[41] In this, his methods were clearly successful. He brought several former professional boxers into the Staff, including "Bombardier" Billy Wells, Jimmy Driscoll, Jimmy Wilde, and Johnny Basham. He used these experts to assist him in developing techniques for hand-to-hand fighting, and he also used their fame to boost the reputation of his school.[42] The demonstrations he put on for students became legendary—both Siegfried Sassoon and Robert Graves described these demonstrations in their wartime remembrances.[43] After hearing Campbell's presentation, Sassoon was even inspired to write his paean to the bayonet, "The Kiss," in which the combined bullet and bayonet practice

---

[38]   Major General Sir Wilmot Herringham KCMG CB, *A Physician in France* (London: Arnold, 1919) pp. 90–91, as quoted in Charles Messenger, *Call to Arms: The British Army 1914–1918* (London: Cassell, 2003), p. 420.

[39]   Oldfield, *History of the Army Physical Training Corps*, p. 28.

[40]   In *Mind, Body and Spirit*, the Royal Army Physical Training Corps regimental journal, the reports of these instructors appear alongside those of their counterparts assigned to schools and line units.

[41]   Campbell later said, "To be truthful, it was all a bit of ballyhoo. Even by 1914 the bayonet was obsolete. The number of men killed by the bayonet on the Western Front was very small, but it was superb as a morale booster ... I found nothing better to introduce recruits to the terrible conditions which awaited the poor devils up the line." See Gray, *Prophet in Plimsoles*, p. 28.

[42]   Ibid., pp. 24–26. See also Oldfield, *History of the Army Physical Training Corps*, p. 25.

[43]   See Robert Graves, *Goodbye To All That* (Garden City, NY: Doubleday & Co., 1957), p. 275, and Siegfried Sassoon, *Memoirs of an Infantry Officer* (London: Faber & Faber, 1930), pp. 11–20.

of the Staff's training is captured in a chilling exhortation to "Brother lead and Sister steel" to help the soldier in his work of killing.[44]

Campbell would use graphic, bloody language to inspire soldiers when giving his demonstrations, exhorting them to kill Germans unhesitatingly and without mercy. His goal was to get them to a fever pitch of excitement, ready to engage in whatever close-quarters combat was necessary to destroy the enemy.[45] His "script" for bayonet training is largely still in use by the U.S. Army: while performing stationary bayonet exercises, soldiers are asked over a loudspeaker by the instructor, "What makes the grass grow?," and they respond in unison, "BLOOD!" When asked, "What is the spirit of the bayonet?," they reply, "TO KILL!"[46]

If the use of the bayonet by the British Army in the First World War did not directly result in many confirmed victories, the morale and fighting spirit engendered by the training program developed and administered by the Staff certainly had a positive effect on the soldiers who benefited from it. After the war, several commanders publicly credited Campbell and his "traveling circus" of instructors with restoring their troops' morale after coming out of the line, and even the Imperial German Army recognized Campbell's importance by placing a bounty on his head.[47] Perhaps the acid test of the success of Campbell's methods,

---

[44]   Siegfried Sassoon, *Collected Poems* (New York: Viking Press, 1949), pp. 15–16.

[45]   See Sassoon, *Memoirs of an Infantry Officer*, pp. 11–20. In this passage Sassoon describes his stay at the "Fourth" Army school at Flixécourt, along with his assessment of Brigadier Kentish: "a tremendous worker and everyone liked him." His experience with the Physical and Bayonet Training Staff is recounted thus: "But the star turn in the school room was a massive sandy-haired Highland Major [Campbell] whose subject was 'The Spirit of the Bayonet' … He spoke with homicidal eloquence, keeping the game alive with genial and well-judged jokes. He had a Sergeant to assist him. The Sergeant, a tall sinewy machine, had been trained to such a pitch of frightfulness that at a moment's warning he could divest himself of all semblance of humanity. With rifle and bayonet he illustrated the Major's ferocious aphorisms, including facial expression … Man, it seemed, had been created to jab the life out of Germans. To hear the Major talk, one might have thought that he did it himself every day before breakfast. His final words were: 'Remember that every Boche you fellows kill brings victory one minute nearer and shortens the war by one minute. Kill them! Kill them! There's only one good Boche, and that's a dead one!'" Sassoon goes on to relate how the class went through the assault course: "Capering over the obstacles of the assault course and prodding sacks of straw was healthy exercise; the admirable sergeant-instructor was polite and unformidable, and as I didn't want him to think me a dud officer, I did my best to become proficient."

[46]   Any soldier who has participated in this training will vividly remember these exhortations—they do, in fact, have the desired effect with most young men.

[47]   Campbell is recognized by several mentions in various documents in Sir Ivor Maxse's papers. See also Grey, *Prophet in Plimsoles*, pp. 26–8.

Figure 11.1 Bayonet Assault Course, France, *c.*1918 (Imperial War Museum)

and the PT and bayonet training programs he oversaw, would be the number of requests the Staff received from British, Commonwealth, and Allied units for instructors and demonstrations, and for student positions at the school. By 1917 the Staff was spending a large part of its time and effort on educating soldiers from outside the British Army, and it is this expansion to Commonwealth and Allied forces of the Army's PT and bayonet training schemes that truly shows their worth, as viewed through contemporary eyes.

The Canadian Expeditionary Forces (CEF) provides a superb example of the manner in which the transfer of physical training systems occurred within the Commonwealth forces. When the Canadian Army was mobilized to fight in 1914, its newly formed battalions were consolidated at a preliminary training camp in Val Cartier, Quebec. There the new soldiers underwent some basic training, including some rudimentary PT, and the units were organized and outfitted with some uniforms and equipment. Later, in 1915, the CEF moved to Britain, where it established itself at Salisbury, and continued its preparation for deployment to France.[48] At Salisbury, the leadership of the CEF, after consulting with their British counterparts, requested a cadre of Gymnastic Staff Instructors to establish and oversee PT and bayonet fighting instruction within the new units of the CEF. The War Office assigned the Canadians five enlisted Staff Instructors and one Officer Superintendent.[49] Almost immediately, Canadian NCOs and officers also began to attend the Staff's schools in Britain. The worth of the training provided by the British instructors was rapidly recognized by the Canadian Army leadership: shortly after the assignment of the British Gymnastic Staff's cadre, the CEF created its own system for supervising physical and bayonet training, closely modeled after the original.

By 1916, when the Canadian Corps was established in France, the CEF had created the position of Director of Physical and Bayonet Training, Canadian Army. In May, and then again in December 1916, the Director, Lieutenant Colonel H.G. Mayes, visited both the British Staff's school at St. Pol and the Canadian Corps at the front. He was impressed enough with the physical and bayonet training systems he saw in France to order forty Canadian Assistant Instructors to France, in order to attend the school at St. Pol and begin running programs for their own troops. These instructors arrived on February 16, 1917.

---

[48]   Colonel A. Fortescue Duguid, *Official History of the Canadian Forces in The Great War 1914–1919, General Series Volume I* (Ottawa: Canadian Ministry of National Defense, 1938), chapters I–IV.

[49]   Ibid., pp. 130–31. See also "Report of the Army Gymnastic Staff, 1916," Royal Army Physical Training Corps Museum file #1664, p. 10, and Starr, "War History of the Army Gymnastic Staff" (second draft), p. 5.

Canadian soldiers continued to attend the British schools throughout the war and were assigned to other Imperial Forces as well, to assist them in their training.[50]

In January 1918, the Canadian Army Gymnastic Staff was officially formed in France, in order to take over supervision of instructor staff already performing duties under the overall control of the British. The first Officer-in-Charge of the Canadian Gymnastic Staff in France was Captain T.B. Colley. His formal instructions were: "In addition to the regular physical training and bayonet fighting the C.A.G.S. [Canadian Army Gymnastic Staff] also instructs in Drill, and in such musketry principles as enter into a combined bullet-bayonet practice. Each instructor is expected to take an active interest in Athletics and promote Recreational Training of all kinds." Colley regularly sent representatives to the monthly Superintendent's conferences, started in January 1917 by the British Staff at St. Pol, in order to maintain uniformity of practice and to participate in decisions about doctrine and other matters.[51]

The Australian and New Zealand Imperial Forces similarly established counterparts to the British Staff, and these organizations also sent representatives to the Superintendents Conferences. The officers in charge of the Australian and New Zealand programs were involved at the outset in the 1918 discussions surrounding the establishment of the British Expeditionary Forces Sports Board, the forerunner to the Army Sport Control Board.[52] Beyond the Commonwealth forces, the British Gymnastic Staff was instrumental in establishing close relations with the U.S. Army early on in its involvement in the war and was one of the key elements in maintaining those close relations through training.

In October 1917, following a request from the military authorities in the United States for assistance with instructors for the full range of required training, the Gymnastic Staff sent a contingent of six officers and nineteen NCO Staff Instructors to Fort Bliss, Texas. These men were assigned to U.S. divisions then being formed and trained, and were charged with both setting up and operating PT and bayonet fighting programs for their American counterparts. They were also charged with teaching American officers and NCOs the fundamentals of the British systems. These men were so popular that in some cases the US divisions refused to release their British instructors when they left for Europe, and brought them to France. A second contingent of Gymnastic

---

50   Starr, "War History of the Army Gymnastic Staff" (first draft), pp. 7, 11.

51   "War Diary of the Army Gymnastic Staff, 1918–1919: Canadian Corps," WO 95/1068, National Archives. Entry dated March 18, 1918, etc.

52   "War Diary of Physical and Bayonet Training Staff," various entries, especially July 31, 1918. See also Starr, "War History of the Army Gymnastic Staff" (first draft), p. 32.

Staff Instructors went to the U.S. in July 1918, including the Staff's only Victoria Cross winner, Captain H. Daniels.[53]

The U.S. Army's plans for training, fielding equipment, and combat employment once they reached France relied heavily on assistance from their Allies; in spite of Commander of the American Expeditionary Force (AEF) General Pershing's insistence on the AEF being maintained intact and given its own sector of the front, he knew that he must use the infrastructure of his allies to complete his soldiers' training.[54] In addition to the British instructors already detailed to the units of the AEF, Lieutenant Colonel Campbell sent two Staff Instructors to work with Major Coulon, the officer in charge of the British contingent assigned to the AEF. The AEF also began sending officers and NCOs to the British Physical and Bayonet Training School at St. Pol as soon as the school was ready to receive them.[55]

The first group of twenty-nine arrived at St. Pol on September 29, 1917, and each class thereafter, for the remainder of the school's existence, had a large percentage of American students. These students engaged in the full range of instruction offered at the school, including formal PT, a boxing tournament, cross-country racing, bayonet fighting and the assault course, and various games and sports. The British Gymnastic Staff's "War History" describes the contacts made with US soldiers at these courses initially as uncomfortable. However, the "History" relates that, soon enough, the barriers of a common language broke down and relations became friendly, with students establishing comradely associations that lasted for the remainder of the war.[56] The training received at the St. Pol school by the US Army representatives, along with the instruction given by the Gymnastic Staff cadres sent to the US, complemented the US Army's existing systems and played an important part in the development of US military physical training doctrine.

As the war progressed and British forces became involved in fighting outside France, the Physical and Bayonet Training Staff sent contingents to many other theaters. There were Physical and Bayonet Training establishments in Egypt, Mesopotamia, Salonika, and Italy. The officer in charge of the Staff's operations in Italy was Major Betts, the first Gymnastic Staff officer to be commissioned from the ranks, and the first Master-at-Arms. Betts had started the war as the Superintendent of Gymnasia at Grantham, but he was subsequently transferred

---

[53]   Starr, "War History of the Army Gymnastic Staff" (second draft), pp. 11–12.

[54]   For a superb overview of the American contribution to the First World War, see Rod Paschall, *The Defeat of Imperial Germany 1917–1918* (Chapel Hill, NC: Algonquin Books, 1989).

[55]   Starr, "War History of the Army Gymnastic Staff" (first draft), p. 17.

[56]   Ibid., pp. 17–18.

to the BEF to take on duties as the Superintendent of Physical and Bayonet Training for the 41st Division. When this division was sent to Italy in 1917 in the wake of the Italian collapse after the Caporetto Offensive, Betts went with it, and by virtue of his seniority became the officer in charge of the Staff's operations there. He was later awarded the Distinguished Service Order for his work in that capacity.[57]

By January 1918, the Physical and Bayonet Training Staff in France consisted of fifty-six officers, mostly the Army and Divisional Superintendents and the staff at the St. Pol headquarters and school. There were additionally 542 enlisted soldiers, the majority of whom were instructors, although since the lean early days after its arrival in France the Staff had managed to accrue nine drivers and thirty-five administrative personnel.[58] Throughout that spring, the Staff entertained numerous deputations and dignitaries, including Colonel Wright the Inspector of Gymnasia, and delegations from the French, Swedish, Siamese, American, Greek, and Portuguese armies. The Portuguese had been sending students to the school since 1917, and were looked at favorably by their British instructors. The Staff was even visited by the Superintendent of the Women's Auxiliary Army Corps (WAAC), "with view to a course of Physical and Recreational Training for the WAAC." The Superintendent, Lieutenant Colonel Campbell, was engaged in speaking tours in Great Britain and throughout France, all designed to encourage the maintenance of PT and bayonet training, and to provide motivation to soldiers about to engage the enemy.[59] All of this institutional structure and activity had been started from nothing in 1916—an explosive development that paralleled the growth of other training, administrative, and logistics structures within the BEF and the Army at home.

The Army Gymnastic Staff during the years between 1916 and 1918 was by any measure enormously successful. In its roles at home in training instructors and soldiers getting ready to deploy to the front, and in its incarnation as part of the BEF's and other theater establishments, where it trained unit leaders and supervised PT and bayonet instruction, the Staff gained for itself an international reputation for professional, practical, and realistic training. From developing specific programs to assist convalescing soldiers, to dealing with the unique

---

[57]   In the Army Physical Training Corps Museum's First World War file (#1664), there is an undated letter from Major Betts to Captain Starr that outlines the contributions and actions of the Physical and Bayonet Training Staff in Italy. It contains much detail, including organizational charts. Starr likely asked for this letter to assist him in compiling the "War History," and many of its details are contained in the various drafts of that document.

[58]   Starr, "War History of the Army Gymnastic Staff" (first draft), p. 22.

[59]   "War Diary of Physical and Bayonet Training Staff," entries dated December 28, 1917 through February 6, 1918.

training challenges of the new Royal Flying Corps and Royal Tank Corps, and finally, working with other Commonwealth and Allied troops to spread the British Army's traditions of physical culture, the Staff perforce became one of the most visible and best recognized formations in the Army.

All of this activity was the culmination of the work begun in 1860. No longer was the head of the Gymnastic Staff in any danger of being "in a position analogous to that of Mr. Angelo, the Fencing Master," as put by Major Hammersley's father when his son applied for the first position of Superintendent in 1860.[60] The dual task of oversight for the Army's physical training, along with supervising and conducting bayonet and fencing instruction, had, by regulation, belonged to the Staff from the beginning.

There was, however, one mission that the Staff had been informally performing throughout its existence, but for which it had never had a formal mandate. That was the task of supervision, coaching, instruction, and overall management of unit games and sport. From the unit-level instructors who took on the job of coaching a tug-of-war team or cricket eleven, to the officer staff of the Headquarters Gymnasium who voluntarily served as Secretaries for the various associations, the Gymnastic Staff had always taken a lead in the conduct and institutionalization of Army sport. At the height of the Staff's influence and credibility during the First World War, that task was finally allotted to the Staff in a formal way. From then on, the Staff was held directly responsible for establishing recreational training and games for all British soldiers, managing competitions, providing uniforms and equipment for teams, supervising the construction of grounds and facilities, and providing for medals and awards. The Staff was also made responsible for writing the official doctrine for the conduct of this kind of training for the entire Army. British and Commonwealth soldiers had, as we have seen, played games and engaged in sport from the beginning of the war. However, it was the final blending of this recreational training function with the older, established mission of physical training that marked the achievement of completion for that task begun by Major Hammersley and his "apostles": institutionalization of the British Army's entire physical culture under the single aegis of the Army Gymnastic Staff.

---

[60]   Oldfield, *History of the Army Physical Training Corps*, p. 2.

Chapter 12

"The Greater Game": Wartime Recreational Training

Too much attention cannot be paid to the part played by games in fostering the fighting spirit. They afford the platoon commander an unrivalled opportunity not only of teaching his men to play for their side and work together in the spirit of self-sacrifice, but of gaining an insight into their characters. He should not only personally and actively arrange for games and competitions for his men, but take part in them himself. If he induces his platoon to be determined to produce the best football team in the battalion, he will have done a great deal to make it the best platoon in every way.

SS 143: *The Training and Employment of Platoons*, 1918[1]

Whenever British soldiers could, they played games. In the early years of the war, the nature of these games was largely determined by that most precious of soldiers' commodities, time. With the frenzied pace of the military buildup and the intense nature of the combat in 1914 and 1915, unofficial sport flourished but was, perforce, haphazard. In spite of the fact that, as one well-known commentator stated during the war, "no British troops ever travel without footballs or the energy to kick them,"[2] battalions in France and other operational theaters were largely left to their own devices when it came to leisure time. The battalions of the New Armies training in Britain, however, had time, and so played games much as their forebears in the Victorian and Edwardian Army had done; the institution of games for new soldiers was, as we have seen, a useful way of assimilating civilian volunteers into the Army, and was an important conduit for passing on the traditions of military physical culture.

By the end of 1915 and into 1916 the situation in the operational theaters began to change. The British front in France had largely stabilized, and the Army avoided any major offensive actions as it prepared for the Somme offensive that would commence in the summer of 1916. These facts allowed for the large-

---

[1]   SS 143, *The Training and Employment of Platoons*, issued by the General Staff, 1918 (papers of General Sir Ivor Maxse, 40/WO/5868, Imperial War Museum Archives).

[2]   "General Jack," in J.G. Fuller, *Troop Morale and Popular Culture in the British and Dominion Armies 1914–1918* (Oxford: Clarendon Press, 1990), p. 85.

scale resumption of organized games and sport among British units; more or less routine periods of trench duty meant the possibility of organized training and leisure schedules. A by-product of these more regularized schedules was the creation of formal schools and training centers, as discussed in the previous chapter. Coupled with improved infrastructure in the rear areas, these more "normal" conditions led to units beginning to engage in more regular recreational training, such that by 1917 the prevalence of military sport and games began at least to equal, if not rival, anything the Army had experienced in the Victorian and Edwardian periods. As with the organization of physical training, the British also shared their games and sports with their imperial partners and allies.

All of these developments would take an unprecedented turn in 1917 that would change recreation for the British soldier forever. Late in 1916, the Physical and Bayonet Training Staff in France proposed a scheme to the leadership of the BEF that would place the responsibility of sponsoring, organizing, and overseeing all sports and games in the Army under the Staff. Additionally, the Staff argued that they alone should be responsible for writing the official doctrine and rules for the conduct of games in the Army, and that they should supervise the construction of grounds, as well as provide uniforms and trophies for unit sports. It would seem logical that the Staff should take on these tasks, as it had, since its creation, been charged with taking care of Tommy Atkins's "mind, body and spirit." When this scheme was approved, British Army physical culture had finally evolved to the point where it had been moving since 1860: a modern, codified system of interrelated activities, from the initial recruit's squad PT, to unit sports championships, all with a written series of rules and doctrine that governed its conduct, managed and promoted by a single body—the Army Physical and Recreational Training Staff.

As stated above, unofficial or spontaneous unit-level games continued to flourish in the Army throughout the early period of the war, in spite of the pace of operations. Whenever possible, commanders encouraged their units to make and receive sporting challenges, and, of course, individual soldiers were never slow to start a game when the chance presented itself. Examples of this kind of activity are legion. Following a lengthy and detailed (and unaccountably uncensored) account of the unit's combat actions up to that time, the October 1915 number of the 11th Hussars regimental journal reported on several sporting events in France. Under the leader "Boxing at the Front," there appeared accounts of matches held in February of that year. Held in the *Estaminet Maison Commune* in Fletres, the matches included novice-level bouts as well as regimental championships. The journal expressed pride and satisfaction in the performance of the Hussars: "If the Germans could have seen the determination of the men, and the way they set about their work, the War would have been over on February 4th!"[3]

The journal also reported on "a most successful football tournament held at the front," in January and February of that year between units in the 1st Cavalry Brigade. Forty-five squadron teams participated in this tournament, which is likely a function of the fact that, by that time in the war, the mounted arm was not as closely engaged in fighting in the trenches as some of their infantry brethren. The journal contained a detailed and lively account of the final matches, the tournament being won by B Squadron of the 11th. A photograph of the winning team accompanies the account—eleven soldiers in uniform breeches and shirtsleeves, looking dirty but proud while standing in a muddy French field under some makeshift goalposts.[4]

This same journal also reported on the extensive sporting activities of the 11th's sister unit, the 12th Reserve Cavalry Regiment. The 12th, while stationed at Aldershot, seemingly did very little other than participate in unit sports days, athletics meets, and football and boxing tournaments. Its journal pages are almost solely devoted to those

> pastimes; during the month of September, 1916, at the height of the Somme offensive, the 12th was heavily engaged in the Aldershot Command Athletics Competition, as well as various football and boxing tournaments. It is not clear what the men of the 12th felt about their missing the "big push" in France, but they certainly seemed to enter into their games with a will.[5]

Sergeant Major H.A. Bangert of the Royal Army Medical Corps recorded several unit-level sporting events that he witnessed in the first years of the war. An old soldier stationed in the rear areas around Rouen, he was more able than many soldiers to witness these kinds of events. His diary describes two events in March 1915. On the fourth he attended a "Box arranged for the men on the square [in Rouen], entered into keenly and caused much fun." On the twelfth, he watched a "Football match at *Parc Des Sports* with No. 14 General Hospital, result 1–1 ... The men sang songs on the return journey, being very pleased with the result of the game." The next month his unit played Rugby at Wimereux and held a unit sports day in July that had to be delayed for two days on account of the rain.[6]

3　*XI Hussar Journal* Vol. VI (October 1915), Double Number, p. 48.
4　Ibid., pp. 42–44.
5　*XI Hussar Journal* Vol. VII No. 2 (September 1916), pp. 32–38.
6　"War Diary of Sergeant Major H.A. Bangert, RAMC," unpublished manuscript, Imperial War Museum Archives, 97/26/1.

Clearly, rear echelon units such as Sergeant Major Bangert's field hospital would be able to have a more varied and extensive games schedule than frontline units, and even cavalry regiments like the 11th Hussars were likely more able to indulge in sports because of their limited utility in static warfare. So what of the infantry? Although there isn't as much evidence before 1916 of infantry units participating in games and sports organized at the same levels as units like hospitals and even the cavalry, the infantry were still able to get some playing done. A soldier in the 1/4th (Dundee) Battalion, The Black Watch, recalled that "most of our men were playing football within half an hour of finishing a heavy march after a fortnight in the trenches."[7] In March of 1915 the 1st Battalion, Northumberland Fusiliers reported in their journal that, "During our periods of inactivity from the trenches, the various officers responsible for the amusements of the Brigade have furnished us with four really good exhibitions of the 'the noble art.'" These fights were popular and well attended, and as in the Hussars the journal writer "left the hall wondering what would happen if any of the doughty warriors meet the 'Huns' at close quarters." Unfortunately the tournament had to be suspended for almost a month when the brigade was moved back into the line. When the boxing was able to start again, it turned out to be "rather an unfortunate show," as many men scheduled to fight didn't turn up and the referee was "missing."[8]

France wasn't the only place where British soldiers continued to play in spite of the war. J.W. Whatley recorded that his Territorial unit played a football tournament almost immediately after arriving at Kingsway Camp in Delhi, India at Christmas 1914. He also recalled that on April 7, 1915 in Dehra Dun, following a training route march in the morning, his unit played several football matches: they beat the 6th Hampshires 2–0, and tied the 2nd Gurkha Rifles twice—the first match 0–0 and the second 1–1.[9] There was even an opportunity for sport at Gallipoli, where there was a football tournament in spite of the fact that almost nowhere on the Peninsula was safe from shellfire,[10] and the ANZAC Corps was bold enough to play a cricket match as a ruse during the evacuation. Australian soldiers played this match just behind the trenches at Shell Green, on December 17, 1915, in order to deceive the Turks into believing that all was normal within the Commonwealth lines.[11]

---

[7]   Fuller, *Troop Morale and Popular Culture*, p. 86.

[8]   *St. George's Gazette* Vol. 33 (March 31, 1915), pp. 41–42.

[9]   "Diary of J.W. Whatley," unpublished manuscript, Imperial War Museum Archives 96/48/1.

[10]   Fuller, *Troop Morale and Popular Culture*, p. 86.

[11]   *Official History of Australia in the War of 1914–1918, Vol. XII, Photographic Record of the War* (Sydney: Angus & Robertson Ltd., 1923), photo number 153 (Australian War

The many battalions of the Northumberland Fusiliers played games all around the war. The 8th (Service) Battalion played football against the 9th Battalion Sherwood Foresters at Christmas 1915, after being evacuated from Suvla Bay in Gallipoli, and went on to play more matches and held a boxing competition in January 1916.[12] The 9th (Service) Battalion, in France, played football in the run-up to the Division Championships, until they were knocked out of the running by the 7th Battalion, York and Lancaster Regiment.[13]

By 1916, with the enormous expansion of the Army in France and elsewhere, the Army was better able to routinize periods of trench duty. This, coupled with the establishment of what amounted to permanent facilities in the rear areas, made the opportunities for recreation more numerous and conducive to regulation. Commanders began more often to encourage sports at brigade and higher levels, and unit gymkhana began to be held in ways not seen since before the war. To some historians this expansion of sport and games has seemed almost incongruous—after all, was not the business of the Army limited to fighting, training, work details, and only occasional recreation? J.G. Fuller, in his important book *Troop Morale and Popular Culture in the British and Dominion Armies 1914–1918*, describes most military sport during the war as "spontaneous and unorganized." He also credits the other ranks and junior officers with the organization of most unit games, and discusses the "extensive coverage" allotted to sport in most unit journals almost as if it was a novelty, with "[o]fficial reaction to the soldiers' enthusiasm for sport" as negative in the first years of the war.[14] Clearly this was not the case. Extensive coverage of unit sports in journals was, if anything, the norm, and at least since the 1870s commanders at the highest levels of the British and Dominion Armies were almost to a man enthusiastic supporters of sport in any form, especially for the soldiers in frontline regiments. Evidence of the emphasis placed on sport by the Army hierarchy as a morale, teambuilding, and leadership development tool is everywhere, with wartime doctrinal literature such as SS 143, quoted at the beginning of this chapter, being just one example.

Without the support and encouragement of sport by commanders at all levels, events like the Brigade and Divisional races reported by the *XI Hussar Journal* in March 1916 could not have taken place. These marathon races involved at least ten officers and soldiers from each squadron in the Cavalry Division, and prizes were presented by the Division Commander himself. As the Divisional race was the culmination of races run since December 1915 at

---

Museum Official Photo No. G1289).

[12]   *St. George's Gazette* Vol. 34 (January 31, 1916), 8th (Svc.) Battalion notes, p. 16.

[13]   Ibid., 9th (Svc.) Battalion notes, p. 16.

[14]   Fuller, *Troop Morale and Popular Culture*, pp. 85–94.

the squadron, battalion, and brigade level, it is clear that the effort and time involved in putting together this event had to involve support at the highest levels from the beginning. This is especially apparent when one considers that, simultaneously with the qualifying races, each troop, squadron, battalion, and brigade in the division was conducting a full football competition schedule, to say nothing of their military duties.[15]

Gymkhana were a superb example of the way in which the Army leadership sponsored and encouraged sport. As we have seen, these events were commonplace before the war, even to the extent that they were considered by many units as the normal culmination of the yearly collective training period. Their reappearance in late 1915 and early 1916 demonstrates not only that the ebb and flow of the war had settled into something more regular but also that the Army's hierarchy was determined to retain the pre-war traditions of sport intact, in spite of the upheavals occasioned by the war. Major General Nicholson recorded in his diary that, when he was a Brigade Commander in March 1916, he scheduled a Brigade gymkhana while the unit was in a rest camp near Calais. Although the event was twice delayed by rain, it was eventually held on March 25. Not only did Nicholson himself judge the horse jumping competition, he won one of the horse racing heats while mounted on his charger.[16]

1st Battalion the Northumberland Fusiliers participated in a Brigade sports day on March 31, 1916, where they competed in cross-country racing, boxing, football, tug-of-war, and a "bombing competition";[17] competitions like these were outlined as potential forms of training and fun in the Physical and Bayonet Training Staff's Special Tables and other pamphlets published during the war. The 8th Battalion of the Fusiliers reported on an imperial-flavored sports day held in Egypt on March 23, where they competed in boxing, obstacle races, and tug-of-war against the New Zealand Sappers, the Bikaner Camel Corps, and the Egyptian Survey.[18] Prior to the spring of 1916, sports days and gymkhana were almost never reported in combat theaters, being almost exclusively held in Britain. Their return to regular practice everywhere in 1916 is a great indicator of how the Army's operational tempo had become settled with static trench fighting.

By 1917, sports days or gymkhana were even more common, and many units began to routinely schedule these events whenever they were out of the line. F.G. Senyard reported on several sports days in his letters home, one in May 1917,

---

[15]   *XI Hussar Journal* Vol. VII No. 2 (September 1916), pp. 14–16, 32–36. Incidentally, B Squadron won the marathon finals too.

[16]   "Diary of Major General Sir (Cecil) Lothian Nicholson KCB CMG," unpublished manuscript, entry dated March 24, 1916, Imperial War Museum Archives 01/14/1.

[17]   *St. George's Gazette* Vol. 34 (March 31, 1916), 1st Battalion notes, p. 49.

[18]   Ibid. (April 29, 1916), 8th (Svc.) Battalion notes, p. 82.

Figure 12.1   Pillow fight, Guards Division sports day, c.1918 (Imperial War Museum)

and another the next month. A year later, he was in training for the upcoming battalion sports, which were to include a "dry boat race," a "klondyke race," an "elephant race," and a "sack melee." Senyard wrote to his wife that the dry boat race consisted of eight men astride a pole running backwards along a course, the klondyke race was a 200-yard dash and then grabbing prizes out of a hole, and the sack melee ("a rather bloodthirsty affair") consisted of men in sacks tied at the neck, charging and trying to drive each other out of a ring:

> The chap who charged me out of it yesterday weighed about 18 stone and he not
> only shot me out of the ring but nearly out of the field as well. I was missing when
> that event came on today. I haven't discovered what the Elephant race is yet, but I
> have made my will and am now prepared for the worst.[19]

Training for Senyard's battalion's sports sounds very much like training for war. In addition to unit sports, large horse racing meets were also common by 1917. The famous unofficial Army newspaper, which was named in succession *The Wipers Times*, *The "New Church" Times*, *The Kemmel Times*, *The Somme Times*, and *The B.E.F. Times*, periodically reported on these sports days and races, even making occasional space for a cricket or football match. It must have been an important event indeed to make the pages of the all-Army newspaper, which was laboriously printed on a portable press by a small, overworked staff in caves, dugouts, and shell holes all over northern France and Flanders.[20]

One of the more interesting phenomena in Army sport during this time was the appearance of nascent professionalism. Prior to the war, there is almost no indication that money prizes or unit specialization in games were common—the public-school ideal of the amateur clearly held sway. But with the influx of civilians into the forces during the war, including many professional athletes, it can be seen as almost inevitable that professionalism in Army sport would begin to appear. When the war prevented units from having the ability to present elaborate cups, medals, or other prizes to victorious units or individuals, many commanders resorted to awarding cash prizes for sports. Given the importance of games to unit pride and tradition, it was only natural, perhaps, that some units would not only try to specialize in particular games, but that they would seek to recruit good athletes, and even former professionals, to serve on their teams. Lieutenant Colonel Campbell's acquisition of his slate of former boxing

---

[19]   "Letters of F.G. Senyard MM," unpublished folio, Imperial War Museum Archives 98/28/1.

[20]   See Lieutenant Colonel F.J. Roberts and Major J.H. Pearson, eds., *The Wipers Times* (London: Eveleigh, Nash & Grayson Ltd., 1930). This book is a complete compilation of all the extant issues of the famous trench magazine.

champions for the Physical and Bayonet Training Staff is just one example of this phenomenon—even though Campbell used these men to assist in training, they also put on exhibition fights at rest camps and convalescent depots, sometimes for money. Money prizes only contributed to what many in the Army's sporting world saw as a terrible danger to the very foundations of military athleticism.

Major T.D. McCarthy of the 2nd Battalion Irish Guards recorded in his diary the result of some of this nascent professionalism in Army sport. On March 11, 1916, when he was still a sergeant, his battalion played the 1st Battalion, Grenadier Guards, in a football match on the Aviation Ground at the rest camp in Calais. McCarthy played right halfback, and his battalion lost the game 4–2 in overtime. He relates how the brigadier praised his battalion team "for our good display," because the Grenadiers had seven former professional footballers on their team.[21] Given the powerful political connections and cachet of a unit like the 1st Battalion Grenadier Guards, it is perhaps unsurprising that they would have the wherewithal to recruit professionals for their unit teams. McCarthy makes no comment on it, but it is highly likely that after the game his unit felt unfairly treated in the sporting spirit by their comrades in the Grenadiers.

There were other, perhaps less insidious results of the practice of awarding cash prizes for sport. In July 1917 Lieutenant Edwin Campion Vaughn recorded his impressions of his unit's intensive training prior to the Third Ypres Campaign. At the end of the training period Vaughn wrote of the culminating event, the regimental sports day, which "went very well." We do not know what the events were, but they most likely consisted of foot races, some military competitions, and, naturally, football and boxing. We do know, thanks to Lieutenant Vaughn, that "the Colonel gave the prizes which were, of course, hard cash." He also recorded that the result of this choice of prize was "a terrific blind," a unit-wide drunk that caused the troops to present "a sorry spectacle" the next morning. A few days later Vaughn's battalion "moved up the line" to begin the offensive.[22]

The rapid growth of unregulated unit sports in the Army after 1916 and the dangers attendant on some of the less savory aspects of these sports were cause for concern by the men who prior to the war had overseen many of the recreational pastimes in the Army. Leaders in the Gymnastic Staff and men like Brigadier Kentish saw both opportunity and potential calamity in this expansion of games. With many units returning to the pre-war practice of conducting training in the mornings and unit sports in the afternoons, the Staff felt that it was incumbent on them to take action designed to establish some

---

[21] "Diary of Major T.D. McCarthy," unpublished manuscript, Imperial War Museum Archives, 92/3/1.

[22] Edwin Campion Vaughn, *Some Desperate Glory: The World War One Diary of a British Officer* (New York: Touchstone, 1981), pp. 176–180.

form of control over these activities, ensuring that through sport the overall goals of soldier fitness and morale could continue to be met.[23] Without some form of oversight for Army sport, there was a danger that not all soldiers would properly benefit from games, and that the basic purpose of military games might be subverted. The aversion to athletic professionalism felt by many in the Army's senior ranks was also a powerful incentive to establish control of some kind.

In June 1916, then Major R.B. Campbell informally approached GHQ, British Expeditionary Forces, with a recommended course of action for the management of Army games. This idea, which was clearly based upon the idea for a Secretariat of Army Games to which Campbell had been a party in 1913, involved establishing a central body for the management of games in the BEF. Campbell and his staff formally presented this scheme in September 1916, with the goal of having games organized for an overall championship of the BEF. The BEF staff, perhaps remembering the debate surrounding this type of scheme before the war, felt that "it was too ambitious for the moment" and rejected it— along with "a good deal of contumely from various quarters accompanying the process!!"[24] At a conference in September 1916 at Auxi-le-Château, Campbell presented a second version of his scheme, in which the Division was the primary training unit for championships. Generals Butler and Burnett-Stuart, both officers on the BEF staff, attended this conference and were in favor of the second scheme. After some discussion, General Butler advised Campbell to obtain approval from all of the Field Army commanders before formally proposing his idea to Field Marshal Haig, and this he accordingly did. Within twenty-four hours he had gained the needed approval, and the scheme went forward to the Chief of Staff of the BEF, General Kigell.[25] It is highly doubtful that Campbell would have been able to secure this acquiescence so rapidly had the Staff not been held in the kind of esteem it was throughout the BEF at this time.

The second idea of a formally sponsored division-level championship for selected sports was ultimately approved, along with funding for equipment and uniforms. The Physical and Bayonet Training Staff was to be the organization responsible for supervising and administering the division-level competitions, and divisions were directed to include their Superintendents of Physical and Bayonet Training on all committees and discussions surrounding the implementation of competitions. Additionally, units were directed to apply through the Staff for the uniforms and equipment that they had been authorized—the goal was to supply at least two footballs, one set of boxing

---

23   Captain F.J. Starr, "War History of the Army Gymnastic Staff," (first draft) unpublished manuscript, Army Physical Training Corps Museum file #1664, p. 6.

24   Ibid., p. 6.

25   Ibid., pp. 6–7.

gloves, and fifty pairs of shorts to each company-sized unit in the BEF. Owing to the initial shortage of funds, however, the Staff was only able to procure seventy-five footballs, fifty sets of gloves, and 2,000 pairs of shorts per division. In addition to their other duties, divisional Superintendents became responsible for maintaining and doling out this equipment to units who wanted it—the Staff were never able to stock enough to meet the demand, and funding for both equipment and sports organization continued to be a problem during the war, as it had been before the war.[26]

With the formal mandate to oversee games and sports in the BEF, the Staff had reached an important milestone. Previous to this decision in late 1916, the leadership of the Gymnastic Staff had only an unofficial role in the conduct of military sport. Now that role was official, and the Staff in France was able to make policy recommendations and doctrinal decisions regarding sport that would be binding on units in the BEF. One of the first targets of the Staff when they gained this authority was the practice of awarding money prizes—in December 1916 the Staff recommended to GHQ that no money prizes be allowed for any recreational training in the BEF. In February 1917 GHQ published a General Routine Order (GRO) banning money prizes in boxing only. As related in the Staff's unpublished "War History,"

> The money question was at first an uphill fight. Nine officers out of every ten contended that men would not box for [non-monetary] prizes; but they were frequently confounded by the boxers themselves, who generally stated a preference for a medal, as a memento of a contest in the battle area. All sorts of subterfuges were resorted to in order to evade the G.R.O.[27]

One of these subterfuges was the practice of awarding boxers non-monetary gifts: Jimmy Wilde, one of the boxers on the Staff, fought Joe Conn in 1918 for a purse of uncut diamonds.[28] J.W. Whatley was still winning cash prizes in 1918 for football and athletics competitions in Palestine.[29] Clearly the amateur ideal was not as widely embraced in the Army as one might have thought, and the Physical and Bayonet Training Staff's writ did not yet run beyond the operational area of the BEF. However, the Staff persisted, and when in the summer of 1917 they finally issued the first official training pamphlet governing sport and games (SS 137, *Recreational Training*), it included an outright ban on money prizes for all

---

[26]   Ibid., pp. 6–7, 9–10.

[27]   Ibid., p. 9.

[28]   Derek Birley, "Sportsmen and the Deadly Game," *British Journal of Sports History* Vol. 3 No. 3 (December 1986), p. 310, note 30.

[29]   "Diary of J.W. Whatley," various entries dated February to September 1918.

Army sports. This ban was only really effective in France, and the Headquarters of the Gymnastic Staff in Britain would continue to struggle with issues of professionalism outside of the BEF throughout the war. Be that as it may, it was a start. Too late, perhaps, to prevent Lieutenant Vaughn's commander from issuing his money prizes in July of 1917 and sending the battalion on a bender, but it was ultimately to be "the death warrant" for professionalism in Army sport.[30]

With the Staff now responsible for Recreational Training throughout the BEF, they required an increase in the number of personnel they had assigned—this accounts for some of the successive increases to the size of the Staff in 1917 and 1918, including an eventual team of six engravers to make medals, shields, and cups for unit sports awards.[31] This expansion was also the reason for the assignment to the Staff of Captain Starr, who in addition to his writing duties was originally detailed as Recreational Training Officer for the entire BEF. In 1917 GHQ directed the Staff to begin including classes in sports organization in its courses at the St. Pol school. This it did, and classes of this kind were also quickly added to the curriculum of the courses at the Headquarters Gymnasium in Aldershot and the other Command Schools in Britain.[32] From that time on all new Superintendents and Staff Instructors would have the grounding necessary to take up their now officially sanctioned sports duties when they reached their new assignments. The Staff had introduced recreational training, to accompany the PT they already conducted, at convalescent depots prior to its official sanctioning, and after 1917 the Adjutant General, Lieutenant General Sir C.F.N. Macready, GCMG, KCB, was one of the most vocal supporters of this form of recovery for soldiers with wounds, both physical and mental.[33]

Along with the task of oversight for games and sports, the Physical and Bayonet Training Staff had necessarily to concern itself with the adequate provision of grounds on which to play. In this project the Staff was greatly assisted by the Army's experience with grounds construction just prior to the war. Similar energies and organization were applied to the construction of grounds in France as had been applied to home stations before the war. In some cases, as with the construction of the gymnasium for the school at St. Pol, German prisoners of war were pressed into service to construct fields, pitches, boxing rings, and

---

[30]   Lieutenant Colonel E.A.L. Oldfield, *History of the Army Physical Training Corps* (Aldershot: Gale & Polden Ltd., 1955), p. 28.

[31]   Starr, "War History of the British Army Gymnastic Staff" (first draft), p. 22.

[32]   See *Training at Home*, issued by the General Staff, 1917 (Maxse papers, File #58, Imperial War Museum Archives), p. 21, and GHQ Training pamphlet SS 152 (*Instructions for the Training of the British Armies in France*), Appendix XXI, p. 82.

[33]   Starr, "War History of the British Army Gymnastic Staff" (first draft), p. 9.

other facilities.[34] In SS 137, the Staff provided detailed specifications for full-size grounds, and for reduced-size fields and other facilities that would allow for units to have games fields even when there wasn't adequate space for a regulation area.[35] This construction program was extended to the Commonwealth forces as well: the area taken over by the 1st Canadian Division in June 1917 boasted "nine baseball fields, one indoor field, three football fields, three tennis courts, one basketball square, and two boxing platforms."[36]

The construction of grounds for recreational training reached the point where it was mandated in the January 1918 edition of the seminal document that guided training for all units in the BEF, SS 152 (*Instructions for the Training of the British Armies in France*). This pamphlet stated that "in forward areas all billets reserved for the use of troops rotating from duty in the trenches shall have connected with them a) Bayonet-fighting courses; b) Ranges of at least 30 yards; c) Bombing trenches; d) Drill grounds; e) Recreation grounds." This same document also mandated not only that physical training never be conducted before breakfast, but that for at least three days per week during rest periods units spend the afternoons playing games.[37] By January of 1918, then, the British Army was requiring that all rest areas and billets have recreation grounds, all divisions in the BEF have competitions in a list of suggested sports leading to a divisional championship, and that half of at least three training days per week while out of the line be spent playing games. Division championships could be held in Assault Training, Athletics, Badminton, Baseball, Basketball, Boxing, Cross-Country Running, Football, Hockey, Shinty, "Tabloid Sports," Tug-of-War, Volleyball, and Wrestling.[38] All this during a time when the Army was engaged in some of the most brutal combat experienced in all of history: the Third Ypres, or Passchendaele campaign, and the Cambrai offensive.

The physical and recreational training systems of the BEF were all put on hold during the crisis occasioned in the spring of 1918 by the German offensives that lasted until early summer. During that time the Staff was forced to abandon the headquarters and school at St. Pol, and to relocate several times. The instructors and students at the school even had to form into two fighting companies during the height of the German advance at the end of March. By May 4, the headquarters had been settled at Hardelot Plage near Boulogne, collocated with the 1st Army

---

[34] Ibid., p. 13.

[35] Each section of this pamphlet dealt with a different sport, and the frontispiece of the pamphlet had specifications for each type of pitch, court or ring.

[36] Fuller, *Troop Morale and Popular Culture*, p. 88.

[37] SS 152, pp. 24, 83, 84.

[38] SS 137, *Recreational Training*, December 1918, p. 4.

School, and the school staff had joined them there by the tenth.[39] Throughout the remainder of that summer, while the Army embarked on its final counterattacks that would ultimately end the war, the Staff restarted its programs and continued to expand its influence. Only one major change to the Army's physical training systems remained to be implemented before the end of the war.

From late 1917 and into 1918 the BEF's Inspectorate General of Training, led first by Lieutenant General Bonham-Carter, and later by Lieutenant General Maxse, had been examining the role that bayonet training had begun to play in the overall rifle training of soldiers. The bayonet assault courses set up by the Staff had evolved to the point where they all included some live-fire practice; soldiers were required not only to engage enemy targets with their bayonets but also to shoot at both close and longer-range targets. For almost a century marksmanship training in the Army had been under the control of the Musketry School at Hythe, and this cooption of marksmanship practice by the Physical and Bayonet Training Staff was not seen by the Inspectorate as entirely logical. Bonham-Carter had instituted some combined bullet-bayonet training competitions where he required that the staffs collaborate,[40] but he did not take the next step to end this anomaly of two different organizations having responsibility for the same kind of training.

Maxse saw things a little differently—soon after taking over as Inspector in July 1918 he embarked on a series of tours of all training establishments, both in France and at home. During that tour he noted deficiencies in how training was being conducted in all of these establishments; "bullet and bayonet" training were just two of these.[41] Based on the results of his initial assessments, Maxse sent a letter to General Wigram at GHQ dated August 20, 1918, asking that Major General Sir P.S. Wilkinson, Inspector of Musketry, come to his headquarters to meet with Lieutenant Colonel Campbell in order to synchronize bayonet and rifle training. In a follow-up to that letter, Wigram noted that GHQ was looking into "schemes about Campbell."[42] What those schemes were, was revealed later that fall when in October the Staff were informed that bayonet training was to be removed as a responsibility of the Staff and transferred to the School of Musketry. In a October 19 letter to the Staff, the Chief of Staff of the BEF stated:

---

[39]   "War Diary of the Physical and Bayonet Training Staff," WO 95/55, National Archives, entries dated March 21–May 11, 1918.

[40]   For example, see Starr, "War History of the British Army Gymnastic Staff" (first draft), p. 15–16.

[41]   "Notes on Inspections August to October 1918" (Maxse papers, File 53/2I),

[42]   Maxse papers, File 58.

It has been decided that the present policy of teaching the use of the rifle at one educational establishment and the use of the bayonet at another shall be discontinued. In future the use of the rifle and the use of the bayonet will be taught as one subject at the present Army Musketry Camps, which will be renamed Army Rifle Training Camps and the training in the use of the bayonet by Physical and Bayonet Training Staffs will be discontinued ... The Physical and Bayonet Training school and the Physical and Bayonet Training Instructors will become the Physical and Recreational School and the Physical and Recreational Training Instructors respectively ... Bayonet training will continue to be taught by the by the P+BT staff until such time as the number of Instructors trained in Rifle Training renders that procedure unnecessary.[43]

By the beginning of November, special classes for Musketry Instructors were being conducted at the Staff's school, and volunteers from the Staff were being transferred to the Musketry School.[44] This change removed the one part of the Staff's mission not wholly connected with physical fitness, and the name change to Physical and Recreational Training Staff spoke volumes about the evolution of that mission since the start of the war.

The story of Army sport during the First World War is one of dramatic change and development but also one of surprising continuity. First World War military sport was, in the end, an expansion (albeit a dramatic one) of pre-war systems and practices, adapted to the environment and circumstances of the war. The major difference between the two is the important development of the Physical and Recreational Training Staff, as the representative overseas of the Gymnastic Staff, finally taking over full control of sports organization and doctrine.

Wartime recreational training continued to serve the same official purposes as Army sport before the war, again, with many of its previously unstated purposes codified and reinforced. It is instructive here to review what was the Army's official doctrine regarding sport, as outlined in SS 137, *Recreational Training*. This pamphlet, updated and reissued four times between the summer of 1917 and December 1918, expressed unequivocally the philosophy underlying the pursuit of games in the Army. There was virtually no difference between this philosophy as expressed in 1918, and what it had been since the earliest days of Victorian Army sport:

> Games offer the best means of keeping men fit in mind and body and cheerful and contented in spirit. Love of games is inherent in the British race. Games recall the

---

[43]   "War Diary of the Physical and Bayonet Training Staff," entry dated October 22, 1918.

[44]   Ibid., entries dated November 3 and 19, 1918.

pleasanter circumstances of man's normal existence ... Games, too, have a moral value, for the man who is training for a competition will be more likely to keep both body and mind under control than he would were such incentive lacking, and he will be less inclined to succumb to vicious temptations. Games are also a process of education, not in the ordinary acceptance of the term, but in the sense of character building and habit formation ... Played in the real games spirit – the amateur spirit – they teach self-sacrifice and self-subordination in the individual, and these develop in time into *esprit de corps*, indispensable to the Army in war or peace ....[45]

Games had always been viewed by the Army as a superb means of developing leadership in soldiers, and especially for young officers. As a consequence, young officers had been encouraged to play games and engage in sport at least since the 1840s, and that, too, had not changed in 1918:

> Officers should take a personal and active interest in the games. They will thereby ensure that they are played in the true sporting spirit, and at the same time will increase the bond of sympathy between themselves and their men. They will gain, too, an insight into the character of their men which they could obtain by no other means.[46]

These aspects of sporting philosophy remained constant throughout the developmental period of the Army's physical culture, and to a great degree remain constant even today. This philosophy and the training programs it engendered set the British Army apart: by placing the British military experience with sport during the war into the context of what was happening in the other major European armies, an interesting and very salient point arises. The British Army was the only one of all the major European armies fighting in the war—French, Russian, German, Austrian, and Italian—that never suffered a major mutiny or collapse between the start of hostilities and the Armistice.[47] The British Army is also the only one of these armies that fostered organized sport and fitness to such an extent.

It is impossible to know for certain, but it is more than likely that the physical and recreational training programs conducted by the British made at least part of the crucial difference in the morale and fighting spirit that kept Tommy Atkins

---

[45]   SS 137, December 1918, p. 3.

[46]   Ibid., p. 3.

[47]   The Russian Army collapsed in 1917 as part of the Revolution; the French Army mutinied in 1917 following the Nivelle Offensive; the Italian Army collapsed after the Caporetto Offensive and had to be shored up by British and French divisions; the German and Austrian armies collapsed in 1918, thus bringing the end of the war.

and his Commonwealth partners in the fight. It was not by accident that SS 137 stated very clearly on the first page, "Games offer the best means of keeping men fit in mind and body and cheerful and contented in spirit." Games, in other words, keep soldiers disciplined and fighting.

As stated in Chapter 1, it is immaterial if we today agree with this philosophy at face value, but it is essential that we understand how this philosophy acted on British fighting men, from the lowest private to the Field Marshal commanding the BEF. The fundamental belief in the games ethic was so ingrained in the contemporary Army that, whether it was openly expressed or not, it is clear that many soldiers sincerely believed that, as they were during the Victorian and Edwardian periods, sport and games were major contributors to the combat effectiveness of the British warrior. As a former Guards Lieutenant stated in 1920, "The British instinct for sport helped materially to win the war. This is admitted by everybody, including the enemy ...."[48] Given the widespread nature of this attitude, it should have been relatively easy for those interested soldiers to consolidate the gains made by the Gymnastic Staff during the war, and to apply Army wide the practices adopted by the BEF in physical training and sports organization. Such a consolidation would dramatically modernize the manner in which all British soldiers' recreation was managed.

With the end of the war in sight, many of the senior leaders at the War Office in London had begun to plan for shaping the Army in the post-war period. In addition to dealing with the enormous task of demobilization, they were concerned about being able to return to an all-volunteer Army while maintaining sufficient forces to police Britain's now greatly expanded Imperial possessions. In these discussions dealing with the issues of voluntary recruiting, the subject of sport inevitably presented itself. The Army had been interested in the use of sport as a recruiting tool for many years, and with the huge expansion of organized sport in the BEF and the positive international reputation of the Physical and Recreational Training Staff, it was only natural that sport would be seen as a potential draw for new volunteers. In order for sport to succeed in attracting men to the colors, however, it was necessary to sustain the progress made during the war in sports organization and training. The manner in which this end was accomplished resulted in the final achievement of the goal so many of the supporters of Army sport had long been working for: the creation of an Army Sport Control Board.

---

[48]   Frank L. Riseley, late Lieutenant Grenadier Guards, in the *Household Brigade Magazine*, Victory Number (1920), p. 92.

Epilogue
"Raise the Tone": The Formation of the Army Sport Control Board[1]

As the end of the war approached in the fall of 1918, and the Gymnastic Staff worked through the process of transferring responsibility for bayonet training to the Musketry Department, moves were afoot that would finally complete the process of modernization for Army Sport. All of these were accomplished in the context of the Army Council's planning for demobilization and the need for retaining control of newly acquired imperial possessions in the Middle East and Africa. The story of how the Sport Control Board came into being is remarkably uncomplicated, given the resistance and ultimate failure encountered by its advocates the first two times similar proposals were made—by the Gymnastic Staff in 1913, and by the Physical and Bayonet Training Staff in France during 1916. The reasons for the ease with which the final proposal was implemented stem from three primary factors. First, pre-war concerns about funding for a sports oversight body were not a consideration in the Army's money-rich environment of 1918. Second, the Army Council was deeply concerned about recruiting sufficient soldiers after the war to maintain the strength levels required for expanded imperial responsibilities, and many felt that the positive image of Army sport would be a powerful tool in that effort.[2] Finally, leadership at all levels in the Army were upset at the festering problem of professionalism in Army sport, and were determined to maintain the Army's amateur athletic traditions intact.

---

[1]   A note about sources: much of the source material for this chapter comes from the uncatalogued files of the Army Sport Control Board (ASCB). I was given access to this material by Major General (retired) S.W. Saint-John Lytle, CB, the current Director of the Board. These papers were in his office, and he was good enough to let me use them—the records contain War Office folios and many loose documents, they are mixed and in no particular order, and there are many unsigned and undated memoranda and letters. I have tried here to be as clear and detailed as possible in describing the nature of these sources.

[2]   See Jeffrey Keith, *The British Army and the Crisis of Empire 1918–1922* (Manchester: Manchester University Press, 1984), especially chapter 2 ("Weakness in the Home Base"), pp. 16–17.

In a way that is quite similar to the effort to establish a board in 1913–1914, the process by which the Army Sport Control Board was ultimately set up in 1918 is highly illustrative of the importance ascribed to soldier recreation and athleticism by the Army. The Board was set up in the midst of the hard fighting through the late summer and fall of 1918 that ended with the Armistice, and during the serious deliberations and planning surrounding demobilization and deployments to Russia, Turkey, Africa, and the Middle East. That the Army Council would spend any time at all during this period considering the proposal for a sports board is a clear indication of the central place held by physical culture in the pantheon of Army values and thinking. This concern demonstrates remarkable development in the fifty years since the formation of the Gymnastic Staff. Clearly, the men who ran the British Army in 1918 were so convinced of the success of physical training and sports programs in achieving their goals—morale, *esprit de corps*, and improving soldier health and fitness—that they were ready to put those programs at the center of plans for recruiting, training, and retaining soldiers who would maintain the Empire at the height of its territorial extent.

Early in 1918, Brigadier Reginald Kentish began to communicate with senior officers of the Gymnastic Staff and their counterparts in the Physical and Bayonet Training Staff in France, about a proposal to get the various Army sporting associations into solvency so they could be prepared to resume operations after the war. He included Lieutenant Colonel Campbell, the Superintendents of the BEF's major subordinate commands, the Commandant of the Army School of Physical Training at Aldershot, Lieutenant Colonel J.S.W. de Joux, and the Superintendents of all the major Home Commands. He suggested that they meet to discuss how this task of fundraising might be accomplished. There is no recorded date for this meeting, but in several letters outlining the genesis of this idea, officers who were there described the results of the meeting: Kentish suggested that the representatives of the various commands begin soliciting money for investment in War Bonds, the proceeds of which could then be used to restore the Football, Boxing, and Athletics Associations to an operating state. This proposal was to be the catalyst for the foundation of the Army Sport Control Board.[3]

At some point later in the year a memo was sent to the Adjutant General at the War Office arguing that the time had come for revisiting the idea of establishing a controlling body for all of Army sport. The exact date and author of

---

[3]   Letter dated September 20, 1918 from Brigadier E.R. Fitzpatrick, Deputy Adjutant General, to Lieutenant General Ernest Hewett, DSO (officer in charge of general policy regarding training, War Office), ASCB files. This letter is attached to several letters from Lieutenant Colonel de Joux and others, including Major J.A. Nixon, Superintendent of Gymnasia, Northern Command. All of these attest to the fact that Kentish was the instigator of the scheme to raise money for the Associations.

this proposal is a mystery, but its connection to Kentish's money-raising scheme is unquestionable—the memo outlining it is attached in the Adjutant General's file in the Board's historical records to other letters that refer directly to Kentish's communications with the Gymnastic Staff and Command Superintendents. It is highly probable that, if the memo was not sent by Kentish, he at least had a hand in it. He was the one who initially raised the question of restarting the various associations, and he was one of the signatories to the original 1913 scheme requesting a controlling body for sport. It is also possible that the memo was drafted by a group of individuals; perhaps it originated in one of the Superintendent's meetings that were routinely being held by the Physical and Bayonet Training Staff in France. Regardless of who the author was, the reasons for establishing such a body that are laid out in the memorandum are very similar to those raised by Colonel Couper in 1913, and they parallel complaints about sporting problems encountered by the Staff in attempting to enforce its policies outside the operational area of the BEF, including in the Home Commands. The arguments presented for a controlling body were:

a. There is no authority to lay down the lines on which Sport and Athletics are to be carried out.
b. The existing Associations are given very little or no encouragement and have no controlling body to refer to or watch over their actions. These are:
c. Army Football Association
d. Navy and Army Boxing Association
e. Army Athletics Association.
f. The soldier is not well catered for with results that tend to discountenance amateur sport in the Army. The soldier is inclined to join the civilian organizations, generally professional.
g. To do away with controversies such as have occurred in cases where soldiers have taken part in professional competitions and receive money prizes. (To the detriment of sport and to the loss of prestige in Army Athletics.)
h. Financial arrangements are bound to be indifferent, and lower organizations badly controlled.
i. To bring all commands and Overseas forces into a sphere after the war that will help the Army and sport.[4]

---

[4]   Memorandum (anonymous, undated), Adjutant General's War Office folder, ASCB files.

It is clear from the existing records that this memorandum was far better received at the War Office than any of the previous attempts by the Gymnastic Staff and others to establish a controlling body for sport. The successful example of sports organization and oversight provided by the Physical and Bayonet Training Staff in France had to be one of the major reasons for the positive reception, as many of the same officers who rejected the first proposal of its kind in 1913 and 1914 were still in the Army Council in 1918—Sir R.H. Brade, Secretary of the War Office, and Lieutenant General Sir Henry Wilson, to name just two.[5]

Some evidence exists of the debate during September and October among the Army Council surrounding the idea, and it is clear that the concerns about funding that ultimately killed the proposal in 1914 were not an issue in 1918. In the environment of total war, it would seem that the Council's traditional cheeseparing had been abandoned. Even the pre-war concern about a disabled or retired officer taking charge of the supervisory body had disappeared, and several officers argued that such a position would be an excellent way for the Army to look after their own when the war ended; the war had also apparently succeeded in breaking down objections as to the "suitability" of certain jobs for officers.[6]

These arguments made by the officers discussing the proposal are helpful in discerning what the Army's senior leaders felt were the most important issues connected with military sport. The discussion most often surrounded the problems of professionalism and the image of Army sport in civilian circles. The Adjutant General was obviously concerned with how the image of Army sport might affect recruiting:

> Recent events, more particularly competitions in connection with boxing, have shewn [*sic*] the necessity of having a central controlling body for the Army, which shall be powerful enough to have a strong influence over sports both within and outside the Army. I consider that a committee organized on the lines of the attached proposal would have this effect.[7]

---

[5]   Army Lists, 1914, 1918, National Army Museum Archives.

[6]   There are several memoranda and letters in the Adjutant General's War Office folder (ASCB files) that accompany the memorandum cited above. Many of these deal with the financial questions about support for the Board, with some baldly suggesting that the Council should quickly take advantage of the funds then available to establish the Board, before they dried up after the war. There are also several letters suggesting that a retired or disabled officer should be retained to run the Board. This is in fact what is currently done: the officers of the Board, including the Director and the Secretary, are retired soldiers. The Secretary at the time I did this research, Lieutenant Colonel (ret.) Barry Lillywhite, was the former Commander of the Army Physical and Adventurous Training Group, in which position he was responsible for running the Army Physical Training Corps School at Aldershot.

[7]   Memorandum dated September 28, 1918, Army Sport Control Board (ACSB) files.

Brigadier Fitzpatrick, the Deputy Adjutant General, was perhaps more interested in ways in which the Army, as the last real remaining bastion of aristocratic control of sport, might hold back the tide of professionalism through the influence it generated from its image and wartime record. He wrote, "I am all for doing anything that will raise the tone of the Civilian Athletic Associations to that which obtains in the Army."[8]

Regardless of individual agendas, there is little evidence of any opposition to creating a supervisory body for sport. While the War Office staff reviewed and discussed the proposal, the Command Superintendents continued their attempts at raising money for the associations. By the beginning of November, however, the Army Council had reached some decisions about the scheme for a controlling board and had begun to formulate ideas as to its structure and function. In a letter to the Headquarters, Eastern Command, Fitzpatrick gave away some of these ideas in an effort to halt the fundraising effort for the associations:

1. With reference to your [memo] E.C. No. 6/32387(A), dated 4th September 1918 ... I am to inform you that an Army Council Instruction will shortly be issued relating to the formation of a Central Board of Control for Sport in the Army.
2. The Board will meet once a month, and will give early consideration to the financial question. In the meantime there is nothing to be gained by appealing to units to subscribe from their Regimental Institute funds, in order to establish funds to support the Army Boxing, Army Football, and Army Athletic Associations.[9]

Soon after Fitzpatrick sent this letter to the Eastern Command, on November 20, 1918 the Army Council indeed issued its landmark communication that was to be the culmination of the process of development and modernization of the Army's physical culture, Army Council Instruction No. 1299 of 1918, which directed the formation of the Army Sport Control Board. This Instruction laid out the basic structure of the Board, along with its functions:

2. The objects of this Board of Control are: -

   (a) To assist the organizations now existing in the Army for the various branches of sport.
   (b) To control the conduct of sport in the Army.

---

8   Minute to September 28, 1918 Macready memo, October 1918, ACSB files.
9   Letter from Brigadier Fitzpatrick to HQ, Eastern Command, ASCB files.

(c) To assist the organizations for sport in the various Commands at Home and Overseas.

(d) To deal with questions arising from organizations outside the Army, in which sport in the Army may be connected.

(e) To maintain the necessary cooperation in sport between the Army and the other Forces of the Crown, both at Home and Overseas ...

3. G.Os. C.-in C., Great Britain, Ireland, and all other theatres will take steps to organize committees on similar lines in each command, with a view to the furtherance of sport on sound lines.[10]

In addition to 1299, there quickly followed other instructions specifying what the nature of command sports boards would be. In a November 25 letter to the Army Council, Major General Sir Henry Cecil Lowther of the General Staff argued for a rapid establishment of these committees. The text of this letter again highlights the philosophy of Army athleticism and how that dovetailed with the Council's concerns:

> The Army Sport Control Board are anxious that, during the process of demobilization and the period which must necessarily elapse between that process and the reorganization of our future Army, the earliest possible efforts should be made to organize sport in all its branches; the intensity of military training carried on throughout the war will, on the conclusion of peace, be considerably relaxed, the leisure of the soldier consequently increased and it is considered that a great part of such leisure cannot be more profitably employed than by the universal participation of all ranks in the National Sports of this country.[11]

The Army Sport Control Board held its first meeting on November 18, 1918, and then held weekly meetings of the Executive Committee after that. Each month there was a full meeting of the Board. In the chair was Major General Harrington, the first Director, and assisting as Vice Chair was Colonel Campbell, who since the end of the war had been promoted and replaced Colonel Wright as Inspector of Gymnasia. Major Betts too, had been promoted, to Lieutenant Colonel, and he took over the Physical and Recreational Training Staff in France just in time to preside over its rapid demobilization. Other members of the Board included representatives (usually the Gymnastic Staff Superintendent) from every Home

---

[10]   Army Council Instruction No. 1299 of 1918, War Office, November 20, 1918, ASCB files.

[11]   Letter dated November 25, 1918 from Major General Sir H.C. Lowther, para. 7, ASCB files.

command, each overseas command, including India, each arm of the service, each sports association, and each overseas Dominion force.[12]

One of the first successes of the Board was in the first full month of its existence. In November and December of 1918, after arguing that the Army philosophy of athleticism was naturally opposed to making sport mandatory for soldiers, the Board asked the Army Council to clearly separate mandatory physical training from voluntary sport. This process would be assisted if the Army ceased using the term "recreational training" and officially changed the name of the BEF fitness organization to the Army Physical Training Staff. The Board also asked that all funds for Army Sport be separated from funds for PT, and that the Board be responsible for sports funds while PT funds be channeled through the Gymnastic Staff.[13] These changes were almost immediately approved, and accordingly the Army Council sent a letter to Field Marshal Haig, which informed him of the changes, and that further, in an effort to separate training from games and sport, they would eliminate the term "Recreational Training."[14]

One of the offshoots of this process was the name change in December 1918 of the entire Gymnastic Staff to the Army Physical Training Staff—during the Second World War it was finally changed to the Army Physical Training Corps.[15] As the sports system directed by the Board took root, the Board turned to other areas that had traditionally been dealt with by volunteers or ad hoc committees. The Board was involved in promoting Army sport and Army athletes, and encouraged units to put sports in the forefront of their recruiting campaigns. One of the most visible results of this emphasis was the central place occupied by sports in period recruiting posters, the most famous example of which is the 1919 poster with the slogan "The Army Isn't ALL Work," painted by Graham Simmons.[16] Another of the areas on which the Board started work almost immediately was Kentish's pre-war project of providing grounds at Army posts all over the Empire. In 1919 Kentish was asked by the Board to return to his project, recover ground lost during the war, and bring it to completion. He

---

[12]   Attendance Book of ASCB meetings, first entry dated December 2, 1918, ASCB files. See also Captain F.J. Starr, "War History of the British Army Gymnastic Staff," (first draft) unpublished manuscript, Army Physical Training Corps Museum File #1664, pp. 31–33, and "War Diary of Physical and Bayonet Training Staff," entries dated November 3, 1918–February 6, 1919, WO 95/55, National Archives.

[13]   Minutes of ASCB meetings November–December 1918, ASCB files.

[14]   Letter from Army Council to Field Marshal Haig, December 1918, ASCB files.

[15]   Lieutenant Colonel E.A.L. Oldfield, *History of the Army Physical Training Corps* (Aldershot: Gale & Polden Ltd., 1955), chapters 3, 4.

[16]   This poster is reproduced at the front of the book.

accepted the task, and between 1919 and his retirement from the Army he was in charge of overseeing this project world wide for the Board.[17]

Among other things he accomplished during this time, Kentish worked to upgrade the Aldershot Athletic Grounds first built under the supervision of Colonel Fox in the 1890s. He eventually had a large grandstand constructed and a modern cinder track installed. Kentish's project, along with his other work in support of Army sport, gave him notoriety throughout the Army and beyond. After he was satisfied that British soldiers were adequately supplied with playing fields, he retired from the Army in 1925 to found the National Playing Fields Association to build fields for underprivileged civilians throughout Britain. His work in support of British games and sport, and as one of the first members of the Army Sport Control Board, won him a position on the British Olympic Committee that he held until old age in the 1930s. He is remembered in the Army with a plaque at the current Aldershot Stadium.[18]

Ronald Bruce Campbell, who spent most of his adult life working for soldier fitness, similarly went on to work for the promotion of athletics and fitness for all Britons. He was promoted to Colonel in late 1918, and was instrumental in organizing the Inter-Allied Games of 1919. Also in that year, Campbell produced a scheme that anticipated imposition of standardized fitness instruction throughout Britain, civilian and military. He advocated one unified system of training using the same words of command, and with the same exercises used throughout. He also advocated that a national central school of physical training be formed, with instructors from the services, and military and civilian instructors from Britain and the Dominions attending.[19] Many of these ideas were ultimately adopted in 1936, when the Board of Education terminology and construction of physical training tables were included in the Army's Manual of Physical Training.[20]

Campbell competed in fencing on the 1920 British Olympic Team, and under his tutelage the British Olympic Modern Pentathlon team began training at the School of Physical Training in Aldershot. Campbell continued to serve as Inspector of Gymnasia until his retirement in 1923, and then went on to a distinguished career at the University of Edinburgh where he taught

---

[17]　　See Basil Kentish, *This Foul Thing Called War: The Life of Brigadier-General R.S. Kentish, CMG, DSO (1876–1956)* (Sussex: The Book Guild, 1997). Kentish regularly attended ASCB Executive Committee meetings until his retirement in 1925—see Attendance Book of ASCB meetings, ASCB files.

[18]　　Kentish, *This Foul Thing Called War*, and unpublished memoir, Kentish papers, Imperial War Museum Archives.

[19]　　Oldfield, *History of the Army Physical Training Corps*, p. 45.

[20]　　Ibid., p. 59.

physical education and remained an influential force in Britain's amateur and international sporting world.[21] Campbell and Kentish are just two of the many former members of the Army's sporting and Physical Training Staff and Corps alumni who have gone on after their time in the military to make names for themselves in the civilian sports establishments.

The action of July 1, 1916, when the 8th Battalion, East Surrey Regiment "kicked off" their attack by booting footballs into "No Man's Land," can be seen in a number of different lights. Many would see that act as a risible gesture that points out the unprofessional and archaic state of Britain's Army, and most especially the backward state of a leadership climate and culture that would foster such behavior. There is, however, another way to view the Surreys' gesture. There can be no doubt that the soldiers who followed those balls into the killing fields were probably naïve about what lay ahead, but they were also well trained, and well aware that many of them would not make it across that space between the trenches. It is highly possible that the symbolic act of following footballs "over the top" has less to do with naiveté, and more to do with defying the horror they faced and maintaining their unit pride, optimism, and morale in the face of imminent death. Soldiers throughout history have made gestures, carried talismans, and acted in ways that help them to face the cruel realities of battle by recalling home, or some aspect of unit history and tradition that maintains their will to fight on.

Soldiers have fought to the death to protect their unit colors, a simple symbol of unit pride and history, and although these flags are no longer carried into battle, they are still treated by most armies as an item of reverence and respect. The British Foot Guards still have the bearskins they were given permission to wear in honor of their defeat of Napoleon's Old Guard at Waterloo. The US Army's Third Infantry Division takes enormous pride in its designation as the "Marne Division," a recognition of its heroic last-ditch defense of that river line in 1918, and the fierce attachment of US Army Rangers to their motto of "Rangers Lead The Way!" recalls their against-all-odds assault up the cliffs at Omaha Beach on June 6, 1944.[22] It is certainly within the realm of possibility,

---

[21] John G. Gray, *Prophet in Plimsoles: An Account of the Life of Colonel Ronald B. Campbell* (Edinburgh: Edina Press, 1977), pp. 38–44, chapter 4.

[22] This motto comes from the following incident: when the 29th Infantry Division's attack off Omaha Beach was stalled and soldiers were pinned down and being cut up at the shore line, the Division Commander, Major General Norman Cota, began to personally piece together an assault force from the disorganized troops on the beach, to break through the beach exits around Vierville. He had in his division's sector several companies of Rangers from the 5th and 2nd Battalions, and when his ad hoc assault force was ready he gave the order to advance, saying, "Rangers, Lead the Way!"

then, that when the Surreys followed footballs into the Somme Offensive, they might have been following symbols of their own unit pride, their own attachment to symbols of home, and what it meant to be a British Soldier. If a motto or a stand of regimental colors can define a unit's sense of itself, is it so far-fetched that another, perhaps more mundane symbol could do the same?

It would certainly be fitting for British soldiers in 1916 to feel that a defiant symbol of Britishness and military *esprit de corps* should be a symbol of something that was so viscerally important to the culture of the British Army— sport. It is also fitting that soldiers would follow into battle a symbol of their fitness training that was so instrumental in transforming them from raw civilian volunteers and conscripts into fit, disciplined fighting men. From 1860 to the First World War, the British Army's physical culture, as defined by its games and PT, was important enough to the lives of its soldiers that it did, in fact, act as a broadly unifying and homogenizing force, and one that did represent for many in the Commonwealth armies all that was best about Britain, and the British Dominions. Just as surely as British soldiers carried their flags and other symbols into battle all over the Empire, they carried their games and gymnastic training as well, and used them to make their surroundings more like home and their subjects more like themselves.

British Army physical culture was a central part of the transformation of that organization between the Crimean and First World Wars. It acted as a significant bridge between the Army and its parent society, over which flowed ideas and values in both directions. It also acted as an important way for soldiers and their leaders to set themselves apart, both from their civilian counterparts in Army sport's continued adherence to the amateur ideal, and from their adversaries in the fundamental Britishness the Army's games implied. British Army physical culture was, and still is, one of the defining characteristics of that organization. Only by appreciating this crucial part of the British Army's history, from its beginnings in the Victorian period to its achievement of fully modern status after the Great War, can one truly understand the vital role Britain's soldiers played in the shaping of both their country's past and the future of much of the rest of the world.

Select Bibliography

Unpublished Sources

Army Physical Training Corps Museum

File #1664

Army Sport Control Board

The Board's historical files are uncatalogued, and unorganized. See footnotes for specific documents referenced.

British Library

Annual Reports of Inspector General of Gymnasia in India 1903–1916, *India Office Records (IOR)* (L/MIL/7/17086)

Imperial War Museum

War Diary of Sergeant Major H.A. Bangert, RAMC (97/26/1)
War letters of Major the Honorable R.E.S. Barrington (PP/MCR/55)
War Memoirs of R.W. Brierley (P191)
Papers of Field Marshal Sir John French (75/46/13)
Papers of Brigadier General Reginald Kentish
Papers of General Sir Ivor Maxse
Diary of Major T.D. McCarthy (92/3/1)
Diary of Major General Sir Cecil Lothian Nicholson KCB CMG (01/14/1)
Letters of F.G. Senyard MM (98/28/1)
Diary of J.W. Whatley (96/48/1)

The National Archives (UK)

WO 279/553: Memorandum on Army Training, During the Individual Training Period 1912–1913
WO 105/45: Papers of Lord Roberts of Kandahar

WO 33/14: Report of the Committee on Gymnastic Training for the Army 1864

WO 33/14: Report on Gymnastic Instruction in the French and Prussian Armies, August 1859

WO 279/48: Report on Physical Capacity of Territorial Forces Troops to Carry out the Work and Endure the Hardships which were Incidental to the Maneuvers of 1910

WO 32/4027: War Diaries of Commandant, Étaples 1917–1919

WO 95/1068: War Diary of the Army Gymnastic Staff, 1918–1919: Canadian Corps

WO 95/55: War Diary of Physical and Bayonet Training Staff

WO 32/5492

WO 32/5493

WO 32/7047, 1903

National Army Museum (UK) Archives

Army Hockey Association: Laws and Rules, Season 1931/32 (Class: 355.545 "1932" acc. #32985)

Cricket, 1900–1920 (acc. #7404-44-2 to 4)

Diary of Corporal Ralph Clark 4th (Territorial Army) Battalion, The Lincolnshire Regiment, July 27, 1914–July 27, 1915 (acc. #7606-45)

Gamebooks, Hodson's Horse (1865–1947)

Hart's Army List, 1869

Hill, Colonel G.V.W. Fifty Years of Sport in the Royal Irish Fusiliers (acc. #7707-45)

Indian Cavalry Polo Tournament Nominees and Runners-Up (1883–1939) (acc. #6112/305)

Polo Rules of the 7th Hussars (acc. #7104-63-1)

Program of Gymnastic Display and Concert (acc. #8010-38)

Regimental Polo Books (1st Battalion, The Suffolk Regiment, 1883–1931) (Suffolk Regiment Museum)

Regimental Polo Books (9th Lancers, 1883–1950) (Home Headquarters, 9th/12th Lancers, Leicester)

Special Tables, Physical Training 1916 (Class. 355.545 acc. #27161)

Supplementary Tables, Physical Training 1916, reprinted with amendments, March, 1917 and Games, Issued by the General Staff, 1917 (Class. 355.545)

Table Card of Exercises (Army Gymnastic Staff, 1907) (Class. 355.545 "1907" acc. #L/63/2601)

The Hunting Diary of General Sir Alexander Wardrop (acc. #6404-81)

Unpublished Manuscripts

Nash, Sylvia. "The History of the Army Rugby Union."

Published Primary Sources

Professional and Regimental/Unit Journals and Magazines:

Aldershot News and Military Gazette
Brigade of Guards Magazine
Mind, Body and Spirit: The Annual Journal of the Royal Army Physical Training Corps
Journal of the United Services Institution of India
National Defense
St. George's Gazette, Journal of the Northumberland Fusiliers
The Black Horse Gazette, Journal of the 7th (Princess Royal's) Dragoon Guards
The Cavalry Journal
The Green Howards Gazette
The Highland Light Infantry Chronicle
The Household Brigade Magazine
The Infantry Journal (US)
The Journal of the Household Brigade
The Journal of the Military Service Institution of the United States
The Journal of the Royal United Services Institution
The Light Bob Gazette
The Star and Crescent, A Quarterly Record of Sport and Soldiering in the 17th Cavalry
The Thin Red Line, Journal of The Argyll and Sutherland Highlanders
The Thistle, Journal of the First Regiment of Foot, The Royal Scots
The United Services Magazine
The XI Hussar Journal

Contemporary Newspapers and Periodicals

Blackwoods Magazine
The Illustrated London News
The London Times
The Nineteenth Century (and Beyond)

Contemporary Journal and Newspaper Articles

"A.L.B." "Reflection on the Training of British and Indian Troops," *Journal of the United Services Institution of India* Vol. 39 No. 178 (1910), pp. 129–130.

"A Staff Corps Captain." "Modern Military Training," *The United Services Magazine* Vol. 23 (1901), pp. 404–407.

Adams, A. Leith (Surgeon-Major, London Recruiting District). "The Recruiting Question, Considered from a Military and a Medical Point of View," *The Journal of the Royal United Services Institution* (1874), pp. 55–98.

"Anonymous." "Battalion Command," *The Journal of the Royal United Services Institution* Vol. 35 No. 163 (September 1891), p. 478.

Brunton, Sir Lander. "Physical Education and Training in Relation to National Defense," *National Defense* Vols. 1–2 (1908), pp. 503–511.

Bullard, Major R.L. and Hawkins, Captain H.S. "Athletics in the Army," *The Journal of the Military Service Institution of the United States* Vol. 37 (1905), pp. 399–409.

Burton, Major R.G. "Shikar as Training for Scouts," *Journal of the United Services Institution of India* Vol. 28 No. 134 (1899), pp. 88–90.

—. "Some Ideas on the Training of an Officer," *The United Services Magazine* Vol. 25 (new series) (1902), pp. 637–642.

—. "The Image of War," *Journal of the United Services Institution of India* Vol. 37 No. 171 (1908), p. 221.

—. "The Strategy and Tactics of Tiger Hunting," *The United Services Magazine* Vol. 28 (new series) (1903–1904), p. 402.

Butts, Lieutenant E.L. "Physical Training of the American Soldier," *The Journal of the Military Service Institution of the United States* Vol. 16 (1895), pp. 499–512.

"Chancton." "The Gymnastic Training of Recruits in the British Army," *The United Services Magazine* Vol. 29 (1904), pp. 66–71.

Chapman, C.R., Major-General C.F. "Citizen Soldiers of the First Class Army Reserve," *The United Services Magazine* Vol. 2 (1890–1891), p. 570.

Dalzell, Major the Honorable A.E. "Special Lecture Transcript," *Journal of the United Services Institution of India* Vol. 22 No. 107 (1893), pp. 362–385.

Donworth, Lieutenant A.B. "Gymnasium Training in the Army," *The Journal of the Military Service Institution of the United States* Vol. 21 (1897), pp. 508–515.

Esher, Viscount. "A Problem in Military Education," *The United Services Magazine* Vol. 34 (1907–1908), p. 484.

"Ex-Non-Com." "The Soldier in Relation to Regimental Sport," *The United Services Magazine* Vol. XL (1909–1910), pp. 32–36.

Ferguson, R. Munro. "Physical Training and Drill in Relation to Compulsory Continuation Classes," *National Defense* Vols. 1–2 (1908), pp. 511–520.

Fox, Colonel Sir Malcolm. "Army and Navy Boxing," *Household Brigade Magazine*, May 1913, pp. 111–112.

"G.A.T. [Major G.A. Trent, Indian Army Inspector of Physical Training]," "Physical Training of the Infantry Soldier in India," *Journal of the United Services Institution of India* Vol. 38 No. 174 (1909), pp. 201–211.

Hardy, Reverend E. "Recreation Workshops for Soldiers," *The United Services Magazine* Vol. 4 (new series [no date]), pp. 368–373.

—. "Tommy Atkins at Play," *The United Services Magazine* Vol. 12 (1895–1896), p. 522.

Hargreaves, Reginald. "Divertissement," *The Cavalry Journal* Vol. 31 (Jan–Nov 1941), pp. 204–225.

Hatchell, Colonel G. "The Training of Our Recruits," *The Journal of the Royal United Services Institution* Vol. 35 No. 163 (September 1891), pp. 958–61.

Hennell, Captain R. "Soldiers' Institutes for the Native Army of India," *Journal of the United Services Institution of India* Vol. 5 (1876), pp. 69–78.

Hovell, Lieutenant Colonel H. de B. "Physical Training in the Army and Navy: Why the Systems Fail in their Object," *The United Services Magazine* Vol. XLVII (1913), pp. 79–83.

Illustrated London News, March 18, 1868, pp. 266–267.

Inscombe, Major H.P.R. "The Australian Commonwealth Forces," *Journal of the United Services Institution of India* Vol. 38 No. 170 (1908), p. 66.

James, Captain W.B. "The Practical Training of British and Native Troops with Reference to the Lessons of the War in South Africa," *Journal of the United Services Institution of India* Vol. 30 No. 144 (1901), pp. 186–212.

Kentish, Brigadier-General Reginald. Letter to the Editor, *Aldershot News and Military Gazette* (February 23, 1945) [no page numbers].

Laing, Captain F.C. "Physical Training in the Native Army," *Journal of the United Services Institution of India* Vol. 29 No. 140 (July 1900) [no page numbers].

—. "The Encouragement of Fencing," *Journal of the United Services Institution of India* Vol. 26 No. 127 (1897), pp. 137–139.

Legge, Captain R.F. "Some Ideas on the Military Education of the Officer," *The United Services Magazine* Vol. 33 (1906), pp. 415–420.

"Linesman." "The British Soldier," *The Journal of the Military Service Institution of the United States* Vol. 26 (1900), pp. 68–80.

Lyons, Joseph. "Sports and the Territorials: How to Popularize the Force," *National Defense* Vol. 3 No. 10 (August 1909), pp. 137–139.

Maguire, Captain C.M. "Organization and Employment in War of Native Cavalry," *Journal of the United Services Institution of India* Vol. 14 No. 81 (1890), p. 241.

Masters, Captain A. "Organization and Employment in War of Native Cavalry," *Journal of the United Services Institution of India* Vol. 14 No. 81 (1890), p. 273.

Mayne, Major C.B. "The Training of Infantry for the Attack," *The United Services Magazine* Vol. 20 (1899–1900), p. 278.

Norman, Lieutenant W.W. "Organization and Employment in War of Native Cavalry," *Journal of the United Services Institution of India* Vol. 14 No. 81 (1890), p. 299.

Pilcher, Captain James E. "The Place of Physical Training in the Military Service," *The Journal of the Military Service Institution of the United States* Vol. 16 (1895), pp. 295–303.

Ranken, Lieutenant Colonel G.P. "The Practical Training of British and Native Troops with Reference to the Lessons of the War in South Africa," *Journal of the United Services Institution of India* Vol. 30 No. 144 (1901), pp. 153–180.

Raper, Colonel A.G. "Notes on Organization and Training by a Regimental Officer," *The Journal of the Royal United Services Institution* Vol. 36 No. 167 (January 1892), p. 12.

"Regulations For Military Gymnasia," *London Times* (May 11, 1865) [no page numbers].

Richardson, Major A.J. "That Idol – Education," *The United Services Magazine* Vol. 31 (1905), p. 545.

Robinson, Major-General C.W. "Some Ideas Upon the Training of an Officer," *The United Services Magazine* Vol. 25 (1902) [no page numbers].

Sandow, Eugene. "Physical Exercise in the Services," *National Defense* Vol. 4 (1910), pp. 295–297.

Taylor, Lieutenant G.A. "Soccer Football for the Army," *The Journal of the Military Service Institution of the United States* Vol. 45 (1909), pp. 158–160.

Taylor, Major J.R.M. "Scheme of Training New British Armies, 1911," *Infantry Journal* (US) Vol. XI No. 5 (Mar.–Apr. 1915), pp. 704–715.

Thomson, A.G. "Hockey with Rajputs," *The United Services Magazine* Vol. 17 (1898), pp. 556–558.

Walton, Captain W.C. "The Practical Training of British and Native Troops with Reference to the Lessons of the War in South Africa," *Journal of the United Services Institution of India* Vol. 30 No. 144 (1901), pp. 261–295.

Whittall, Major F.V. "The Training of the Native Infantry Recruit," *Journal of the United Services Institution of India* Vol. 32 No. 152 (1903), pp. 267–271.

Will, Surgeon-Captain J. "The Recruit and his Physical Training," *The United Services Magazine* Vol. 17 (1898), pp. 628–651.

Wood, Lieutenant Colonel Evelyn. "Mounted Riflemen," *The Journal of the Royal United Services Institution* Vol. XVIII No. LXXIX (March 4, 1874), p. 17.

Woodhull, Lieutenant Colonel A.A. "Recruiting and Physical Training in the British Army," *The Journal of the Military Service Institution of the United States* Vol. 16 (1895), pp. 37–47.

Woodyat, Major Nigel. "Notes on Hill Training," *Journal of the United Services Institution of India* Vol. 36 No. 166 (1907), pp. 155–157.

British Library

Atkins, John B. *National Physical Training: An Open Debate* (acc. #7404.d.21).

Gordon, Sergeant Major William. *Physical Training Without Arms* (1890), with translations into Urdu and Nagri (shelfmark 8830.a70).

"'The physical training of the recruit and drilled soldier,' with practical illustrations by squads, by Lieutenant Colonel G.M. Fox … on Tuesday, December 15, 1891, in the Prince Consort's and Military Society's Library, South Camp" (Aldershot: Gale and Polden, 1891), lecture #36 (shelfmark C.193.a.257[36]).

Government Publications

Australia
Official History of Australia in the War of 1914–1918, Vol. XII, Photographic Record of the War (Sydney: Angus & Robertson Ltd., 1923).

Canada
Duguid, Colonel A. Fortescue. *Official History of the Canadian Forces in The Great War 1914–1919, General Series Volume I* (Ottawa: Canadian Ministry of Defense, 1938).

India
Manual of Physical Training for the Indian Army 1918 (Calcutta: Superintendent, Government Printing, India, 1918).

United Kingdom
Army Lists
Army Sport Records, 1880–1939 (published by The Army Sport Control Board, War Office, 1939).

Games and Sports in the Army, 1932–33 (published by The Army Sport Control Board, War Office, 1933).

King's Regulations (1901, 1904, 1908, 1912).

Manual of Physical Training (1908).

Parliamentary Papers, "Report of the Director of Gymnastics, on the Gymnastic Instruction of the Army, for the year 1869," 1869–1870, pp. 575–581.

Parliamentary Papers, "Report of Royal Commission on Physical Training (Scotland)," Vol. I (1903), Cd. 1507 xxx. 1., p. 10.

Queen's Regulations (1859, 1865, 1873, 1898).

SS 137, *Recreational Training* (first issued 1917, reprints October 1917, May 1918, December 1918).

SS 143, *The Training and Employment of Platoons* (issued by the General Staff, 1918).

SS 152, *Instructions for the Training of the British Armies in France*.

United States

Army Field Manual 21–150, *Combatives*.

Contemporary Books and Memoirs

Arnold-Forster, Hon. H.O. *The Army in 1906: A Policy and a Vindication* (New York: E.P. Dutton & Co., 1906).

Baden Powell, Lieutenant General Lord R.S.S. *Aids to Scouting to NCOs and Men (Reprint of the Original Edition of 1899)* (Houston, TX: The Journal of Scouting History, 1994).

—. *Indian Memories* (London: Herbert Jenkins Ltd., 1915).

—. *Pigsticking or Hog Hunting* (London: Jenkins, 1924).

—. *Scouting for Boys, Part IV* (London: Horace Cox, 1908).

—. *Sport In War* (Toronto: George Morang & Co., 1900).

Bradley, Alfred. *Physical Training for Boy Scouts* (Glasgow: J. Brown & Son, 1916).

Brodribb, Thomas. *Military Training for our Schoolboys* (Melbourne: [n.p.], 1909).

Churchill, Sir Winston S. *A Roving Commission: My Early Life* (New York: Charles Scribner's Sons, 1930).

—. *The Boer War: London to Ladysmith via Pretoria, Ian Hamilton's March* (New York: Dorset Press, 1991).

French, Field Marshal Viscount. *1914* (London: Constable & Co. Ltd., 1919).

Godley, General Sir Alexander. *Life of an Irish Soldier* (New York: E.P. Dutton & Co., 1939).

Graves, Robert. *Goodbye to All That* (Garden City, NY: Doubleday & Co., 1957).

Kipling, Rudyard. *The Barrack-Room Ballads* (Munslow: Hearthstone Publications, 1995).

Liddell Hart, Captain Basil H. *The Real War 1914–1918* (Boston: Little, Brown & Co., 1930).

Roberts, Lieutenant Colonel F.J. and Pearson, Major J.H., eds. *The Wipers Times* (London: Eveleigh, Nash & Grayson, Ltd., 1930).

Robertson, Colonel J.P. *Personal Adventures and Anecdotes of an Old Officer* (London: Edward Arnold, 1906).

Sassoon, Siegfried. *Collected Poems* (New York: Viking Press, 1949).

—. *Memoirs of an Infantry Officer* (London: Faber & Faber, 1930).

Vaughn, Edwin Campion. *Some Desperate Glory: The World War One Diary of a British Officer* (New York: Touchstone, 1981).

Wardrop, General Sir Alexander. *Modern Pigsticking* (London: Macmillan, 1914).

Secondary Sources

Radio/Films

"A Bridge Too Far" (Joseph E. Levine Productions, 1977).

Simon, Scott. "Soccer in Afghanistan," *National Public Radio Weekend Edition Saturday*, March 2, 2002.

Online Sources

Army. "Sport." At: http://www.army.mod.uk/events/sport/default.aspx (accessed: May 18, 2012).

Bangladesh Army. At: http://www.army.mil.bd/node/81 (accessed: May 18, 2012).

BBC. "Army targets recruits with contact sport," November 25, 2007. At: http://news.bbc.co.uk/2/hi/7110012.stm (accessed: May 18, 2012).

Indian Army. "Army Institute of Physical Training." At: http://indianarmy.nic. in/Site/FormTemplete/frmTempSimple.aspx?MnId=186vVOHbgS1sAcy gzDuO4w==&ParentID=6zS1jQNgsFAAoUM6utUurg==&flag=Y0UY NTCHdHYbdCZT4Hjveg== (accessed: June 10, 2012).

Pakistan Army. "Army School of Physical Training." At: http://www.pakistanarmy. gov.pk/AWPReview/TextContent.aspx?pId=286&rnd=490 (accessed: May 18, 2012).

Sri Lanka Army. "Sports." At: http://www.army.lk/sports.php (accessed: May 18. 2012).

UK Royal Army Physical Training Corps. At: http://www.army.mod.uk/aptc/default.aspx (accessed: June 10, 2012).

Journal Articles

Birley, Derek. "Sportsmen and the Deadly Game," *British Journal of Sports History* Vol. 3 No. 3 (December 1986), pp. 289–310.

Bond, Brian. "The Late Victorian Army," *History Today* Vol. II No. 9 (September 1961), pp. 616–624.

Phillips, Murray G. "Sport, War, and Gender Images: The Australian Sportsmen's Battalions and the First World War," *The International Journal of the History of Sport* Vol. 14 No. 1 (April 1997), pp. 78–96.

Books

Akiyama, Yuriko. *Feeding the Nation: Nutrition and Health in Britain before World War One* (London: Taurus Academic Studies, 2008).

Allen, Charles. *Plain Tales from the Raj* (London: Abacus, 1994).

Axtell, James. *The European and the Indian* (Oxford: Oxford University Press, 1982).

Baker, William and Mangan, J.A., eds. *Sport in Africa* (New York and London: Africana Publishing Co., 1987).

Barnett, Corelli. *The Swordbearers* (Bloomington, IN: University of Indiana Press, 1963).

Beckett, Ian F.W. *The Victorians at War* (London: Hambledon and London, 2003).

Birley, Sir Derek. *Land of Sport and Glory: Sport and British Society 1887–1910* (Manchester: Manchester University Press, 1995).

Blake, Robert, ed. *The Private Papers of Douglas Haig, 1914–1919* (London: Eyre & Spottiswoode, 1952).

Bond, Brian. *The Victorian Army and the Staff College 1854–1914* (London: Eyre Methuen, 1972).

Brown, Malcolm. *Tommy Goes to War* (London: J.M. Dent & Sons Ltd., 1978).

Dawson, Lionel. *Sport In War* (London: Collins, 1936).

Eksteins, Modris. *Rites of Spring: The Great War and the Birth of the Modern Age* (New York: Anchor Books, 1989).

Elliot, Major General J.G. *Field Sports in India 1800–1947* (London: Gentry Books, 1973).

Farrar-Hockley, Anthony. *The Death of an Army* (New York: Wm. Morrow & Co., 1968).

Farwell, Byron. *Armies of the Raj from the Great Indian Mutiny to Independence: 1858–1947* (New York: W.W. Norton & Co., 1989).

—. *Eminent Victorian Soldiers* (New York: W.W. Norton & Co., 1985).

—. *Mr. Kipling's Army* (New York: W.W. Norton & Co., 1981).

—. *Queen Victoria's Little Wars* (New York: W.W. Norton & Co., 1972).

Fuller, J.G. *Troop Morale and Popular Culture in the British and Dominion Armies 1914–1918* (Oxford: Clarendon Press, 1990).

Furgesson, Sir James. *The Curragh Incident* (London: Faber & Faber, 1964).

Fussell, Paul. *The Great War and Modern Memory* (New York: Oxford University Press, 1975).

Gat, Azar. *The Development of Military Thought: The Nineteenth Century* (Oxford: Clarendon Press, 1992).

Gill, Douglas and Dallas, Gloden. *The Unknown Army* (London: Thetford Press, 1985).

Gray, John G. *Prophet in Plimsoles: An Account of the Life of Colonel Ronald B. Campbell* (Edinburgh: Edina Press, 1977).

Green, Geoffrey. *The Official History of the F.A. Cup* (London: The Naldrett Press, 1949).

Guttmann, Allen. *From Ritual to Record: The Nature of Modern Sport* (New York: Columbia University Press, 1978).

—. *Games and Empires: Modern Sports and Cultural Imperialism* (New York: Columbia University Press, 1994).

Hargreaves, Reginald. *The Enemy at the Gate* (London: Macdonald & Co. Ltd. [no date]).

Harries-Jenkins, Gwyn. *The Army in Victorian Society* (London: Routledge and Kegan Paul, 1977).

Heathcote, T.A. *The Military in British India: The Development of British Land Forces in South Asia, 1600–1947* (Manchester: Manchester University Press, 1995).

Henderson, Diana. *Highland Soldier: A Social Study of the Highland Regiments 1820–1920* (Edinburgh: John Donald Publishers Ltd., 1989).

Holmes, Richard. *Sahib: The British Soldier in India 1750–1914* (London: Harper Press, 2005).

Hurley, Elspeth. *Florence Nightingale* (New York: G.P. Putnam's Sons, 1975).

Jeal, Tim. *The Boy-Man: The Life of Lord Baden-Powell* (New York: Wm. Morrow & Co., 1990).

Keegan, John. *A History of Warfare* (New York: Vintage Books, 1993).

—. *Opening Moves: August, 1914* (New York: Ballantine Books, 1971).

Keith, Jeffrey. *The British Army and the Crisis of Empire 1918–1922* (Manchester: Manchester University Press, 1984).

Kentish, Basil. *This Foul Thing Called War: The Life of Brigadier-General Reginald Kentish, CMG, DSO (1876–1956)* (Sussex: The Book Guild, 1997).

Killingray, David and Omissi, David, eds. *Guardians of Empire, The Armed Forces of the Colonial Powers c. 1700–1964* (Manchester: Manchester University Press, 1999).

Laffaye, Horatio A. in *The Encyclopedia of World Sport*, 3 vols., ed. David Levinson and Karen Christensen (Santa Barbara, CA: ABC-CLIO, 1996), II.

Livesey, Anthony. *Great Battles of World War I* (London: Marshall Editions Ltd., 1989).

Lomas, David. *Mons 1914: The BEF's Tactical Triumph* (London: Osprey, 1997).

Luvaas, Jay. *The Education of an Army: British Military Thought, 1815–1940* (Chicago, IL: University of Chicago Press, 1964).

Lynch, John William. *Princess Patricia's Canadian Light Infantry, 1917–1919* (Hicksville, NY: Expedition Press, 1976).

Macdonald, Lyn. *1914* (New York: Atheneum, 1988).

—. *1915: The Death of Innocence* (Baltimore, MD: Johns Hopkins University Press, 1993).

—. *Somme* (New York: Atheneum, 1989).

—. *They Called It Passchendaele* (London: Joseph, 1978).

—. *To the Last Man: Spring 1918* (New York: Carroll & Graf, 1999).

Magnus, Philip. *Kitchener: Portrait of an Imperialist* (New York: E.P. Dutton & Co., 1959).

Mangan, J.A. *Athleticism in the Victorian and Edwardian Public School* (Cambridge: Cambridge University Press, 1981).

—. *The Games Ethic and Imperialism* (New York: Viking, 1986).

—, ed. *The Cultural Bond: Sport, Empire, Society* (London: Frank Cass, 1991).

Marston, Daniel P. and Sundaram, Chandar S., eds., *A Military History of India and South Asia, from the East India Company to the Nuclear Era* (Bloomington, IN: Indiana University Press, 2007).

Mason, Tony and Riedi, Eliza. *Sport and the Military: The British Armed Forces 1880–1960* (Cambridge: Cambridge University Press, 2010).

McCulloch, Ian M. *Sons of the Mountains: The Highland Regiments in the French and Indian War, 1756–1767* (Fort Ticonderoga, NY: Purple Mountain Press, 2006).

Messenger, Charles. *Call-to-Arms: The British Army 1914–1918* (London: Cassell, 2005).

Mollo, Boris. *The British Army from Old Photographs* (London: J.M. Dent & Sons Ltd., 1975).

Mortimer, Gavin. *Fields of Glory: The Extraordinary Lives of 16 Warrior Sportsmen* (London: André Deutsch, 2001).

Oldfield, Lieutenant Colonel E.A.L. *History of the Army Physical Training Corps* (Aldershot: Gale and Polden Ltd., 1955).

Omissi, David. *The Sepoy and the Raj: The Indian Army, 1860–1940* (London: Macmillan, 1994).

Parker, Eric. *The History of Cricket* (London: Seely Service & Co. Ltd., 1950).

Paschall, Rod. *The Defeat of Imperial Germany 1917–1918* (Chapel Hill, NC: Algonquin Books, 1989).

Ramsay-Skelly, Alan. *The Victorian Army at Home: The Recruitment and Terms and Conditions of the British Regular 1859–1899* (London: Croom Helm, 1977).

Raugh, Harold E., ed. *The British Army 1815–1914* (Aldershot: Ashgate, 2006).

Simkins, Peter. *Kitchener's Army: The Raising of the New Armies, 1914–1916* (Manchester: Manchester University Press, 1988).

Slim, Field Marshal the Viscount. *Defeat into Victory* (London: Cassell & Co., Ltd., 1956).

Smith, F.B. *Florence Nightingale: Reputation and Power* (New York: St. Martin's Press, 1982).

Spiers, Edward. *Haldane: An Army Reformer* (Edinburgh: Edinburgh University Press, 1980).

—. *The Army and Society 1815–1914* (London: Longman Group Ltd., 1980).

—. *The Late Victorian Army* (Manchester: Manchester University Press, 1992).

—. *The Victorian Soldier in Africa* (Manchester: Manchester University Press, 2004).

Strachan, Hew. *European Armies and the Conduct of War* (London: George Allen and Unwin, 1983).

—. *From Waterloo to Balaclava: Tactics, Technology, and the British Army, 1815–1854* (Cambridge: Cambridge University Press, 1985).

Strachey, Lytton. *Eminent Victorians* (New York: Harcourt, Brace and Co., 1918).

Streets, Heather. *Martial Races: The Military, Race and Masculinity in British Imperial Culture, 1857–1914* (Manchester: Manchester University Press, 2004).

Sweetman, John. *War and Administration: The Significance of the Crimean War for the British Army* (Edinburgh: Scottish Academic Press, 1984).

Terraine, John. *Mons, the Retreat to Victory* (London: B.T. Batsford Ltd., 1960).

Thomas, Hugh. *The Story of Sandhurst* (London: Hutchinson & Co., 1961).

Thompson, F.M.L. *English Landed Society in the Nineteenth Century* (London: Routledge and Kegan Paul, 1963).

Tuchman, Barbara W. *The Guns of August* (New York: The Macmillan Co., 1962).

Walvin, James. *The People's Game* (London: Penguin Books Ltd., 1975).

Warner, Phillip. *Army Life in the '90's* (London: Hemlyn Publishing Group Ltd. [Country Life Books], 1975).

Weintraub, Stanley. *Silent Night: The Story of the World War I Christmas Truce* (New York: Penguin Putnam Inc., 2001).

Welch, M.D. *Science and the British Officer: The Early Days of the Royal United Army Services Institute for Defense Studies (1829–1869)* (London: The Royal United Services Institute for Defense Studies, 1998).

Yong, Tan Tai. *The Garrison State: The Military, Government and Society in Colonial Punjab, 1849–1947* (New Delhi: Sage Publications, 2005).

Young, Percy. *A History of British Football* (London: Stanley Paul & Co. Ltd., 1968).

Index

Abu Clea, Battle of 19
Adjutant General, British Army 186,
    194–195
Afghan War 42–43
Afghanistan 43–80
Africa
    hunting, sport 10–13, 60–61, 63,
        70–73, 77–81, 121–122, 193–194
Aldershot 15, 21, 28, 34–39, 44, 54–63,
    74, 93, 105–106, 114, 116, 118,
    120–122, 132–134, 147–150, 158,
    161, 177, 186, 194
Aldershot Athletic Grounds 202
Allenby, General Sir Edmund 160, 162
Amateur Athletic Association 5, 37, 42–43
amateurism 37, 41, 65, 182, 185, 190, 193,
    195, 202; see also athleticism, games
    ethic
American Expeditionary Force
    relation to British Army 172
    training 172
Army Athletic Association 120, 122, 197
    formation 118, 120, 122, 195, 197
Army Boxing Association, championships
    74, 195
Army Council 62, 114, 116, 118, 120–123,
    131, 193–199
Army Football Association 71, 113, 116,
    122, 195, 197
Army Medical Corps 25, 56, 177
Army Sanitary Commission 24–26; see also
    barracks, Florence Nightingale,
    reform
Army School of Physical Training 57, 194

Army Sport Control Board 66, 74,
    112–113, 117, 123, 159, 171, 191,
    193–198, 200
army temperance movement 28–29
artillery 40, 42, 48, 87, 94, 104, 108, 133,
    148, 160
assault course 106–107, 146, 162, 165, 169,
    172, 188; see also bayonet training
athleticism 2, 4, 5, 18–20, 31, 41, 44, 80,
    86, 90, 97, 99, 109, 140, 183, 194–
    195, 198–200; see also amateurism,
    games ethic
athletics 17, 37, 43, 51, 63, 67, 70–71, 75,
    77, 83, 94, 112, 117–118, 120,
    122, 151, 154, 171, 177, 185, 187,
    194–195, 200
Australian Army 80, 154–155, 158, 171,
    178

Baden-Powell, Sir Robert 12–13, 16, 18,
    21, 41, 97, 103, 109, 124–125; see
    also Boy Scouts
Bangladesh Army 82
barracks, military see also Army Sanitary
    Commission, Florence Nightingale,
    reform
    construction 24–25, 150
    sanitation 25
bayonet training 43, 55–56, 105, 130, 174
Bengal Army 89
Betts, Major J.L. 105, 133, 172–173, 198
    big game hunting 12–13, 20; see also
        field sports, shikar, shooting,
        shooting expeditions
billiards 67, 113, 118
Boer War 124; see also South African War

Bombay Army 87

boxing 35, 52, 55, 58, 67, 74–76, 117, 120, 154, 167, 172, 176–187, 194–197

Boy Scouts 13, 103,109; *see also* Baden-Powell, Sir Robert

brevets 34, 71–72

Bridges, Sir Thomas 138–140

British Army units

10th Hussars 15

11th Hussars 15, 176–178

14th (King's) Hussars 15, 115

18th Division 151

20th Hussars 52

21st Foot 49

3rd Hussars 14

3rd Imperial Yeomanry 73

46th (North Midland) Divisional Training Battery, Royal Field Artillery 148

4th Dragoon Guards 138–139

4th Hussars 12, 16

7th Dragoon Guards (Princess Royal's) 71, 96, 115, 119

94th Regiment 42

Argyll and Sutherland Highlanders 42, 48, 68, 126

Blues and Royals 75, 149

Brigade of Guards 16, 42, 71, 73–75, 136, 151; *see also* Household Brigade

Buckinghamshire Regiment (14th Foot) 34

Coldstream Guards 40, 43, 70, 125

Durham Light Infantry 164

East Surrey Regiment 1, 201

East Yorkshire Regiment (15th Foot) 9, 12, 154

Essex Regiment 151

Gordon Highlanders 13, 58, 161

Grenadier Guards 40, 72, 75, 183

Highland Brigade 52

Highland Light Infantry 147

Household Brigade 16, 17, 40, 71, 73–75; *see also* Brigade of Guards

Household Cavalry 40

Irish Guards 183

King Edward's Horse 14

Leinster Regiment 21

Lincolnshire Regiment 150, 152

London Irish Rifles 2

Lovat's Scouts 73

Middlesex Regiment 154

North Lancashire Regiment 49

Northumberland Fusiliers 2, 15, 71, 73, 77, 126, 129, 145, 149, 154, 178–180

Northumberland Hussars 14

Nottinghamshire and Derbyshire Regiment (Sherwood Foresters) 10, 137, 179

Paget's Horse 73

Parachute Regiment 55, 125

Rifle Brigade 40, 73, 118

Royal Army Medical Corps 177

Royal Army Physical Training Corps xi, 83, 167

Royal Artillery 40, 42

Royal East Kent Regiment (the Buffs) 42

Royal Engineers 5, 40, 42, 60, 71, 116

Royal Flying Corps 163, 174

Royal Fusiliers 14

Royal Hampshire Regiment 67, 178

Royal Irish Fusiliers 114

Royal Scots 21, 68, 70–71, 73–74

Royal Sussex Regiment 139–140

Royal Tank Corps 174

Scots Guards 73

Scottish Horse (Territorial Army) 148

South Wales Borderers 48

The Black Watch (Royal Highland Regiment) 52, 178

West India Regiment 54

West Yorkshire Regiment 154

York and Lancaster Regiment 105, 179

British Expeditionary Force 1, 2, 104, 126, 128–129, 131, 134, 138–141, 156, 159–165, 173, 176, 185–188, 191, 194–195, 199

British Expeditionary Force Sports Board 171

British Navy 16, 30, 44, 74, 118; *see also* Royal Navy

British Olympic Committee 200

brothels, regimental 30; *see also* Contagious Diseases Acts, prostitution, venereal disease

Burton, Major R.G. 20–21, 97, 99

Calcutta Cup 42

Cambridge, Duke of 16, 28

Campbell, Colonel R.B. 120, 157, 161–168, 172–173, 182–184, 188, 194, 198, 200–201

Campbell, Lieutenant Colonel John 125

Canadian Army 158, 170–171, 187

canteens 30, 75, 122–123; *see also* drinking, drunkenness, morality

Cape Foxhounds 10–11, 13

Cardwell, Sir Edward 26

caste differences *see* "class company" regiments

Caton Woodville, Richard 1

cavalry 15–16, 29, 35, 37, 42, 48, 82, 88–89, 93–96, 104, 138–139, 196–197, 200

Cavan, Earl of 136

Chatham Barracks 28, 35–36

children, in barracks 25

Christmas Truce, 1914 136–138

Churchill, Winston 12, 16

civilian-military relations 104, 109, 111–112, 117, 120, 141, 146–147, 196–197, 200

"class company" regiments 94

Cleather, Lieutenant Colonel W.B.G. 49, 51–52, 56

Colley, Captain T.B. 171

colors, unit 48, 201–202

Commander in Chief 16, 58

Commander in Chief, India 85

commanding officers 11, 21, 27, 34, 37, 50–51, 55, 63, 74, 87–88, 95, 106, 108, 146–147, 151–154, 160–163, 168, 176, 179–180, 182, 184

Committee on the Education and Training of Officers 20

Committee on Gymnastic Instruction for the Army 37

Commonwealth Forces 4, 170–171, 187

Connaught Shield 106–107

Connaught, Duke of 106

conscription 109

Contagious Diseases Acts 30

convalescence camps, PT in 163, 166–167, 173, 183, 186

Couper, Colonel V.A. 118, 120–122, 130, 164, 195

cricket 9, 11–12, 15–16, 19, 40–42, 51, 66–74, 80, 94–96, 115–118, 123–125, 139–140, 178–182

Crimean War 3, 4, 11, 22–27, 34, 43, 107

cross-country running 35, 60, 103, 106, 118, 154, 172, 167, 180, 187

The Curragh 11, 35, 118

Dalzell, Major the Honorable A.E. 89–90

Daniels, Captain H. VC 172

Danish Army, gymnastics 63–105

de Joux, Lieutenant Colonel J.S.W. 194

degeneration, racial/national 102, 111–112

Delany, Captain W. 164

depots, training and replacement 159–160, 162

   Étaples 159, 187, 162

   Le Havre 161

   Rouen 161, 166, 177

regimental 87–88, 131–132, 145, 148, 152, 154
disease 23–28, 30, 114, 116
doctrine, military 2, 82, 104, 128, 141, 159, 171–172, 174, 176, 189
Dormer, Sir James 21
drill 31, 34, 37, 51, 61, 107, 111, 117, 145–146, 148, 171
drill, physical 27, 35, 52, 91, 108
drinking, drunkenness 2, 3, 24, 27–29, 114, 116, 183; see also morality
dumbbells, weight training 38, 52, 68

East India Company 81
East Kent Fox Hounds 17
Edgeworth-Johnstone, Captain Walter 54, 55, 58, 74
education 4, 5, 20, 23, 24, 29, 109, 190, 200
Egypt, sport in 60, 77–78, 172, 180
English Amateur Athletic Association 5, 37, 42–43
enlistment, terms of 27, 29–30
Esher, Viscount 22
esprit de corps 3, 20, 22, 41, 78, 94, 128, 137, 140, 146–147, 190, 194, 202; see also morale
Ewart, Lieutenant General Sir J.S. 121–122

FA Cup 42; see also Football Association
family connections of senior officers 18
fencing 31, 35, 37, 54–56, 105, 124, 130, 174, 200; see swordsmanship
Fenians 29
festival celebrations, Indian 94–95
field hospitals PT in; see convalescence camps
field P.T. 104, 106–107, 155
field sports 10, 11, 15–16, 20, 22, 82, 97, 134–136; see also hunting, shooting, shooting expeditions, fox hunting, shikar, big game hunting
fishing 10–12

Foch, Field Marshal Ferdinand 162
food, soldiers' 25, 139, 141, 145
football 1, 2, 15, 39, 41–43, 51, 61, 65–74, 77–78, 80, 90, 92, 96, 113–117, 119–120, 127, 130, 136–137, 146, 152–155, 166–167, 175, 178–187, 201–202
Football Association 5, 41, 137
footmarching 63, 90, 105; see also route marching, marching drill
Fox Gymnasium 36, 55
fox hunting 10–11, 14, 18, 139–140; see also field sports
    clubs 10–11, 13, 17
Fox Lines 55
Fox, Colonel George Malcolm 52, 54–60, 74–75, 90, 109, 161, 200
French Army 10, 30
    First World War 3, 14, 130, 137, 139, 141, 173, 190
    gymnastics 27, 31, 62
French, Field Marshal Sir John 121–122, 131–132

Gallipoli 148, 178–179
games; see regimental sport, recreational training
game books 13
games ethic 19, 41, 94, 99, 137–138, 191; see also athleticism, muscular Christianity
gender images 86, 155
German Army 14, 49
    First World War 104, 131, 136–138, 140–141, 168, 186–187, 190
    gymnastics 62
Gildea, Major G.F. 44, 49
Godley, General Sir Alexander 12–14
Goodlake, Colonel Alexander 43
Graves, Robert 167
Green Howard Hounds 10
Gurkhas 85, 96, 178

Gymkhana 15, 43, 67, 75, 77, 88, 96, 106, 179–180; *see also* sports days, military tournaments

Haig, Field Marshal Sir Douglas 131, 162, 184, 199
Haldane, Lord Richard 48, 103
Hammersley, Sir Frederick 31, 34–43, 49, 54, 86, 159, 174
Harington, General Sir Charles 198
Havelock, Sir Henry 28
Headquarters Gymnasium, Aldershot 54, 58, 106, 120, 132–134, 150, 174, 186; *see also* Fox Lines
Herbert, Sir Sidney 24
Highland Regiments 26, 85; *see also* British Army units
Hill, Lieutenant Colonel E. Cleary 92–93
hockey 61, 67, 90, 92, 96, 113, 118, 120, 187
horse racing 10, 16, 71, 77, 124, 180, 182
horseback wrestling 82, 84; *see also* silladar cavalry
hospitals 23, 31, 160, 166, 178; *see also* convalescence camps
hunting 10–11, 71, 124; *see also* field sports, fox hunting, hunting, *shikar*, pig sticking, shooting
 in Africa 11, 13
 big game 13
 expeditions 21
 during wartime 11, 13
 in India 12–13
 in Ireland 11
 as training 20–22, 97, 99
hunting estates 10
Hyderabad Contingent 88, 92, 97

identities, gender, racial 4, 84–86, 96–97, 99, 103, 189, 155
Imperial General Staff 118, 160
Imperialism, cultural 79–83, 95

India, sport in 12–13, 15–16, 21, 42, 68, 71, 75; *see also* big game hunting, hunting, pig sticking, *shikar*, shooting
Indian Army units
 12th Bengal Native Infantry 79, 90
 1st Infantry, Hyderabad Contingent 92
 2nd Bengal Lancers 92
 2nd Cavalry, Hyderabad Contingent 88
 2nd Punjab Cavalry 89
 46th Punjab Infantry 91
 4th Bombay Rifles 97
 Central India Horse 88
 Prince of Wales' Own Bengal Lancers 43
Indian Mutiny, military consequences of 82, 84, 85, 87, 92
Inter-Allied Games 75, 200
Iraq; *see* Mesopotamia
Ireland, sport in 10–12, 42–43; *see also* fishing, hunting
Italy 172–173; *see also* Betts, Major J.L.

kabbadi 83
Kabul Stadium, football game 2002 80
Kentish, Brigadier General Sir Reginald 114–117, 120–122, 162, 165–166, 183, 194–195, 199–201
King's African Rifles 81
Kipling, Rudyard 2, 27, 66
Kitchener, Sir Herbert 40, 130–131

lancers 43, 88, 138; *see also uhlans*
libraries, regimental 28–29
Ling System 51–52, 56, 63, 105
linked battalion system 48
literacy 29, 58

Madras Army 21
Mafeking, Siege of 124
Malta 37, 41

manliness 19, 83, 95, 125; *see also* games ethic, gender images
Manual of Physical Training 31, 49, 55, 63, 78, 94, 103–105, 112, 200
Manual of Physical Training, Indian Army 83, 94
marching drill 108; *see also* footmarching, route marching
Marindin, Major Francis, 42, 71
Marne, Battle of the 130, 139, 201
martial race theory 84–85, 99
Maxse, General Sir Ivor 151, 162, 165, 188
May, Sir Edward 11
McLaren, Archibald 31
Memoranda on Army Training 108–109
Mesopotamia 3, 172
mess, officers' 19
military tournaments 5, 16, 39, 43–44, 51, 54, 56, 58, 60, 66–67, 71, 73–77, 88, 96, 118, 140, 172, 177–178; *see also* Gymkhana, sports days
militia 26
missionary, missionaries 79
Modern Pentathlon 200
money prizes 182–186, 195; *see also* professionalism (in sport)
Mons, retreat from 130, 138–140
Moore, Sir John 60
morale, military 3, 6, 31, 44, 78, 86, 99, 106, 134, 137–138, 140, 146–147, 154, 158, 160–161, 166–168, 179, 184, 190, 194, 201; *see also esprit de corps*
morality 23, 27–31, 44, 116
muscular Christianity 81; *see also* games ethic, athleticism
musketry 34, 37, 48, 50–51, 62, 104, 171, 188–189

Napier, Colonel John S. 58, 60, 63
National Olympian Association 37, 42
National Playing Fields Association 200

National Service League 109–112
Neville, Captain W.P. 1
New Zealand Army 111, 158, 171, 180
Newbolt, Sir Henry 19, 124
Nightingale, Florence 24
Nineteenth Century (and beyond) 111
North-West Frontier
     Russian threat towards 84, 87

Officer Training Corps (OTC) 132
Officer-men relations 40–41, 71, 94–99
Old Contemptibles 1, 3, 141
Olympic Games 67, 77, 200
Onslow, Colonel G.M. 52, 54

Pakistan Army 82
Pashtuns 85
Peninsular War 10, 62
Pershing, General John 172
Peshawar Vale Hunt Club 10
pig sticking 12, 18, 21, 82, 140; *see also* field sports, hunting, *shikar*
playing fields 114, 116–117, 122, 200
polo 11–18, 21, 42, 71, 82, 96, 117
Polygon Wood 136
Portsmouth
     Soldiers' Home 28
     Physical Training School 150, 158
Prince of Wales 16, 28
prisoners of war, German 138, 186
professionalism (in sport) 182–184, 186, 193, 196–197
promotion, military 18, 35
prostitution 30, 28; *see also* Contagious Diseases Acts, brothels, regimental
public schools 5, 18–19, 33, 42, 66, 73, 91, 109, 123, 132, 182
Punch 155
Punjab, soldiers 85–86, 94
purchase system 18–23; *see also* promotion, military

Queen's Regulations 3, 34–35, 51

race, race relations 4, 84–86, 96–99, 103,
    189; *see also* martial race theory
rackets 9, 67, 113, 117–118
Rangers, US Army 201
recreational training 34, 79, 80–83, 87,
    94–95, 99, 102, 120–123, 130, 134,
    156, 164, 171–176, 179, 183–191,
    194, 199; *see also* regimental sport
recruitment, military 23, 26–27, 82–86,
    120–122, 154–155, 159, 191–194,
    196, 199
Red Cross 160; *see also* Nightingale,
    Florence
reform
    Army 4, 6, 22–28, 48–49, 60, 84, 103
    social 23, 28, 44
regiments, British Army; *see* British Army
    units
regiments, Indian Army; *see* Indian Army
    units
regimental sport 11, 16, 30, 41–44, 66–73,
    77, 94, 96, 114, 162, 176, 183; *see*
    also recreational training
religious differences 86, 94; *see also* class
    company regiments
Richards, Frank 29
Roberts, Sir Frederick 60, 62–63, 85,
    111–112
Robertson, Colonel J.P. 11
Robertson, Field Marshal Sir William 40
Rolt, Brigadier S.P. 105
route marching 55, 134, 148, 150, 178; *see*
    also foot marching, marching drill
Royal Military Academy, Woolwich 42,
    130, 133
Royal Military College, Sandhurst 19, 86,
    130, 133
Royal Navy 16, 30, 44, 74, 118; *see also*
    British Navy
Royal Tournament 39, 43–44

Royal United Services Institution of India
    87–88, 91, 95, 99
Royal United Services Institution 50
rugby 15, 39, 42, 113, 177
    Rugby Union 41–42, 118
Russia 3, 84, 87, 91, 124, 190, 194

Salisbury Camp 170
Salonika 172
Sassoon, Siegfreid 167
School of Musketry, Hythe 62, 188–189
School of Physical and Bayonet Training
    150
    St. Pol 163, 170–173, 186–187
sepoys 82, 87, 90–91, 94–99
Sherer, Major John F. 15
shikar 97; see shooting, hunting, pig
    sticking
shooting, shooting expeditions 10–15,
    21–22, 136
short service 26–30
Sikhs 85, 94, 98
silladar cavalry 82; *see also* horseback
    wrestling
Smith-Dorrien, Sir Horace 116
soldiers' homes, institutes 28–30
Somme, Battle of 1–2, 125, 175, 177, 202
South African War 11, 48, 60, 62, 77, 90,
    124, 138, 148; *see also* Boer War
sowars 87–90
swordsmanship 35, 37, 54, 90, 93; *see also*
    fencing
sport and war, connections 20–22, 97,
    124–126
sports days 5, 44, 67, 77–78, 98, 106, 113,
    126, 154, 177, 180–183; *see also*
    Gymkhana, military tournaments
sportsmanship 41, 96–97, 100, 138
Sportsmen's Battalions
    Australia 155
    United Kingdom 154
Sri Lanka Army 82

Starr, Captain Frank J. 164, 186
Sudan, the Nile Campaign 19, 60, 77–78
Swedish Army gymnastics 51–52, 58, 105,
    166, 173
swimming 48, 58, 88, 90, 123

Tanet Side Harriers 125
Tel el Kebir, battle of 52
tennis 11, 118, 187
tent-pegging 43, 77, 88, 96
Territorial Army 78, 106, 108, 111, 113,
    126, 131, 148
Third Army School 161–163
tiger hunting 20–21, 97; see also big game
    hunting, field sports, shikar,
    shooting
trench digging practice, as physical training
    146
troopships, training on board 148
tug of war 43, 72, 77, 92, 98, 148, 174, 180,
    187

uhlans 138; see also lancers
Unites States Army 49, 104, 158, 168,
    171–172

Val Cartier Camp, Quebec 170

venereal disease 27, 30, 114, 116; see also
    brothels, Contagious Diseases Acts,
    prostitution

Ward, Sir Edward 116, 120–121
Wardrop, General Sir Alexander 21
Wellington, Duke of 10–27
Wells, "Bombadier" Billy 167
Whigham, Colonel R.D. 136
Wiart, Sir Adrian Carton de 12
William II, Kaiser 2
Wilkinson, Johnson 9, 12
Wolseley, Sir Garnet 9, 14, 51, 58, 74
Women's Auxiliary Army Corps (WAAC),
    PT 173
Wood, Sir Evelyn 10
wounded, care of, recovery 166
Wright, Colonel Walter 120, 130–133,
    147, 149, 161, 173, 198

yeomanry 73
Ypres, First Battle 3, 130, 136, 140, 141,
    159, 161

Zulu War 48